What Her
Body Thought

ALSO BY SUSAN GRIFFIN

Bending Home

The Eros of Everyday Life

A Chorus of Stones

Unremembered Country

Made from This Earth

Pornography and Silence: Culture's Revenge Against Nature

Rape: The Politics of Consciousness

Woman and Nature: The Roaring Inside Her

Like the Iris of an Eye

Voices

What Her
Body Thought

A JOURNEY INTO THE SHADOWS

SUSAN GRIFFIN

📖 HarperSanFrancisco
A Division of HarperCollins*Publishers*

HarperCollins books may be purchased for educational, business, or sales promotional use. For information please write: Special Markets Department, HarperCollins Publishers, 10 East 53rd Street, New York, NY 10022.

HarperCollins Web Site: http://www.harpercollins.com
HarperCollins®, 📖 ®, and HarperSanFrancisco™ are trademarks of
HarperCollins Publishers Inc.

FIRST EDITION

Book design by Helene Wald Berinsky

Library of Congress Cataloging-in-Publication Data
Griffin, Susan.
What her body thought : a journey into the shadows / Susan Griffin. —1st ed.
ISBN 0-06-251435-0 (cloth)
ISBN 0-06-251436-9 (pbk.)
I. Title.
PS3557.R48913W45   1999
818'.5409—dc21   98-43253

99 00 01 02 03 ❖/RRD(H)10 9 8 7 6 5 4 3 2

For my mother
Sarah Emily Colvin Williamson
1914–1992

and to the memory of
Marie Duplessis
1824–1847

I have never had the impression that
my experience is entirely my own,
and it often seems . . . that it preceded me.

JOHN BERGER

CONTENTS

One

TWO STORIES ▪ 7

A CHILD'S BODY ▪ 51

Two

SUSTENANCE ▪ 83

THE SOCIAL BODY ▪ 161

Three

THEATER ▪ 187

EROTIC BODIES ▪ 245

Four

DEMOCRACY ▪ 271

THE BODY ELECTRIC ▪ 321

What Her Body Thought: A Journey into the Shadows is a companion volume to *A Chorus of Stones: The Private Life of War*. Both books are part of a series entitled This Common Body: A Social Autobiography.

ACKNOWLEDGMENTS

I would like to thank the many people and institutions who helped me to complete this work. Civitella Ranieri Center, the writer's retreat, housed me in the converted granary of a beautiful castle in Umbria for several weeks. The attendants at the Museum at Gacé in Normandy devoted to the life of Marie Duplessis were kind and helpful. I thank the Bibliothèque Nationale for letting me see the original manuscripts of *La dame aux camélias* and the Bibliothèque Historique de la Ville de Paris for letting me study pamphlets from the eighteenth and nineteenth century that they have preserved. The Théâtre des Variétés sent me materials about the theater. In addition, the Théâtre de la Ville, which was at one time the Théâtre Sarah Bernhardt, allowed me to see Bernhardt's old dressing room, which has been preserved there. My visit to the museum at the restored Château du Monte Cristo was also helpful, as were my visits to the Musée Carnavalet and the Musée de l'Assistance Publique. I am indebted to the Travelers for allowing me to see Paiva's famous mansion, and to my generous guide there. Special thanks must go to The Jockey Club, also in Paris, and to baron du Cassagne, who spent several hours helping me to understand the period and milieu in which Marie Duplessis lived.

Let me also thank Madame la baronne Elie de Rothschilde for our conversation. I also thank Micheline Boudet for our brief conversation and for her book, *La Fleur du Mal,* on the life of Marie

Duplessis. Isabelle Villaud was very helpful both directly and because she facilitated communication with Christian Roy-Camille, who very generously shared with me his considerable knowledge and understanding of both Marie Duplessis and *La dame aux camélias* and whose passion for the subject gave me courage. Agnes Montenay directed me to certain important locations in the ninth arrondisement and Alberto Manguel accompanied me to the Bibliothèque Historique, helping me with the procedures there and, even more important, gave me an invaluable reading list of French novels and plays written on the subject of courtesans. Odile Hellier was always present to help me with my questions and I also thank her not only for founding The Village Voice, one of my favorite bookstores in any city, but also for providing in it a center and meeting place in Paris for readers and writers of all nationalities.

Daniel Meyers, Marlotte Reinharez, Judith Oringer, Carol Spindel, and John Levy helped me with many practical concerns in Paris. The actor and teacher Madeline Barchevska very kindly sent me a videotape containing fragments of performances by Sarah Bernhardt. Leonard Pitt was a companion in his enthusiasm for Paris and introduced me to several very important texts on the history of the city. Odette Meyers, my good friend and constant French teacher, continuously helped me with French texts whenever my own knowledge failed me. And, along with Rapheal Balmes, to whom I am also grateful, she accompanied me to the museum at Gace, helping me with questions there. I also want to thank Margot Hackett for providing me with texts on courtesans and for, along with her husband, Bob, organizing and hosting Odette's classes at their home and feeding us all so well. Both Lise Huerelle and Lea Mendelovitz provided important help with translations. And above all I want to thank my friend of many years Edith Sorel for her countless insights, her wit, her guidance, her inexhaustible knowledge of Paris, and her feeling for life, which makes everything, in the end, worthwhile.

I want to thank many of my friends prominent in the field of somatics, who have so generously shared their knowledge and work with me. Don Johnson has been an illuminating commentator and companion for many years, guiding me through this field. Emilie Conrad's work has been revelatory, transformational, and essential both to this work and my own health. Bonnie Bainbridge Cohen gave me valuable knowledge both directly and through her writing about her extraordinary work. I thank Candace Perth for her courageous and insightful work. And I thank the Esalen Institute, including its founder Micheal Murphy, for making it possible for me to encounter so many extraordinary somatic practitioners and thinkers.

I am deeply grateful to Jan Montgomery and Marya Grambs for their work to improve the lot of those of us who are ill and for helping me in so many ways. I am grateful to the San Francisco CFIDS Foundation, which during the years that it existed was so helpful to me. I also want to thank the late Randy Shilts for opening up so many new paths of knowledge about illness. And I thank Hilary Johnson for her brilliant and thorough book on CFIDS, *Osler's Web*. Conversations with Joan Sutherland, Joanna Macy, Ruth Escobar, Daniel Boyarin, Anita Barrows, Georgia Kelly, Ty Cashman, J. Puett Morgan, Ariel Parkinson, Mary Swig, Alev Croutier, Mayumi Oda, Jill Lessing, Marilyn Yalom, Glen Reeder, Paul R. Brenner, Joe Wemple, Sandra Sharpe, Sandra Gilbert, Mary Felstiner, and Carolyn Kizer enriched this work. I thank Mikhail Gorbachev, Jim Garrison, and Sam Keane for inviting me to the State of the World Conference, where I participated in more than one educational seminar on economics, health, and environment. I also thank Grazia Borrini, Sheldon Margen, and the Department of Public Health at the University of California at Berkeley for inviting me to several colloquia on the subject of health, which have proved influential and significant to this work in more ways than I can name. I thank Naropa Institute and The Center for Research on Women at Stanford for hosting programs on this book while it was in process. And Susan Groag Bell and Karen Offen for giving me a copy of their important work *Women, the Family and Freedom: The Debate in Documents*. I would also like to thank Angie Theriot, not only for my conversations with her about patients' rights but for her groundbreaking work in that field, including the founding of Planetree, a research center for patients. Let me also give a well-deserved expression of gratitude to the many friends who have helped and sustained me through my illness, and especially to a group of women with whom I met for many years, Joan Sutherland, Mimi Sternberg, Cornelia Schultz, Lenore Friedman, Naomi Newman, and Ruth Zaporah. And I warmly thank Jill Davey and Joan Miller, Joan Lester, and Carole Johnson for their very crucial and kind support in a difficult time.

In the period of writing the book I met with two groups of writers that included Alev Croutier, Vijaya Najaran, Noelle Oxenhandler, Maxine Hong-Kingston, Nina Wise, Bokara Legendre, Don Johnson, Daidie Donnelly, and Pamela Westfall-Bochte. Both groups were very helpful and encouraging. Alev alerted me to many references. Daidie also read the manuscript and I am grateful not only for her subtly intelligent response but for the sensitive and abiding support she has given me in more than one time of crisis. I thank Joanna Macy too for her reading of the book and for her sustaining friendship and inspiring presence in my life. Anita Barrows also gave this manuscript a careful and insightful reading, and she and Joanne Yeaton helped me survive many events, including a sprained ankle. My friend Nina Wise heard many paragraphs on the telephone just after they were written and received them with a quick-witted wisdom. Dorian Ross read the first half of an early version of the manuscript and responded with a heartwarming enthusiasm. Honor Moore heard a section of the book and was also warmly encouraging. My longtime friend Kirsten Grimstad gave the manuscript a close and deeply intelligent reading, as did my old friend Moira Roth, both bringing a wonderful combination of scholarship and perspicacity to bear. Let me also thank my friend Sandra Sharpe for her very insightful, subtle, and intelligent reading.

I thank my friend Jodie Evans for her carefully intelligent reading of the manuscript, for her loving wisdom and support during the last year of its completion, and for the largesse of her soul, which in itself is an inspiration. Let me also thank Brad Bunin and the Author's Guild for helping me through a crisis with this publication. Roger Scholes believed in this book at its inception. Caroline Pincus contributed a critical awareness. I am grateful for Liz Perle's editorship, which has been graceful and creative, at the end of the project, for Lisa Zuniga's work in production, Priscilla Stuckey in copyediting, and Helene Berinsky, the designer of this book. And finally, my deep gratitude goes to Katinka Matson, whose integrity, perceptive intelligence, courage, kindness, and even valor in the representation of this book have all been remarkable.

One

While I retreated down to lower ground,
before my eyes there suddenly appeared
one who seemed faint because of the long
silence.

DANTE, *Inferno*

Yes, this is the dangerous, lucid hour.

COLETTE

NOVEMBER

That sense of descent, hurtling downward toward the original image of all that is fundamentally bad, a body in pain. And always accompanied by fear, the nearness of death, or other endings, the termination of capabilities, lost limbs, eyesight, hearing, hair, skin erupting, blood appearing, breath disappearing, menacing sights, sounds, smells, the unavoidable presence of what is unpleasant, disagreeable, unlucky, even evil. This palpable badness having invaded or mysteriously appeared from somewhere or come about from some heretofore unsuspected cause. Or in its own way, just as terrible, a known cause that could not be prevented, despite every effort, the secret failure, the failure that cannot be hidden.

How do you dare speak of this?

JANUARY

And now, just as you prepare to tell your own story, you hear another story, one you know will be with you as you make your descent.

Two Stories

I know I am here to tell a story. And perhaps it is for this reason that as I ride on the Métro, on the second day after my arrival in Paris, I am acutely aware that all around me, in a language that is still not fluent for me, stories are being told. A group of girls speak almost at once, each giving a different piece of an event they experienced together. An older woman, perhaps a mother, listens as a younger woman, perhaps her daughter, recounts what happened to her that morning. A man sits reading a newspaper filled with reports from all over the world. In my purse I carry a *Pariscope*, the weekly publication that lists hundreds of movies; compelling tales are being unreeled all day in theaters all over the city. And sitting alone for two brief stops between Châtelet and Hôtel de Ville, I am composing a little story now, not only imagining the lives of those around me, but configuring myself in the narrative I call my life. The subterranean depths of the Métro seem fitting. My story is immersed in the body. And it is also right that I should be in this city. The story I will tell alongside my own was set here. As I wander the streets for the flavor of this history, just as certainly as I have entered Paris, the body of the city has entered me.

The tale I tell from my own life concerns an episode in an illness I have had for more than a decade. Over a period of three years I was very ill. Now, though several years have passed since I got back on my feet, and though I have regained most of my strength, something else inside me has not recovered. An affliction remains that may seem ephemeral compared to fevers or tremors yet nevertheless acts powerfully in my life. The dimensions of memory loom large for me. I am still afraid. And this is why I have decided to move toward rather than away from a terrain of suffering I might otherwise just as well forget. There is a part of myself caught in this underworld, a crucial fragment of being that, only because I have grown stronger in body and soul, I am able to rescue now. Something else, still molten, remains to be discovered in my past.

The memory frightens me. Still I am drawn not only by the hope of staring down this fear but by something else, almost outside the ken of my own story, there in the background, dim but still signaling to me now. Illness is often treated as an isolated event, an island of suffering significant only in itself. Yes, there is drama in disease; in fact, cast as it is between life and death, what more could one ask from a good story? A woman struggles valiantly for years before she succumbs to a little-known disease that turns all her tissue to a stonelike hardness. A celebrated writer laughs his way to health. No longer able to pitch a ball over the plate, a famous and beloved baseball player discovers he has a fatal illness that will soon make him helpless and dependent.

But I have begun to look beyond the solitary figure, toward a background that has all but faded into obscurity. It is there outside the sickroom, outside even the house, occupied as it may be by worried friends and family; it is also in the streets, the town, the city, society. And if illness is already understood by some as a social problem, I am beginning to see it as a source of vision too, a new lens through which one can see society more clearly. Just now, I find myself transfixed by a slight glimmer of promise at the edges of my story, barely discernible traces of a new way of seeing.

The glimmer only grows more intense when I add a second story to my own. Just as I was emerging from the worst episode of my illness and preparing to tell the tale, an older story, legendary in my childhood, caught my attention. Though I had nearly forgotten it, this story took on such a powerful life in my thinking that soon I found I had taken on a companion for my descent into memory. And now it seems entirely natural to me that I should tell it along with mine.

The presence of this tale has widened the scope of my vision by over a century. Known in America as *Camille,* the older story that accompanies mine, though fictional, is based on a true story that took place almost one hundred years before my birth. This was a time of titanic events. A revolution had recently occurred. There were high hopes for democracy, equality, justice. And yet in the same period, while great fortunes were being made, poverty and destitution grew large. Along with the physical body, the social body will appear in these pages now. And with this appearance, the subject of money, which before seemed only tangential to illness (though it never was to mine), how it is gained and how it is spent, is moving steadily toward the center of the narrative.

Whether you are well or ill, getting and spending are crucial to surviving in modern times. Though, as I write now about economy and exchange, I have this thought: in giving away cash or a meal or a horse or an automobile, a dress, a bracelet, a pot, you are usually relinquishing something that, had you kept it, would have been useful to you. But there is one gift that has no value until it is given. And that is a story.

Mingled, stories more than double in value. When one story meets another, the consequences can be surprisingly intense. The architects of the French Revolution, for instance, exchanged tales of tyranny as they made their plans. The effect, not just of the telling but of the mix, must have been remarkable. To see the larger patterns into which one's own life, one's own suffering fall like missing pieces, ciphers crucial to a greater meaning.

Like most Americans of my generation, I was first exposed to *Camille* through the dazzling film directed by George Cukor. Greta Garbo plays the title role, a youngish courtesan who is ill with tuberculosis. Though the film was made before I was born, I saw it on television when I was eleven or twelve. Through all the years since that first view, one scene remains vivid. It occurs near the end of the plot. As Camille lies in her bedroom slowly dying, her grand salon, which entertained so many lovers, is filled now by her creditors waiting to profit by her death.

I was grateful to find the theme of economic failure in this classic story of illness. Once a novel, then a play, afterward an opera, and finally at least four different films, it was until very recently perhaps the most popular story about illness that existed in modern times. One would mention the name, do a gentle mime of a swoon or a slight cough, and in this way evoke the idea of melodrama. Yet despite the story's reputation for mawkish sentimentality, tough realism lies at its core, a realism missing in contemporary accounts of physical decline. Poverty is often caused by illness. Unable to work much or at all, one who is ill watches resources dwindle and costs rise. And if living at a level of subsistence can be a stimulating challenge for those who are well, it is a cruelty to one who seeks aid and comfort to shore up a fragile body.

The true story beyond the legend is even more occupied by the uncomfortable subject of money. Peering into the background of *Camille*, one will encounter desperate circumstances. The low wages of working women in the last century, long hours of hard work without even a subsistence wage, hunger, homelessness, the silent ground of prostitution.

In *La dame aux camélias*, the original novel and the play written by Alexandre Dumas *fils*, as in *La Traviata*, the opera Verdi wrote after he saw the play, this harrowing background is never shown. But for nineteenth-century audiences the shadow of such poverty would have fallen across the stage, almost like a glimpse, from the corner of your eye, of slums in another direction than the one in which you walk. Though you walk away from what you have seen, the shadow of it stays with you.

The story appears to be about a lighter subject, which is love. Yet this is an impossible love whose unacceptability is woven from the harsher cloth of class and survival. The tragedy turns on the social inequities of the nineteenth century. A respectable young man from the rising classes falls in love with a fallen woman. Dumas *fils* based the story on a love affair he had had with a famous courtesan. The plot is simple. Armand courts Marguerite (called Camille in Cukor's movie), who against her better judgment returns his love. Their passion is glorious but brief. Patriarchal disapproval arrests the progress of their romance. The lovers are parted, only to meet again in the last moments of the play. But then it is too late. Coughing desperately, she recites a moving farewell and dies in Armand's arms. Met with the fusion of love and loss, impossible desires and inevitable endings, I find it impossible not to cry when I am watching the final scene. Yet I like these tears. They take me into a larger region of grief, one that is hard to name, except to say this is a place of a terrible dividedness—of the powerful from the humbled, the rich from the poor—and it is also, I suspect, a place of lost visions too.

But it is not only a resonance with suffering that draws me to this story. *Camille* has a certain *joie de vivre* that I recognize. And this too is part of my story. If you are lucky enough to recover, illness will bring you to cherish life. Surviving serious illness, all your senses will seem newly awake, every experience vibrant. *Camille* fairly overflows with the feeling. In my imagination, this tale has become a kind of angel, who transports me with tragic but also sumptuous, wild, and laughing revelation.

One has only to think of Paris, where the tale is set, or the demimonde of the nineteenth century, in whose glamorous atmosphere the action proceeds. There are the glittering rooms whose silk and satin surfaces are lit by hundreds of candles, the flames mirrored in the many facets of the sparkling jewels worn by exquisite women, kept—but this is also part of the charm—illicitly by men of wealth and fame. There are the gilded coaches lined with velvet and the resplendent dresses concealing embroidered lingerie. There are cascading flowers and slow sensuous scenes of love in the countryside, near the Seine, under the lacy trees of Ile-de-France.

Even the death, sad as it is, is also glamorous. Though, except for the very end, this death is depicted as lonely, the scene has been watched with close and hushed attention countless times by large audiences in grand theaters all over the world. There is something redemptive in the witness. And it has been placed before our eyes so skillfully. The great actress Sarah Bernhardt, festooned with white camellias, was famous for performing the heroine's last breath in a manner said to be so effective that occasionally very sensitive women in the audience fainted. She was loved for the way she expired. On her American tours alone, it earned her millions of dollars. Even today, Garbo's performance in *Camille* is luminous and enchanting while it makes you cry. And once I found myself alternately laughing and sobbing at the end of a performance in which Charles Ludlam, middle-aged, paunchy, and balding, played the part of Camille in drag.

Like countless others before me, I have become captivated by this story even as it gives me the courage to tell my own. I have become fascinated with its author, tracking his life story. I have gone to the village at the edge of the Seine where Armand and

Marguerite lived for a few months. I have stood in the theater where Armand met Marguerite. I have traveled the streets of Paris where the famous courtesans once lived. And on more than one afternoon, tired from the illness that is still with me in a more subtle form, I have stood like a weary suppliant, a pilgrim hungering for history, staring toward the offices of British Air on the boulevard de la Madeleine because, by several reports, Marie Duplessis lived upstairs in that building, and she was the celebrated woman who was once a lover to Dumas *fils* and whose death, at the age of twenty-three, inspired the story he told.

I know I am not the only one who is captivated. A tourist map of Paris still points out the site of the young courtesan's grave in the Cimetière Montmartre. Though the novel does not enjoy the esteem of literary critics any longer, it remains in print in over eight languages. When *La dame aux camélias* first opened in Paris, in 1852 (just a few years after the brief but fiery revolution of 1848), the theater was packed to the gills. It made Dumas *fils* famous all over the world. For a period of over fifty years, to play this role was both the ambition and the crowning achievement of great actresses on both sides of the Atlantic. Like Hamlet, the part has a nearly mystical grandeur that is at the same time erotic. One can see the effect today in *La Traviata*. It is based on *La dame aux camélias,* though the heroine has another name here. The number of names she has bears testament to her appeal: Marguerite Gautier, Camille, Violetta Valery. Whomever plays her well attains her own celebrity. The great fame of Maria Callas cannot be separated from her wrenching depiction of Violetta, her voice plumbing the depths of soul and loss.

Because there is this too in *Camille:* along with the quaint notion of woman as fragile, I have found an altogether different appeal, the shimmering power of the real woman, still visible in her fictional likeness, who though she was desperately ill nevertheless claimed the right to live with full intensity. The vividness of her presence is threaded through every scene, whether it is a lavish late-night party, a passionate embrace, or illness and death. Like all the great courtesans, Camille plays the part of a goddess, a goddess of sensuality, sexuality, and of life itself.

Because my story is not so dazzling, I welcome the vibrancy. As I begin to write, I am aware that illicit love is just one of many secrets in the life of the body, some that one wants to know and some that one would rather forget. The subject of illness can be tedious. All of us have had to listen at least once to an overlong and lackluster complaint about the vicissitudes of flesh. Telling a story of illness, one pulls a thread through a narrow opening flanked on one side by shame and the other by trivia.

Still, stories about physical trials of any kind, even including lingering illness, are compelling. In a sense, the drama of the body provides the model for all narrative. As far as I can surmise, the mysterious need for narration is seated in the body. What else is a cry of pain or pleasure but a small story? But mere expression is not enough. One likes to see the shape of a plot emerge from suffering, the curve of suspense and significance that creates a recognizable shape of events. It is as if the innermost soul, though weeping as Camille dies, also says, "What a wonderful story!"

Now as I write, not just the content of the story but the art of telling become the inner lining of the process of recovery on which I have embarked. And as the events of my life turn into the common cloth of narration, plot, and denouement, I am beginning to experience yet another change that gives me courage. It is said that through art you can accomplish distance from events that have at one time defeated you. But this is only because a precise distance is achieved, the exact measurement that is needed to weave the events of one's own life into a shared fabric, a story that suddenly and miraculously belongs to the social body.

■ ■ ■

My story begins quietly. It was several years ago, during the visit of two friends just after Christmas, that my health began to fail. Northern California often has a brief warm spell in the early winter when the sun shines, and this bright light falling when it does seems especially beautiful. For my friends, coming out of the heavy snows of Minnesota, the day was especially welcome.

We spent a few leisurely hours wandering over Berkeley; I was acting as a tour guide, displaying my favorite places. The pace was slow. We stopped for lunch and tea. It was what anyone would describe as a vacation for all of us. But near the end of the day, I began to feel a very deep exhaustion. And as I slid into the car, I remember feeling a pain so sharp on the site of an old infection that I could scarcely drive. Still I pushed the pain away and said nothing about it.

The response is familiar to me. I do not act this way from bravery. Rather, this is just one among many strategies for keeping illness at bay. I reason that if no one else knows about my symptoms, I can perhaps escape the consequences of them. A high-spirited person, I have what Buddhism calls a greed for experience. I wanted to go out that night with my friends. We had a wonderful meal planned at a well-praised restaurant in San Francisco where I had not eaten before. Like many northern Californians, I regard eating as more than an act of survival. Here, finding good food can be another kind of pilgrimage, albeit more sensual in nature. And later we had tickets for a performance, one that at the time seemed crucial to me to witness, though now I cannot remember what it was or why.

When we returned, I went upstairs to take a brief nap. But my fatigue would not ease into rest, and the pain continued, joined now by a dull ache over the rest of my body. I decided that a bath might relax or even revive me, and once I was in the water, the heat did abate some of the pain, but as the water cooled and it was time for me to leave, I found it alarmingly difficult even to stand.

Even so, I was planning what I would wear, which for me is never an easy task.

Paradoxically—but anyone who has been seriously ill can tell you this—whatever ghosts inhabit your psyche become most fierce when you are physically weak. I am never casual about dressing. But when I am exhausted, the simple act of getting dressed, burdened as it is with self-doubt and vanity, suddenly becomes overwhelming.

And another difficulty dogged me that early evening as it still does in a chronic way today. The more fatigued I am, the more diminished is my ability to think clearly. When the symptoms are mild, the effect on the mind is subtle and can be written off as the consequence of tiredness. I enter what many others with my illness have described in themselves as a kind of fog. In a more severe collapse, the effect is not subtle at all. I remember three occasions in particular. Once, driving a car, I could not remember if a red light meant to stop or to go. Another time, I was holding a large pot of hot water, too heavy for my weakened muscles, and suddenly I lost the ability to figure out where I ought to put it. And still another time, as I approached a doorway, my hand automatically surrounded the doorknob, but for five or six terrifying seconds, strange as it sounds, I could not remember that one must turn a doorknob to open a door.

But this is leaping ahead in the story. On that night I had not delineated the territory of my illness so clearly. I simply realized as I lay on my bed, unable to rest, my strength not returning, and the pain still present, that I did not want to stand up, and in any case I was incapable of dressing. (How I thought I would be able to drive a car over the Bay Bridge is another question.) In fact, as I lay there, it began to dawn on me that I lacked the strength to go downstairs to tell my friends that I would not be able to go out with them.

I called downstairs to them, but because my voice had grown

weak, they did not hear me. With all my effort, I could not seem to make it louder. Then, suddenly aware of how sick I really was, I began to weep; I suppose I cried at the frustration of having to stay home, of being helpless or sick at all. But above all, what I remember was the sensation of relief that comes from surrendering. I had given up a long struggle, waged over the last several months, to resist despair over my worsening health, to stay on my feet and continue my life as if I were well. And now, at least for the moment, the pretense was over.

With arduous effort, I pulled myself out of bed and went halfway down the stairs to call to them. As soon as they knew, the starkness of the situation faded for me. Added to my own longing to go out was my reluctance to disappoint them, and in my ghost-ridden, confused state of mind, I even imagined they might be angry with me. But they were not. In fact, we all made a good night of it. They went out for dinner, returning with food for all of us and a rented film. As the evening continued, I lost myself in the wonderful brand of self-reproducing laughter that women who are friends will sometimes share. Forgetting my brief moment of insight, I told myself I would be fine in the morning.

As pernicious as it sometimes is, denial has its uses. Wrapping yourself in the comfort of small illusions, you will be able to fall asleep or navigate the course of a day, focusing on whatever you must do to survive while your fear is kept at bay. My fear was not exactly of bodily suffering itself. Having been seriously ill before, I knew I could survive this kind of trial. It was another specter that confronted me. Since I was a writer, always at the edge of my resources, if I did not recover soon, how would I be able to pay my bills? In this sense of the word, how would I *survive*?

The question was not new. In the waning part of the day, it would pose itself as part of a fatigue that seemed to worsen as the afternoon continued. Barely able to make myself a meal and get into bed, aware that too many days had gone by without enough pages produced, I found myself repeating the half-conscious refrain, *I'm not going to make it.* But when, on the next day, my energy returned, I would rebuke myself for my despair, as if that mood had only been a shadowy aberration.

The struggle of the sick and disabled to earn a living is one you will rarely see depicted, even in all the memoirs by the ill and formerly ill. In one episode of ER, a weekly television program set in an emergency room, a nurse actually follows a patient to his temporary home under a bridge so that she can give him a blanket. He has just been discharged, and the weather is icy. The camera does not stay long with him. Though in one sense, it hardly needs to; this image, or the image of a room in a cheap pensioner's hotel, is at the back of most of our minds. I, for one, was relieved not to have to spend the evening with him out in the cold. At least, not just before I hoped to sleep.

It is this region of thought, the fearful territory I had consigned to the margins of my waking mind, that is so gracefully swept up into the story of Camille. Money, bills, creditors, class, social standing, who is acceptable and who not, who is to be protected and who abandoned. That Marguerite has no resources of her own besides what she is given by the men who are her lovers is the unstated ground upon which the entire action of the plot will be played.

The drama opens on a scene of dazzling, almost decadent, luxury. Yet every lavish display of abundance—gilded coaches, boxes at the opera, brilliant parties—is partnered with the possibility of penury. The heightened gaiety, the laughing guests, their lavish dress, the glittering mirrors, candelabras everywhere shedding their light, the celebrated, wealthy men whose extravagance graces the bodies of beautiful women, almost floating as if in bevies about the room, the flowing wine, the feast laid on a long table. This is all captured beautifully in Verdi's music, pulsing with the rhythms of a cancan. But it is interrupted by a sadder theme, the courtesan's cough, a harbinger, for all those who know the rules, not just of death, but of her coming financial descent should illness make her too unattractive for the attention of her benefactors. Burning her candles at both ends, she seems almost like a bullfighter in her bravado, turning elegantly to avoid each sign of the fate that awaits her.

I practiced my own more prosaic brand of avoidance. Though the same pain, fatigue, and confusion continued for nearly three weeks, slowly I began to improve. Telling myself I had just had a mild relapse of an earlier infection, bit by bit I eased myself back into normal life again. With no disruption in my former direction, I continued as I had before, sustaining myself with vague optimism and the sense once more that a complete recovery waited for me in the near future.

But this time the illusion was short-lived. The way I learned the nature of what had been laying siege to my body for several years was almost accidental. A few weeks after I was out of bed, I ran into an acquaintance in the market where I shop. Marya is a thin, quick, handsome woman with a face that might have belonged to an Italian noblewoman of the sixteenth century. She has not, however, led a sheltered life. Politically and practically wise, she is responsible for the existence of nearly a dozen foundations, institutions, and programs. Her worldly skills are fabled.

I knew that her lover, Jan, a banker before she met Marya, a fund-raiser of equally astonishing talents afterward, had been ill for several years with a new and barely understood illness and that she had recently had a serious relapse. When I asked Marya about her, she told me a story that was frightening. After being bedridden for some time, Jan had had a series of seizures. She was hospitalized with heart problems and would slip into a comalike state for days on end. Now she was in a slight remission but still terribly ill.

"And how are you?" Marya asked me.

Not wanting to say much about what seemed to me a minor episode compared to her lover's treacherous decline, I mumbled something quickly, but Marya, with her intense and direct intelligence, began to ask me pointed questions. Listing my symptoms, I offered the explanation I had given myself, that it was just the return of an old infection, yet Marya, never one to be deterred by irrelevant conversation, stopped me.

"I hate to tell you this," she said, "but when Jan first became ill, those are exactly the symptoms she presented."

Stricken, yet not entirely admitting my terror to myself, I murmured my wishes that Jan get better soon and moved my cart down another aisle. I must have turned visibly pale, because shortly afterward I ran into another friend who asked if something was wrong. But I shook my head and, after exchanging the usual polite greetings, moved away quickly again.

I knew that no cure existed for the illness Jan had, but I had not known before how serious it could be. For a time, the illness was mistakenly confused with Epstein-Barr virus. Roughly two months earlier, I had been told by my doctor, a sensitive and intelligent woman close to my age, that though I did not test positive for Epstein-Barr, she thought that I had a similar virus, if not the same condition. She had done tests for Epstein-Barr virus, but since I had had mononucleosis as a very young woman, the results were not clear. She said the symptoms I had experienced for several years indicated the presence of a similar kind of virus, and she suggested I try a new and promising drug that had had some success. In passing, she told me the drug affected the DNA of certain viruses directly.

Though I left with a prescription, I kept delaying a trip to the pharmacist. I did not want to experiment with a substance that might alter the genetic makeup of my cells. In fact, time has proven me right about my hesitation. The drug was eventually proven to be ineffectual, and there is evidence that those who used it worsened. But the capacity of the mind to obscure and confuse issues is powerful. On the telephone, a friend who agreed with me that I should not take this drug also suggested that there was no proof I had this illness. I leapt to adopt her logic as a solution. The drug was wrong and so was the diagnosis. Yet underneath lay another logic: the illness had no cure, so I could not possibly have it.

Why did the meeting in the market that day break through my defense? Certainly there was something in the clarity of Marya's thought and the unstinting tone of her delivery. And yet as I write I become aware of another reason. When I told her my symptoms, I saw an immediate look of comprehension move over her face. She recognized what I was feeling.

Coming home after my meeting with Marya, I struggled with myself for a day or two, and finally I called. I wanted to know more. As fearful as I was, from this small taste of comprehension I found a hunger to have what I felt be named and understood. Marya suggested I speak with Jan, but Jan was too ill to speak at any length. She told me to read Randy Shilts's book *And the Band Played On.* "It will be frightening," she cautioned, "but you need to read it." I had been able to work again, writing and seeing some students in the morning, but by most afternoons my energy would drain from my body. So it was in this state that I lay on the couch in my living room, where I had a view of the bay as it turned silver heading toward evening, and began to read Randy's book.

Even on the first page I found a passage that made me go cold with fear. "Grethe again felt the familiar fatigue wash over her," he wrote. "She had spent the last two years haunted by weariness, and by now, she knew she couldn't fight it." This was exactly what I had been feeling. I was stunned. Page after page of the book painstakingly described the effects of a compromised immune system, and the symptoms were unnervingly familiar to me. In addition to fatigue and general malaise, I had had swollen and painful lymph glands, terrible headaches, weight loss, mental confusion, memory loss, a white blood cell count low at times despite other signs of infection, disturbed sleep, night sweats. Was it possible that this was the reason my infections had continued for so long?

And in an uncanny way, the similarity went further. Though my illness is not often terminal, it has a moribund quality. Each day when I would slide into the downward spiral of my symptoms, I felt as if I were suspended at the edge of death. As if I were perpetually dying.

One after another, pieces of what had been a fragmented experience began to fall into place. After a few weeks I had the first of what would be countless long conversations with Jan. The illness she had and that I was beginning to acknowledge that I had too was now called chronic fatigue immune dysfunction syndrome (CFIDS). As so often with AIDS, it was now understood that the Epstein-Barr virus my doctor had tested me for was an opportunistic infection, present in many people with impaired immunity. What transpired was an odd mixture of validation and panic. I was emerging from a long bardo of isolation, a period in which what occurred in my body had no language. Though I had sympathetic friends, virtually no one I had spoken with before seemed to have felt what I felt in my body. Coming out of this void, I was astonished to hear a description of what I had long experienced. Odd prickling, legs, arms, face numb like a foot gone to sleep, only lasting all day. Strange lack of balance, a kind of swimming in the head. A feeling of pressure, as if the brain were swelling. And the inevitable collapse—*fatigue* is too mild a word—that seemed to be coming earlier and earlier every day.

Jan had a wealth of information. She was organizing patients with this disease, spreading information that the average doctor did not have. I learned, for instance, that researchers had found lesions on the brain, along with abnormalities of the immune system and, as with MS, degeneration of the myelin sheath that surrounds the nerves in patients with CFIDS.

This data belied an impression created by the earlier skepticism of the National Institutes of Health and that, despite public reversals of policy, persisted in the press, that the disease was largely a figment of neurosis. Abetted by the slang term "yuppie flu" as well as the first medical name, "chronic fatigue," when a cluster of the illness broke out among children in a small New England town, officials responded by calling the incident mass hysteria. The story Shilts had told about the agonizing slowness of society to recognize a serious disease was happening again with CFIDS.

Public denial had a palpable effect on my life. Even as one kind of emotional isolation was being broken, another form of loneliness appeared. Few among my friends grasped the dimensions of what I had learned. Glad though I was to have a name for this illness, I was devastated. Looking back at the history of my symptoms, I realized I had had the illness for five years. Over all of that time, I expected that eventually I would get well. I had had a series of curable conditions. Yes, there were relapses, but over time, I would regain my health. Now certainty weighed more in the direction of an illness that would continue and perhaps even get worse. Yet among my friends, besides those who also had the disease, there was almost no one who comprehended the gravity of what I had learned.

Northern California is home to a community of unusually responsive people. The art of sympathy is cultivated here (though, as in postwar culture in general, this cultivation is also a sign of an earlier ability having waned). The atmosphere of caring this produces can be oppressive to some. A friend from the East Coast who had had breast cancer complained that, at a time when she was past her grief, everyone here seemed very eager to cry with her.

Though the response from many of my friends was sympathetic, each time I told anyone I was ill, an account was required. The story, not only of the illness, its endless symptoms, and its mysterious etiology, but also of the political wars that surrounded it had to be told. And in this telling, the rite of passage that occurs between friends, by which suffering is acknowledged and even held, was somehow interrupted. And then as time moved on, there would be some who asked the inevitable questions, often accompanied by citations from newspaper articles or quotations from television doctors implying that the illness was more attitude than flesh.

Of course, even with a disease such as cancer, which is commonly understood as serious, the responses of others are not always helpful. Regarding illness, there will always be those who are stricken with terror at the thought of it in themselves or others. And because the feeling is not an entirely acceptable one, it must be masked. My friend from the East was lucky she did not have another classic Californian encounter with a friendly interrogator who would be quick to ask her what she felt she learned from her disease.

But my difficulty was not simply with the failure of understanding in others. My compassion toward myself was eroded by the same public image. I have been taught to think of the soul as solitary in its struggles. Long used to being a rebel, I have more than once too easily dismissed the effect of public opinion on my inner life. In fact, in a vacuum of public recognition, the outlines of my dilemma were less clear to me. Without the presence of public definition, I could not dwell with my own realization for very long, much less attend to the pain of it. That I needed time to grieve, to adjust to a different prognosis, is something I can say now easily. But I did not understand this then. Such an act requires courage and clarity. Yet during those months it was as if in my own consciousness, the graciousness necessary for this kind of quiet reckoning did not exist. Instead, I felt embattled, assaulted from every side, my body betraying me on one flank and society attacking from another.

Instead of reflection, my mind darted continually toward survival. I was pulled then, as I often am now, in two contradictory directions, toward concealment and revelation. To reveal the frayed state of my body might lessen the nightmarish quality of illness, smooth the rougher edges of my fear, and blend it into a landscape more generous than my besieged soul could supply. But as much as I wanted to be seen, I also wanted to pass as well. Those who are ill learn to fear rejection from the fit. Expressions of frailty, pain, despair are not always welcome. They will perhaps be politely tolerated or ignored or explained away by sententious advice, as, all the while, in the arena of discourse, you can almost feel the distance between yourself and others grow.

There is a crucial moment in *Camille* when Marguerite, unable to contain the violence of her coughing, rushes from the room. The party continues robustly without her. Except that Armand has followed her into her bedroom. Discovering her there, he embraces her and declares his love. Her coughing helps us to believe that it is a grand love he confesses, one that has overcome the sight of blood and spit. In the opera this passage is sung to some of the most beautiful music ever composed. *Dell' universo intero,* the hero sings, arguing that his love is as large as the entire universe. The grand theme starts and then stops, as slowly the woman he woos ponders his sincerity. She is tempted to trust him, you feel it in her voice. And yet, she is also drawn in another direction, back to the high life, which, even if it abandons her, is a life she knows.

Despite a perilously maudlin quality, the scene always moves me. It reaches into some fiery center for which no barrier exists to love and through which suffering is merely a path to greater love. To be reminded of this passion offers a compensation to the daily life of illness, which is hard and unlovely. Illness is as often a barrier to intimacy as it is a bond between lovers. When ill yourself or faced with someone else's illness, you can easily panic. The descent into ignoble moments of denial and blame can be swift. One night, I made such a descent through a long and tortuous telephone call with a woman who until recently had been my lover. She is a kind and sensitive woman, and months later she would be kind again, bringing me a meal, helping me with housework. But now the shock was hers as well as mine. At first she did not want to believe either the diagnosis or the seriousness of the illness. "What about a test?" she asked. I told her what I had just learned myself. "There is no test," I said. "It can only be diagnosed through symptoms." I was disappointed with her questions. I wanted her voice to pale as I had paled that day in the market, to feel, even over the lines of the telephone, a sympathetic shudder run through her body. But instead she continued in the direction of doubt. "You don't know for certain," she argued.

Then somewhere in the midst of answers, the course of her inquiry shifted. "Why weren't you concerned about exposing me?" she asked with some anger. This unleashed a fury in me. Shouting over the telephone, I exposed the contradictions in her logic. Either she believed I had the illness or she did not. If she did not, she had no cause to worry. If she did, where was her concern for me? Forgetting any concern for her, I argued logically as if logic alone were all I had left. And that, in a sense, was true.

Or rather, I felt I had to fight to hold onto my perceptions. Clarity, I have come to see, is not as easily achieved in isolation as I once thought. Even the vaunted ivory towers of monastic life existed as part of a communal life with a common philosophy. The calm of that atmosphere created a congenial solitude. If reflection was turbulent, such as in the thoughts of a St. John or a St. Teresa, this inner life was mirrored by an architecture that echoed and supported it. Lacking any social structure of this kind, the desire to perceive and know your own experience founders on the desire for communion. The choice between truth and society is harsh. Abandoned by the social body, you may be tempted to abandon yourself, but the consequence of this is an even more subtle inner abandonment. Despite temporary respites of small denials, the soul is bound up with honesty in some way that cannot, except at great cost, be violated.

Even what remains unspoken can, by omission, create a perilous divide in consciousness. Suddenly without an echo to remind you of yourself, you find it easier to deny what you know to be true. Being ill with an illness unrecognized, I could not fall back on society's knowledge of my condition whenever my own clarity failed me. But fail me it did, even when I most needed it. Over the spring, as I regained strength, I hoped against hope that I would be well enough to travel. I had been invited to lecture in Germany at a large gathering of scientists and philosophers convening to discuss nature and spirit. So much of my work had addressed this subject. And I was eager to hear the work of others that would be presented. In a sense, I knew only too well the condition of my health. Yes, I was on my feet, but I was walking on the thinnest ice. The least mishap could make me fall through the brittle skin of my resilience. And the trip was filled with mishaps. A train reservation scheduled too early. Two planes missed. A pattern not entirely haphazard, the mistakes themselves the products of exhaustion.

Like the famous frog that slowly adjusts its temperature to water that grows progressively hotter until it is cooked, in time I learned to ignore fatigue, fever, pain, pushing my body to the edge of collapse. As I grew more ill, I lost the perspective of wellness, the simple ability to know how sick I was, and with fatigue my capacity to make intelligent plans also diminished. Since I was one of a very few women presenting, to assuage complaints of women in the audience, the directors of the conference wanted me to appear more often. I did not say no, as I should have. My exhaustion grew when my sleep was interrupted by a companion who had gone to a late-night party.

Illness creates a different geography in the body, one with its own natural laws. The more ill I am, or the more fatigued, the less I am able to sleep. In a state of extreme exhaustion, my ability to sleep grows more and more fragile. If I am awakened, the chances are I will not be able to fall asleep again at all. Paradoxically, at least to the rest of humanity, I have to be rested in order to rest. As I moderated an early-morning panel, my hands, face, and arms began to numb, and I found myself making tense efforts to cover the fact that, try as I did, I could not remember most of the panelists' names.

When the rhythms of the body are played out in such eccentric measures, altering that commonality through which others might be able to imagine what you experience, you will often be ashamed for feeling as you do. Shame is almost always a response to the judgments that others make, though the origin may be more in your past than in the present moment of your embarrassment. Although it was less true for my generation than my mother's, in my childhood the body was still the site of a form of social warfare. As children, we were shamed into controlling our bodies—where we touched ourselves, where and when we shat or farted, how well we washed.

Of course, in a certain sense I renounced that early shame, accepting my body with all its liquids and all its desires. But in another sense it is still with me, experienced even as part of bone, tissue, blood. From memory and experience, a subtle structure of shame has been built within my body. My child's misbehaving body, the shame of having divorced parents, or an alcoholic mother, the shame of becoming a lesbian, the shame of being ill and edging so close to poverty—all these half-conscious recriminations mix and conflate within me so that, without great effort, I can no longer discern the taste and texture of one from another.

Given the social stigma of prostitution, it is not surprising that shame is one of the emotions Garbo includes in the marvelously complex layers she portrays as Camille, first frivolous and mocking, then wanting to believe, and then believing, responds to Armand's declaration of love. Mockery, of course, is the fallen woman's best defense against society's judgment. Yet a watchful eye can detect the shame beneath. And just underneath this shame there must be a very old sadness. Though it is not written into the script, you can feel an old history between the lines. An earlier innocence. And a trust that has been betrayed.

The sense of an earlier innocence and of betrayal redeems the shame—not only the courtesan's but your own—through all its archaeological layers. Garbo is breathtaking, as slowly her sophistication peels back to reveal a desire to be loved and an ability to love, both left as if untouched since childhood. While Armand holds her in his arms, the delicacy of her emerging ability to trust his love appears to be woven from the same fabric as her physical fragility.

As if to protect the delicacy of their attachment, the lovers escape to the countryside. In Franco Zeffirelli's production of *Traviata,* they hole up in an elegant country home, with high ceilings and glass walls crowded by gigantic green plants, a cross between an Italianate villa and a greenhouse. The setting in George Cukor's film is gentler. Fruit trees in blossom, an unmade bed, flowing with white, lacy sheets from which Marguerite rises into a stream of light, as if into health itself. Nanine, Marguerite's faithful servant, fawns over her, glad to see her mistress so happy, as she brings breakfast to her bed. Garbo is radiant. She almost floats, her head thrown back, the long, swanlike throat showing white. Even before Armand's father appears to break the couple apart, you can sense the tenuousness of her state, and you are afraid for her. It is not that she is holding back emotion now. Indeed, she seems to swim in feeling; she is nearly drowning in it. And despite the robust and erotic pink of her cheeks, her body, as if knowing somehow the risk in opening her heart so wide, seems almost to quiver, like a lamb newly shorn.

The whole shape of the story is there in her gestures. You know that the nakedness of her feelings will soon be turned against her. When Armand's father tries to bribe her to leave his son, she turns him down. But quickly perceiving the depth of her love, he uses this love against her, telling her that she is ruining Armand's reputation and his sister's chances of a respectable marriage. As Camille comes to understand that her love is harmful to the man she loves and ruinous to his family, Garbo's face collapses into a resigned and terrible grief. She agrees to part from Armand. If she trusted the world to allow her love, now that trust has been betrayed.

In the nineteenth-century version, despite the tragedy, the play ended with a redemption. Through the sacrifice of her own desire, Marguerite was saving her soul. But twentieth-century drama rarely focuses so directly on the progress of the spirit. Betrayal, however, would have been a compelling theme then. A collective innocence was being lost. The film was made in 1936, only three years after Hitler's ascent to power. Cukor himself had just fled Germany, though I doubt the film was meant to comment on that history. Rather, both hope and betrayal would have been felt silently, in the body.

In my own body, but for different reasons, I experience a similar movement, a shift from hope to betrayal, almost daily. Whenever I feel well for a period, my days seem to glisten like a pastoral idyll photographed through a soft lens. Even now, used to years of fluctuations, with each remission I am given to believe that the failures of my body are gone and I will be well forever. The temptation is to believe that finally I am in control, that I have taken on the right attitude, assumed a posture of strength, and cured myself. Only later, like a lover who is seduced and abandoned, am I dismayed, as slowly in the course of an hour, a day, or a week my symptoms gradually reappear. Then it is wellness that seems an illusion.

It was on the last evening of the conference that I collapsed. A friend and I were walking back to my hotel room. Because I had grown so weak, we chose a shortcut through the park that surrounded the conference building. But after we had walked a short distance, we found a locked gate across our path. We would have to walk another two blocks around to the front door. Sitting, then lying down on the grass, I began to weep. I felt I could go no farther.

Somehow with the help of my friend, I got into my room and into bed. Still, I had not yet confronted the extent of my decline. The next morning I was drawn to the conference, which in the fog of my awareness had taken on a blazing significance. And though after the first session I began to realize I should be in bed, my attendance was requested for a gathering of women who wanted to honor the women speakers. This gathering was a short walk away in the new building, but it felt like an impossible distance to me, so finally I requested a wheelchair.

The assembled women applauded us and gave us flowers. Yet that does not alter the sense I still have in my memory of these small events as a kind of waking nightmare. Though I seldom have had to use a wheelchair since, and I told myself the use of it was temporary, in a silent and inward way, I was startled to find myself sitting waist high as the chair careened through crowds of people who could walk and stand with ease.

And, visible as one aspect of my vulnerability had become, for other reasons altogether I felt an interior panic in my body I could not describe. A few years earlier I had helped to care for a friend who had had a concussion. Now I was glad I had heard her describe what she felt, the aftershocks of transient brain damage. She could not tolerate bright light or loud sounds, the presence of more than one person in a room or the fast movements of cars. In such a state one learns a great respect for the nervous system. That the sorting of many stimuli into one understandable reality is actually a form of work, a physical act, that the brain performs, was a novel idea to me. When over time I began to be able to delineate my own impairment, I became fascinated. But now, newly stripped of the soothing sheet of order I was used to wrapping around my senses, I was in a state of shock. Indeed, inside I felt like a cartoon figure of an electrocuted cat I once saw, eyes spinning, hair standing on end.

The symptoms of this illness make for a very long list that one does not always want to recite, much less hear. Despite all my awareness, I find myself afraid that I sound like an old lady obsessed with her body. Though as I write this, I am aware of a plethora of prejudices implied in such a simile, the humiliation that is a humiliation of the flesh being perhaps the most cruel.

And the life of the body is at the heart of my story. Besides suffering insomnia and exhaustion, I was in pain, an ache in my muscles as if I had a terrible flu, a sharp arthritic pain in all my joints, a burning pain down my spine. But it was the shooting pains in my chest, together with palpitations (perhaps the least serious of my symptoms), that alarmed a friend. German, she had a German friend at the conference who had been cured by a physician who was in southern Germany, and together they called this doctor. She knew of the illness and urged me to stop working immediately. She said if I went on I was in danger of doing permanent damage to my body. And she thought she might be able to help me.

Since I followed her advice, I have revisited the decision many times. Perhaps this is a way my own mind has of denying the level

of collapse my body suffered. Many times in my imagination I have
watched myself ignoring her advice, skipping over my illness as if it
were simply an annoying impediment to my plans, and traveling
on, north to Hamburg, a city I have always wanted to see, where I
had a speaking engagement. Then after that to Norway to visit a
friend who perhaps would have taken me to Samiland, a place of
midnight suns and reindeer, which I wanted to see with an even
greater passion.

Did the German doctor help me? Yes, she did, though the
effects did not survive my arduous plane trip home. She prescribed organic food and massage, gave me injections, drops, oint-
ments. Improving by small increments, I was able to take short
walks. And there was something else she did, less for my body
than for my mind. Like Marya and Jan had, but through a medical
lens, she saw what was happening in my body and let me know
that she did. She was not sentimental; she had a scientific interest
in my condition, and this made her sympathy precise. She was
almost ninety, and her kindness had that air of sternness common
in German authority figures from her generation. With a delicately
subtle intelligence, her face registered an understanding of what I
was feeling. The questions and her comments were like probes into
my own bodily knowledge. It was as if a prisoner long held in
solitude were suddenly invited to enter a brilliantly revealing conversation. Though I was grateful that she was able to get me well
enough to fly home, more than anything she did, I found the
sharp dexterity of her mind healing. She had borne witness to my
experience.

As with most of us, I have always felt a powerful need to be known
and understood as I really am. Being misunderstood, either in negative or positive ways, is more than painful for me. At times I have
even felt myself close to deranged by such misperceptions. This is
perhaps why I find the second act of *Camille* nearly unbearable to

watch, though of course I know the outcome. Convinced by Armand's father that she must leave him, Marguerite tells him a lie. In a letter she will send him after she departs, she writes that she is bored with their life together and has chosen to return to the wealthy man who supported her in the past. Since Armand thinks that she is just leaving him for a short visit to Paris, he is perplexed by her mood. Garbo's performance is excruciating to watch. She swings from pretended gaiety to desperately tearful expressions of love, all the while betraying her heart.

The next time they see each other, Armand has a different idea of who she is. He believes the lies she has told him. The lovers appear at a party together but, as in a dance, with different partners. Yet the electricity of their love can still be felt in the room. Except now Armand's passion is expressed as hatred. Blinded by his rage, he cannot see the posture of love in Marguerite's body nor that she is grief-stricken. Gambling recklessly and winning, he insults her by throwing his gains at her feet.

As I describe the scene, I am impressed with how intricately the issue of money is woven with shame throughout the story. Armand's shame at being supported by Marguerite, which fuses with his grief and his rage. Marguerite's shame over being a courtesan, accepting money for love. The shame Armand's father fears will be cast over his family. And finally the shame of thinking about money at all, which, like sex, is a subject banished from polite society.

Yet, though *Camille* is a love story, without money there would be no plot. The subject is everywhere in the play. The bribe from Armand's father, which Marguerite will not accept. That she sells her possessions to pay the rent for their country house. That he borrows heavily against his inheritance. The creditors that occupy her house as she is dying. All the wages of flesh are there, the need for food and shelter mixed in equal proportion with erotic desire.

■   ■   ■

One other aspect of my German sojourn remains to be told. I was so thin—I weighed about a hundred pounds—that my sitting bones were painful against the hard surface of the enamel bath, and because of this and the tendency of my illness to make one hypersensitive to cold, I was constantly shivering. It was an unseasonably cold late spring. But though she was kind in her manner, the landlady from whom my German friend had rented a room could or perhaps would not find a way to give us enough heat. This memory mixes with another that remains indelible, of images made using the beautiful and delicate petals from the spring flowers blooming everywhere. Fashioned by the women of the village where I was staying, these designs appeared on all the pathways during the celebration of Corpus Christi. Among them, I was stunned to see floral representations of instruments of torture—whips, clubs, a rack and screws. These were supposed to recall the sufferings of Christ, but because the instruments were medieval, they reminded me more of witch burnings, and of course the Holocaust came to mind. It was southern Germany that, despite a more gentle appearance, provided the birthing ground of the Nazi movement. Since I was weak and relatively helpless, unable to speak the language, my knowledge of this past gave all my perceptions an eerie and frightening quality.

Though it seemed an interminable period, I was in the Black Forest for just two weeks, and because a kind woman, a professor, invited my friend and me to stay at her warmer, more comfortable apartment in the village, the second week was easier. Then it all ended. My doctor finding me well enough to fly, we took a train to Frankfurt and the next morning boarded a plane to San Francisco.

I was glad finally to be home, where I understood the language and could interpret the more subtle signs of discourse. Still, the dissonance that unnerved me so in Germany was not gone from my life. I felt safer here, and yet this apparent safety had a hidden inner lining, the continual presence of a fear that seemed to intensify because it did not belong with the sunny image America has of itself. This is the fear that springs from knowing, as most everyone does, that it is dangerous to be ill for very long here. Lack of decent care, economic ruin, homelessness—these were the specters that haunted my return.

My awareness of this menace mixed freely with my alarm over the changes in my body, making both more intense. For the first several months, exertion of any kind would set off a fearsome series of physical torments. As I look back, the disrepair of my nervous system is frightening to consider. I cannot reproduce in myself now a complete sensual memory of what it was like. I can only reconstruct the feeling from memory and circumstance. One day, for example, a good friend who lived nearby invited me to watch a video on the Australian rain forest at a gathering at her house. Though I was dubious about the prospect, my friend hoped it might do me some good to be out, and I was lonely. Someone was sent to help me down the stairs and take me there, and once arrived I was treated with care, seated on the couch where I could stretch out my legs, given tea to drink. But try as I did, I simply could not follow the logical sequences of the video. And as the camera moved over rushing water or captured light dappling off leaves, I could scarcely bear to look at the screen. Because music was played in the background, the narrator's voice was indecipherable to me, and the rapid spin of images played havoc with my nerves. I tried putting my head lower, tried averting my eyes from the flashing light, tried blocking the video out entirely. But in my peripheral vision I would catch the casual motion of others in the room, and this alone overwhelmed me. The whole sensual kaleidoscope was just short of torture. I endured it as long as I could and then asked to be brought home again.

Quieter at home, I noticed that symptoms I had had in a more subtle form months earlier had grown to a gargantuan size now. Where once I was easily tired, now I lacked the strength to sit in bed and read. Sitting up, I would feel dizzy or I would begin to have a fierce headache, coupled with an overwhelming need to lie flat again. But in that position, you will have to hold up a book to read it, and for the first few weeks, even the lightest paperback books were too heavy. Where once I felt a slight numbness in my hands and feet, now most of my body felt oddly numb with a pins-and-needles sensation. And my memory worsened to the point of absurdity. Trying to think through a practical problem—to remember, for instance, the names of vegetables I wanted friends to purchase when they went shopping for me—seemed beyond my intellectual powers. Finally, after a month of blank spaces in my mind, I began to compile a list of all the food I used to buy when I could shop for myself and all the things that I might, at one time or another, need from the market. Making the list was a slow, painstaking labor. Over several days, each time the name of something—orange juice or zucchini—came to mind, I would write it down. I can still remember with clarity the joy I felt every time I captured a once familiar name on paper.

Clearly, some aspects of my ability to think were affected more than others. What I found was that much of the time I could think lucidly and even creatively if I let my mind wander wherever it wanted. But questions were difficult to answer. It was as if the memory and knowledge existed, but my mind could not locate them. I experienced the attempt to do so as very tiring, so much so that once when a visiting friend kept asking questions, I burst into tears from the effort to answer her.

There were many other symptoms. The medical inventory is so long it verges on the comical. The image that comes to mind is of a dilapidated house whose every system fails; the same night that a pipe bursts, the electricity short-circuits, and besides the darkness, there is no way to power a pump or even, given that telephones require electricity, call for help.

I felt like I lived in such a house, but it was my body, a place I could not, except in dreams, leave. On more than one occasion every system appeared to break down. The dull ache in my muscles that I had experienced before my collapse had become constant pain, sharp in my joints, strong in my bones, and up and down my spine, heavily burdensome in my flesh. Since conventional medicine had at that date very little to offer me, I had decided to use homeopathic remedies, and both of my homeopathic doctors discouraged the use of pain medication, except on the days when the pain was too severe to bear.

On one of those days the nausea that was frequently with me resolved itself, in the early hours of the morning, into such violent vomiting I feared I would faint. Every time I was sick to my stomach, my heart skipped beats and my head began to swim, and because I could not keep anything down, I could not take anything for the pain, which had become excruciating.

In hindsight, I see I was afraid somehow of dying that morning. Not that I hadn't thought of death before. In Germany as I got thinner and thinner, it occurred to me I might waste away. But this was a peaceful thought, a slow ebbing, with the promise at least of an end to suffering. Yet at the same time, while I was in Germany, even though I had come to accept the possibility of death, I clamored to find a way to keep warm. The abstract thought of cessation is far different from the agonies of dying. Coming anywhere close to this process, the body rallies its own forces. Even in your flesh itself, you will feel panicked and alarmed.

Now, depicting every aspect of this memory brings me to what was probably the central difficulty of my convalescence. On that early morning when I was so violently ill and every system in my body seemed to fail so miserably, I could find no one to help me. In the year that I fell seriously ill I was single and living alone, with no one steadily present to care for me or oversee my care. Such is the case, I have learned since, for countless people who have disabling chronic illness. Calling around for help, I discovered that unless you are indigent and have used up every financial resource, no governmental or charitable agency exists to help the chronically ill with daily nursing or the domestic tasks of survival.

I was more fortunate than many who find themselves ill and alone. In the first two weeks after my return from Germany, my friends organized a schedule of residence. The kindness shown me was overwhelming. Every afternoon a new friend would appear to prepare my meals for that evening and the next day and to spend the night in the guest bedroom. In the beginning, no one felt I should be left alone. In that first period, I awakened in the middle of the night more than once with strange and terrifying dreams that I was dying or had died. In one I actually left my body and, flying upward, found myself looking down on it, crumbled, inert, vulnerable. After the first two weeks my friends would bring meals, at first lunch and dinner, and then, as I got stronger and more able to fend for myself, just dinner. People I had only barely known came to my house to help me. Old friends extended themselves beyond measure, appearing and reappearing with plates of food, stories to tell, and, as I got more able to watch them, rented movies. One friend, a historian of Japanese prints, brought me a modified version of a *kai seki* dinner one night, a traditional Japanese meal served in several delicately beautiful courses. He dressed for the occasion in a tuxedo and pink, high-topped tennis shoes. Another friend, ill with the disease herself but more well then than I, held me in her arms one morning and told me astonishing and exotic stories from her life before I met her. Others spent hours on the telephone organizing a schedule of caretakers. One friend, the owner of a bookstore, held a benefit reading to raise money for my medical bills. And much later another group of friends helped to raise funds for my care in the larger community. The depth and extent of the help I received, given with a love that moved me deeply, was far more than anyone in any single life could repay.

And yet, here is the substance of the shadow that holds a part of my soul in captivity now. Though I felt and still feel that too much was asked for and too much was given by my friends, it was not enough to shelter me from that harrowing feeling of fear and anguish that is a consequence of being ill without the safe ground that comes only with predictable care. Friends would call at the last minute saying they could not come. Several times no one could be found to do the difficult work of scheduling help. And so much effort was expended on bringing me meals that I could not bring myself to ask for help with other tasks. Though I was in bed for most of the day, my sheets went unchanged for weeks, my laundry unwashed. For a brief two days someone whom I hoped could exchange rent for care came to stay in my house, but she proved to be disturbed. Her legacy was a kitchen in disarray I did not have the strength to repair. It would be two years before I could put it back in order.

Once an old friend, an actress who had been in Europe touring for months, asked when she came to visit what she could do. Since she had not been present for earlier efforts, she had a fresh energy to contribute. I felt enormously grateful when she went to my refrigerator and, discovering that it badly needed cleaning, set herself to the task. At times a friend delivering a meal would come in looking visibly fatigued, and this was one of the moments when I would feel a thick guilt and, along with this, a subtle form of panic. A seemingly implacable logic framed the failure of my body. If I continued to need care, I would lose the love of my caregivers, many of whom were also strained as time wore on. Yet without rest, I would not recover. Very late at night or in the early hours of the morning, in a state of worried wakefulness, I would repeat the steps of this reasoning to myself.

These nights made the days when I would make calls for help seem perilous to my soul. In my dependency I had descended into an older territory of my psyche, the region of my childhood. There was a circumstance in my childhood that my present circumstances echoed. During the years when a child is dependent on adults for the meeting of bodily needs, I was often neglected by an alcoholic mother. Too frequently I was left alone, given no dinner, only later to be kept awake by my mother's drunken return. This memory, which had become as if part of my cells, made my nights alone more treacherous, awakening as it did the fears of a helpless child.

Even without such a childhood memory, a precise sorrow rises up in the psyche in response to abandonment. On some nearly inaccessible level of the psyche, I would read the lack of care as a sign of disapproval of my need. Failing to make my needs go away, I felt trapped in an impossible dilemma. Because I was in need, I felt inordinately dependent on the goodwill of others and yet at the same time feared that my needs would forever alienate my friends. In my darkest moments, I translated this impasse as a sign that the world did not wish for my life to continue.

More than once I contemplated suicide. In desperate moments, late at night, calling for help and reaching what seemed like the end of all possibilities, I felt as if ending my life were the only choice I had left. To remain ill for very long without the care I needed would be too torturous. A life I simply did not want. And there was this too: a few times, calling for help, I had lost control, panicked, wept, which led to the deepening of a humiliation I already felt in a measure almost too great to bear. The damp pallor of my body, its weakness, the frightened tremulous state of my psyche, even when I did not express my feelings, the fact that I was alone, without a lover or mate to care for me, made for a formidable mixture, the proof, in the unassailable logic of certain emotions, of my unworthiness. That the logic was circular did not matter. What I have learned from this experience is that in the psyche reason does not always matter. And that certain circumstances can convince you of any supposition.

It is this kind of humiliation—a woman weeping, calling too much attention to herself—that the name *Camille* had come to signify by the time I reached adulthood. Yet oddly, as I review the play, I see that Marguerite was hardly exorbitant in her demand for attention. It is true that both Bernhardt and Callas, so famous for playing the role that they were confused with it, had the reputation of exaggerated passions. But the character of Marguerite is defined less by the extravagance of her demands than by her sacrifice.

Yet, still again, when Bernhardt played the role, letting her head fall slowly backward with grief, as I have seen in still photographs or the brief film clips that remain, her vividness, a truly lavish vitality, is visible. Powerhouse that she was, a genius at her art, prodigiously talented and ambitious, intelligent businesswoman, entrepreneur of her own performances, a millionaire by the age of fifty, with a steady stream of lovers, Bernhardt must have poured all this forcefulness into that pivotal moment the courtesan renounced her own passionate love for the sake of the one she loved. Though, through some mysterious alchemy, her strength only makes the moment more believable. Could anyone doubt that the consequence of such a tumultuous resolution would have to be death?

Power, as much as frailty, seems to be the hallmark of the role. And this is understandable when you know that under the skin of the sacrificial lamb is a woman who has had to struggle mightily to survive. Any courtesan would have had to fight to win her position. Listening to the penetrating layers of passion and grief in Callas's voice, her own combination of frailty and will bending the music, I am strung between weeping and awe as I hear her sing out Violetta's answer to Rudolfo's father:

Tell your daughter, so lovely and pure,
that a poor and wretched woman,
who has but one precious thing in life
will sacrifice it for her—and then will die.

And if the sheer power of such a voice would perhaps seem too much for a character who is dying, the truth is that illness itself uncovers hidden reserves of strength. Though I thought of suicide, another intention had me in its grip. Exhausted, ashamed, at the end of my capacities, still at some of my lowest points I could feel an astonishing power well up in me, as if from my body itself, pushing through embarrassment and fatigue to continue to call for help—the last reserve of an athlete, or a warrior, grabbing at survival.

The fading, quiet invalid of popular imagination is unrealistic in another way too. For one who is well, the idea of being sent to bed can seem like an idyllic respite. But the symptoms of illness will more often than not frustrate every attempt you make to get rest. Seriously ill, instead of repose you will find yourself in a pitched battle. You must fight for a few hours of sleep, to gain even a short respite from pain, to breathe easily or accomplish the simplest bodily chores—brushing your teeth, cleaning your nails, washing your hair.

During the months I spent in bed, as my condition improved slowly, I would set myself little tasks, goals that set my life, even if by the smallest increments, above subsistence. When I could do it, I tried to read seven pages a day. Though the number sounds absurdly small now, using moments of relative wellness to read, it would take me the better part of a day. Yet the progress I would make through a book began to shape my time to another scale of meaning.

I did not read to forget my illness. It was less escape I sought than significance. In what I read I found passages that seemed to echo my own experiences, just as they enlarged the field of my understanding. Reading John Berger's *Pig Earth,* his portrait of life in a peasant village in Alpine France, I found I was drawn to his description of peasant thinking: "The peasant ideal of equality recognizes a world of scarcity, and its promise is for mutual fraternal aid in struggling against this scarcity. . . ." Ill, struggling each day simply to survive, I felt a kinship with this thought. In the isolation of my circumstances, it was as if I had made a close friend, someone else who witnessed an elemental struggle for survival.

Regarding isolation and struggle, another book became equally important to me. A work I never would have suspected I would like, Gabriel García Marquez's *The Story of a Shipwrecked Sailor.* I chose it for its author and because it was brief and light in my hands. But since, even when healthy, I am not given to physically rigorous adventure, the subject matter did not interest me. Until, that is, I began to read. Then I found another soul mate in this sailor, the lone survivor of a shipwreck, as he spent seemingly endless days and nights at sea defending himself against a blistering sun or terrible storms, the unpredictable attacks of sharks, withering hunger, thirst, and his own despair.

Years would pass before I encountered still another resonance. A harrowing despair punctuated by moments of hope and revelation, all accompanied with the rawest struggle for survival ends Marguerite Gautier's life in *La dame aux camélias,* the novel that Dumas *fils* wrote three years before the famous play was to open. In this version Armand reads of Marguerite's physical suffering through a series of letters. "I never knew how much pain our bodies can give us," she writes. She describes being up night after night, unable to sleep, unable to breathe, coughing with the violence of tuberculosis, gripped by high fevers and racking chills.

Though all her physical needs are met by her kind servant Nanine, and occasional friends spend an afternoon here and there, her rooms are relatively empty except when they are filled with creditors. As she declines, her suitors lose their ardor. "Men who buy love always inspect the goods before taking delivery of them. In Paris, there were many women whose health was better and who had better figures than mine. I began to be overlooked. . . ."

In his lavish production of *La Traviata,* Zeffirelli captures the contrast between her earlier popularity and the loneliness of her illness. The first frames of the film, accompanying the music of the overture, show Violetta, a wraith clad in white, wandering through cavernous, dimly lit rooms. The furniture, also draped in white dust cloth, is being assessed already by her creditors. With the ravages of death blazing from her eyes, she surveys the site of her former life. And then, as a shadow here and there comes to life and the sepulchral brown of her empty salon, the mystic blue of her bedroom, turns to the golden glow of candlelight, as the walls take on a fiery warmth and the murmur of voices and laughter that once filled her life return, the story begins. But every love scene that follows will be tinted by sadness.

The end of the novel is more cruel than the play. As the last pages of her life are turned, Marguerite loses the strength to write any longer. Then she goes blind. A friend continues the correspondence, noting that even with her last breaths, Marguerite cries out for Armand. But her letters reach him too late.

The play is kinder. Perhaps because theater favors presence more than absence, hearing the truth of her sacrifice earlier, Armand manages to arrive on the day of her death. Ecstatic, she rises from her bed with a sudden burst of energy. Not grasping the gravity of her condition, Armand begins to rhapsodize about the future they will have together. But this flowering is her final bloom. In a few moments she is gone.

Sitting in a darkened theater, as Garbo alternately smiles radiantly then lets a premonition of her fate ripple over her face, or listening to Verdi's melodies, one full of the rhythms of the dance, the other majestically tragic, even now, taking notes, trying to cast a cold eye on the contents, I am shaken. I ease myself back to ordinary life with a shudder. Death looms larger here, and with it another realm of knowledge appears, one I cannot yet describe. As if I had been plunged into unexplored depths and found a vast subterranean landscape, of which the modern sensibility seems ignorant, I have come back too stunned to be able to draw a map of where I have been.

Even so, I can detect this vaster landscape at the edges of my own story now. Knowledge of this kind is often called transcendent, as if the numinous may be found only through a miraculous escape from the body's needs. But what I have learned from illness came to me in and through my body—through suffering, yes, but also through the answering of need.

There was, for instance, that morning when I was afraid I was dying as every system in my body seemed to sicken. I remember feeling a longing for help then with a force that would not release me. Shaking, dizzy, afraid I would pass out in my own vomit, with a terrible pain in my spine that seemed to increase by the moment, I waited for the first light and then for the clock to reach a reasonable hour before I made several calls to friends. But no one was available to come. And because I was exhausted, having reached that point, different for everyone, when I felt I could not go on, every moment seemed torturously long.

Even to repeat the story brings me a feeling of shame. Is it because I needed help? That I wanted comfort? Because I was sick at all? Certainly illness made me exaggerate rejection in my mind when no one seemed able to come over. And then there is this too: like Camille, I was a woman outside the protective ken of a family, a state of aloneness that by itself is a source of embarrassment.

But someone did come that morning. I had met her several months earlier when I was outside weeding the garden. She was walking with a neighbor, Cynthia, who wanted to introduce her to me. Laurie had read a book I wrote so many years ago I hardly thought about it any longer. My neighbor had given her the book after she was hospitalized for an emotional breakdown, and Laurie felt that reading it had helped her. Late in life, when she was married and had two children, memories of having been raped by her father had returned to her, and her mind could not hold what she remembered. She developed several other personalities. One was an extremely shy and vulnerable child who would invariably drift toward men who would abuse her. Together the two women told me just some of Laurie's story, and then Laurie, who was timid even in her adult personality, thanked me profusely for having written the book.

That was our first meeting. Later, when attempts were made to find enough friends who could help me with meals and other needs, my neighbor suggested that Laurie would like to bring me breakfast every day. She was staying with Cynthia while recovering from her last hospitalization. I was moved by her offer to help me and at the same time hesitant. What if she became another person while she was caring for me? What if she broke down and began to act irrationally? I felt too weak to be able to cope with these possibilities. But I was assured nothing like this would happen with me. Laurie had enough control, Cynthia said, to prevent it.

And so she began to come every morning, shyly asking me what I wanted. She was assertive to a small degree. She decided I needed to gain weight (I weighed only 105 pounds) and made me try to eat more for breakfast. Slowly, carefully, the way one does with a child who is afraid or has been badly treated, I befriended her. Sometimes she would bring me small pieces she had written about her experiences. Because it was difficult for me to read, tentatively and in a small voice she read them aloud to me. I was relieved and excited to find the writing very good and began to talk with her about her writing and how she could go on with it.

Usually she came at ten in the morning. This gave me time to catch up on sleep, if I could, sleep that I lost in the middle of the night with bouts of pain and fever and terrified wakefulness. But on this particular morning, since I had been up vomiting and in intense pain most of the night, it seemed like hours until she arrived. I did not anticipate that she could do anything for me. I could neither eat nor hold down pain medication. I simply wanted someone to be present, even if only briefly. Though normally I considered myself to be the stronger one, I played a role with her, which she both elicited and accepted, of an older, wiser sister.

But today something else was to take place. When she came into the room, I could see immediately that she recognized the state that gripped me. Under a thin veneer, I was the abused child now, locked outside an empty house until three in the morning, cold, hungry, or left in a car in the parking lot of a bar or curled up half asleep on the Naugahyde seats of a booth in the bar my mother would frequent that served food and so allowed the presence of minors. No doubt she could see the shame in my eyes, which is unavoidably felt by children whose needs are not met, as if to want or to need is an embarrassment that cannot be controlled.

Immediately she did what she could, bringing me tea she said I should try to sip, straightening up the room around me. She had to go out for another appointment, she said, but she would come back at lunchtime. And though I had no practical need for her, I wanted her to return.

In the time she was gone the pain I had been feeling in all my joints and up and down my spine steadily increased. No position I took in bed offered me rest. And as the feeling of nausea continued unabated, every defense I had against bodily suffering began to disintegrate. An hour before she returned, I felt like an exhausted swimmer, caught in waters too deep, close to drowning.

What is bearable to one person defeats another. I can abide pain much more than nausea; the sensation unnerves me so much that with it I lose my courage altogether. As short as an hour can seem, it can also be interminable.

When Laurie arrived I was past the point of social pretense. She asked me how I was, and, trying to respond, I burst into tears. My physical state, as Dumas *fils* wrote of Marguerite, had left me "open to sensation and vulnerable to feelings." But to my relief and gratitude, Laurie was not embarrassed by my anguish. Nor did she tell me there was no reason to cry. Instead, the tone of her voice and the look on her face both registered recognition. She knew I was in trouble. She had brought some broth, which she warmed, encouraging me to sip small spoonfuls of it. And then, sitting with me in my bedroom, watching me turn again and again to find some viable position, she climbed into my bed and, taking my head on her lap, began to stroke my back, up and down my spine, where the pain was worst. For the first time in hours I experienced some relief. The pain remained steady, but with her touch I could bear it. And after some time, the strength of the pain was met by another strength, the force of the sweetness in her touch, a sweetness I felt radiate through my body, like light or warmth, and that made for a closeness between us. I began to rest, and no doubt she could feel my body relax, when she asked me if I would like to hear her story.

She told me what had happened to her since her first breakdown. The resurfacing of memories she could not suppress. A necessary separation from her children and her husband. The many hospitalizations. Nurses who belittled or disbelieved her terrifying memories. Times when, attempting to escape, she was put in restraints. Times when she was drugged. A tough-girl personality that would take her over and place her into combat with the orderlies, some of whom were cruel—one who used such occasions as an excuse to beat her—and one, a large, burly man, who put his arms around her with tenderness as he arrested her violence.

Yet as she told me her history a kind of miracle did occur, a transformation. By the strange paradox at the heart of all stories, what might usually separate us, the stigma of mental breakdown, the isolation of illness, had become a form of intimacy. And over the course of the afternoon still another story was passing wordlessly between us, that in different ways we had both been deprived of a resting place and of a love we could trust, a love that, at least in this moment, we were giving to each other.

A Child's Body

For it always happened that when I awoke like this, and my mind struggled in an unsuccessful attempt to discover where I was, everything revolved around me through the darkness: things, places, years.

MARCEL PROUST, *The Remembrance of Things Past*

HANDS

My mother is kneading something in her hands. It is margarine through which a bright yellow, almost orange pocket of color begins to spread as she works. I watch with an intensity that is absolute. I want this heavy bag in my hands, to rub my fingers over the spreading warm color. It is perhaps also that I want my mother's body in this way, or to be in her hands in this way, or to be her, and also, that the same eros that pulls me toward her pulls me toward pleasure of all kinds. Butter. Brightness. A frank desire in the palms of my hands.

THUMB

Then there is the desire I have toward my hands. My right hand especially. And in particular the thumb of this hand. I have found a way to put it in my mouth, pressing the soft inner flesh against my palate, squeezing my mouth around it and sucking upward. At the same time, I curl the index finger of this hand around my nose. It rests on the soft fine hairs just between my eyebrows. They are nearly invisible, these hairs, you can only see them if you stare, but they are delicious to touch, deliciously soft to my finger, which sends shoots of a soothing pleasure starting with the skin of my forehead and soon circulating through my whole body. The remaining three fingers of my hand rest lightly, tenderly over my mouth, and I press them inward from time to time so that my hand sinks into the more opulent flesh of my cheeks, giving me this pleasure too.

MOUTH

Sitting quietly, my thumb in my mouth, I enter a state somewhere between waking and sleep, profoundly safe, genuinely peaceful; wanting for nothing more than I have at this moment, I have dissolved into that state of self-love that has nothing to do with image or admiration, a love that is wordless and need not be translated into any gesture because it already exists in the body, in the flesh.

TEARS

My family has done everything they can think of to make me stop putting my right thumb into my mouth. My mother paints a sticky substance with a terrible taste on this thumb. But hate it as I do, I lick it off and spit it out. My father ties a mitten on my hand. But still I put the gloved thumb in my mouth. And when they tie the mittened hand to my high chair or to my crib, I bang myself with wrathful tears against the bar of the crib or topple my high chair over.

TRIANGLE

My right hand again, usually, though sometimes the left, if for instance I am eating an ice cream cone with the right hand, forms a cup over my vulva. My grandmother calls it holding myself. *Stop holding yourself,* she says.

There is a simple purpose for this act. I do not want to run all the way into the house and then down the long dark hallway to the toilet. I am bargaining for more time. Putting the departure off.

But the hand rests on a triangle of pleasure. As the pressure of warm pee floods this basin, little flurries of delight shoot through me. I am touching myself somehow at the root. I can feel my own aliveness here. It is in this region, midway between my navel and the base of my spine, that my body seems to know endless possibilities. And despite every injury or insult, a sense of humor is softly sequestered in this place. Cupping my hand over this gateway to inner miracles, I discover where laughter and expansiveness reside.

THERE

But of course I cannot be allowed to go on holding myself like this. My grandmother takes me to my room to tell me that I must not put my hand *there,* especially in the company of men. The saturating tone of shame in her voice floods my body almost along the same paths that pleasure has taken. My hand stops making its familiar arc to this once-welcoming place. Instead, there is just the beginning of a movement, a muscle tensing, then still, in the midst of action. The impulse hidden. Eventually even the thought of this movement seems to vanish.

SKIN

In the same room, while I am undressing, my grandmother tells me I must shut the blinds. Otherwise strange men might see me unclothed. This time her voice is edged with a tone that runs through me like a chill. A world of terrors opens up before me, images of girls lured into cars with promises of candy, of a young woman found dead, buried in an unmarked, hidden grave. Religiously, before I take off my clothes to reveal the whiter skin of my small chest, the pink of my pubis with its two almond halves not yet covered with hair, I pull the cords that will shut the blinds.

EYES

My room is at the end of a long hallway facing the back of the house. Its windows look down to our yard and into the back of the neighbor's yard. In the daytime I can see a narrow incinerator, almost the height of a grown man, which stands facing my room. But in the dark a stranger stands there who is turned toward my window.

FEET

The best, of course, is green grass, not freshly cut, but slightly overgrown so it is long enough to lie flat under the foot but not so long as to graze the calves or to have gone to seed, with the soil not wet but holding water, a moisture on the edge of palpable, and preferably shaded, near evening, when the air is still hot but the grass beginning to cool. The feel is slippery and smooth and pliant with that texture of a living thing, as if the very greenness of the grass can enter your skin and nourish your feet. While you stand or walk or run, a high, clear whistle of joy shoots up your legs, and you feel familiar with trees.

For such grass I need no calluses. But freshly cut lawns, the ones that have gotten too dry or yellowed, or the tall grasses gone to seed require them. And for dirt and mud I need them too, because no matter how silty or soft, rocks and pebbles can unexpectedly be found there. The mud is an indescribable pleasure, like chocolate pudding; it spreads in a smooth and clinging embrace over the tops of my feet, in between my toes, around my ankles. And sand has its own mesmerizing charm, covering and falling away, the infinitely small fragments felt together as one choir, yet vaguely perceptible as tiny points of intimacy, a complex and tactile pointillism available with each slight motion, intensely hot, warm or cool, wet and gritty, a vast education in the possibilities of weather coming to me with each step.

THROAT

My grandfather made it, and it smells of wood polish. I never know when it will be, but sometimes the drawers are opened. I am not supposed to open them myself. I have tried, but the drawer I want to open, the one with the family photographs, sticks as I pull at it. I linger near the desk, fingering the brass. My throat is tight. I want to try to break in, but I am afraid I will be caught.

EYELASHES

My mother is a beautiful woman. Her thin eyebrows, the dark line of her lashes, the finely drawn lines of her face, are exquisite. I swim in her beauty, which is like water to me, sometimes dark, sometimes pellucid like crystal.

NAUSEA

Just before I turn six years old I am told there will be a divorce. I'm not certain what this means, but the news makes me feel sick. On my birthday my mother makes Mexican food, which is my favorite. Tacos and enchiladas. But this time I get sick after eating them, and I will not be allowed to eat the offending food again. Whenever I am carsick I make a popping sound with my lips. Concentrating on this music, controlling the rhythm, I can almost block out the sensation altogether.

NAILS

One night when it is still light out and I am supposed to be asleep, I accidentally scratch my fingernails against the wall. It is at this precise moment that I discover a sensation that fills me with dread. Only later will I learn that others too have felt the same.

LIGHT

My grandmother says she has something to show me. I can scarcely believe my eyes. It is like magic. Countless tiny living stars flit through the night air. Little flies bright with light. As I watch I can feel small sparks ignite inside me.

KNEES

Sliding over the ground, I get large and bloody scrapes on both of my knees. I run howling to the principal's office. Then there is the scalding intensity of iodine. A day later the clinging gauze has to be pulled off, though I plead and cry and try to defend myself against it.

FEVER

Hot in my bed, I watch the air start to waver before my eyes, and soon I find myself immersed in a swelling dune of sand. While the dune threatens to engulf me, I engage in a nearly hopeless struggle to escape. But just as I am almost free, another great mound of sand comes washing over me. Then, surrendering but against my will, I become the sand, my body undulating like the Sahara, waves of heat rising as I rise, a motion that seems to be carrying me away even before I can summon a cry of panic.

PAIN

The doctor wants to make a puncture in my finger. He says it will not hurt very much. But I know it will. I hold out my hand. When I feel the prick of his instrument, I am proud that I do not utter a cry. Afterward, as a sign of courage, I have my wound, the blood seeping into the bandage. I accept the grape-colored ball of candy the doctor gives me like a medal.

TONGUE

I am the only one who can do it. Using my tongue, I save the cream in between the two chocolate wafers until the very last, rolling it up in a long cylinder on my tongue, preserving as I go.

ARMS

All of us love to climb. Martha, the girl who lives next door, is better than me at jumping. Whenever the distance seems too far to the ground, I am afraid to jump. But she can jump one story from the balcony at the back of her house to her yard. One day I climb with my grandfather to the top of the garage, where he is fixing the roof. He goes to the yard and, stretching out his arms, tells me to jump. After I have landed, I am happy for weeks.

LEGS

Sitting in the bathtub, I notice my legs. It is as if they have grown overnight. And I am astonished. They are so long. So much like adult legs, real legs. Mine.

SMELL

I do not like the smell. On the nights my mother is drinking and the mornings after, stale ash and spilled beer surround her. And sometimes there is the faint stench of vomit.

FACE

I am standing, small in my powder blue pajamas, in the doorway to my room, the flowered blue wallpaper behind me, looking through the cramped hallway at her. Her lids half closed, she holds a cup filled with rancid coffee brewed hours ago. Bright red lipstick makes a ring on the cup, while silently I take her into myself. I step back into the blue walls and curl my face into the soft surface of my flannel pajamas.

EARS

I like to lie near the waves and hear them as they sigh and roar, close and then far, far and then close, the sun penetrating my body, bright against the sand, the blue of the water deepening as it recedes, turning white where, once I have risen, I place my foot, slapping against my knees, pulling me in, rushing past as I pull my head under the water, the roar in my ears, and then quiet as I swim out, quiet as the dark of the ocean curls over me, and I turn and stretch myself into the path of where it will break, a sound like collapsing wind as it takes me into it, all my body become water and wave, then the roar and the sigh and a shimmering glide to land.

Two

. . . there are temptations, misfortunes and a fatality
in the life of the poor which the rich can never
understand, any more than a blind man can conceive
colors.

GEORGE SAND, *Histoire de ma vie*

MAY

Just beyond your own body you can feel the presence of another body, amorphous but massive as it surrounds you. A body made up of trees and sidewalks and idea, of oceans and the sound of your neighbor's voice, of the taste of strawberries and the memory of the first strawberries you ate, of what your grandmother said to you when you were six years old and what you read in the newspapers this morning. This body presses into you, becomes you.

Sustenance

I have been in Italy for just one week when, together with a group of companions from the writer's retreat where we are staying, we visit two small towns. We drive across a beautiful countryside filled with groves of olive trees, lines of cypress and poplar, occasional stone farmhouses, ocher-colored fields of wheat where the harvested hay lies in huge round wheels, green fields of oats dotted with bright red poppies, floating like small silk parasols in the wind; the roads and hills are lined with ginestra in bloom, an intense lemon yellow that almost glows, and while we drive through small villages, roses of a deep, almost black, burgundy color climb lushly over fences and balustrades.

As the Italian landscape swims by, I am aware that in the decades just before *Camille* appeared, this was the country of dreams, the site for the best and last hopes for revolution. And that the same land inspired another less tumultuous movement. Though this movement transformed the way we see. You can find the bare beginnings of this perceptual change in the paintings Corot did when he was in Italy, those luminous works that preceded and inspired impressionism. In the universe that he painted, a warm light embraces everything as it seems to enter you.

Now near the end of the twentieth century, I find a similar embrace here, and I am even deciphering signs of hope for my own

life. As my companions and I begin to walk through the first village we enter, we are surprised to find the surrounding landscape
repeat itself in patterns that are being carefully laid over the narrow streets. Women kneel on the asphalt delicately filling in outlines drawn in chalk with the petals of flowers. It is a familiar sight
to me. This is the same celebration I witnessed eight years earlier in
Germany in the month I fell seriously ill. The day of Corpus Christi.
But the feeling could not be more different. I walk easily up the
street now; this is a warmer country, even the flowers seem
brighter, more brilliantly colored and somehow hardier. The jubi-
lant patterns bear no resemblance to instruments of torture. There
is an exhilarating chalice that reminds me more of wine and its
soft roll over the tongue than dolorous and bloody tortures. There
are stars made of ginestra floating in seas of fennel, small daisies
assembled into larger daisies against a background of grass cut-
tings, other lush blossoms made from red rose petals, bordered and
filled at the center with coffee ground to that fine soft brown dust
required for espresso. And in the second city we visit, known for its
beautiful, delicately painted ceramics, as we climb the hill to the
Piazza del Consoli, we are obliged to walk around a long, beautifully petaled panel depicting a chalice that looks just like the cones
of delicious gelato which are to be found everywhere.

Ice cream. Flowers. Wine. The communion is sweet. Because these
designs are so different in spirit from the images that startled me in
Germany, I have taken this coincidence as auspicious. I am fashioning a story from this encounter now. Lately, something has begun to
alter in me. I have a new awareness of an exhausting anxiety I
carry with me, as if without continual vigilance I will not survive.
In my private iconography I read these playful designs as a promise
of healing, if not the trouble in my body, at least the distrustful
mood of my soul. I have come to the right place for such a vision.

■   ■   ■

What Alexandre Dumas wrote of Naples is true of all Italy. It is voluptuous. Here even the austerities of Catholicism are over-whelmed by an earlier pagan delight in natural life. On another day of celebration in Gubbio, huge candles, looking more like phalluses than symbols of spiritual ascension, will be carried by teams of men who race up the steep incline of the small green mountain into which the city is nestled.

The countryside still inspires pastoral reveries. The land is such a vivid presence here. In America one thinks of grandeur, but though in the Alps and the Dolomites there is grandeur too, the abiding word here is sensuality. A gentle but persistent sensuality that will slowly but steadily saturate your mood. Subtly seductive, it catches you sleeping, and you wake to an unexpected part of yourself.

A century ago, the sensual pull of this landscape merged with the great desire for democracy sweeping Europe. I can imagine the sensation of it. The wide, enchanting landscape around you, you would feel yourself expand into the warm air, scented with hay and flowers. Immersed in sensation, liberated from the constric-tions of cold weather and the formal manners that signal social position, you would find the words *freedom* and *equality* sliding easily from your tongue.

A few years after Corot brought his luminescent paintings back from Italy, Garibaldi began his struggle to free the country from two forms of tyranny, papal control and the Spanish occupation. In the small towns of Umbria you can always find a street and often a square named after Garibaldi. And through the strange and wind-ing labyrinth of history, Garibaldi, as it turns out, is part of the story that accompanies mine. I found him lurking in the back-ground of *Camille;* he was a friend of the playwright's father. Among those who took up Garibaldi's cause, Dumas *père* spent weeks with the Italian revolutionary in Naples before writing a book titled strangely, as if author and subject had become one, *The Memoirs of Garibaldi.*

More than once Dumas took his son with him on his journeys. But Dumas *fils* would prove to be less interested in the wide brush strokes of history than was his father. He focused on smaller scenes from private life. Instead of charting the rise and fall of nations, kings, or ministers, as his father did, he filled his canvas with the little dramas that occur between men and women, affairs of the heart.

He was not alone in this choice. Swashbuckling novels that rendered sweeping panoramas of society would soon be replaced in the public favor by more intimate fare, the story of one provincial woman, for instance, whose suffocated longings led to her death, as told in *Madame Bovary.* This literary taste was still in style when I came of age. Heroic novels have never been my favorites. Like many women, I am fascinated by private lives, love, intimacy, tempest, and resolution in relationships between lovers, husbands and wives, daughters, sons.

I have not studied the choice until now, when, reading the history more closely, I sense traces of grief in the shift. Is it a coincidence that stories from the private life became more popular just as the grand hope for public redemption through revolution was beginning to sour? I witnessed a similar shift in taste in my own time. In the 1960s, while a hopeful vision of a just society arose again, countless poems and plays concerning politics and public life were written, read, and performed. But after the hope diminished and public life seemed less and less trustworthy, this subject was less in style.

The dream of justice and equality had been failing for decades when Dumas *fils* wrote *La dame aux camélias.* Napoleon, once the greatest democratic hero, ended his reign by crowning himself emperor. And in the end, with each revolution, the poor, who had built the barricades, were always forgotten by the bourgeoisie who used their new liberties to accumulate more and more wealth. Even the small revolution of 1848 concluded with the crowning of still another emperor.

In the beginning, this revolution looked as if it might really help the poor. Louis Philippe fled, and a second republic was declared. A man with high ideals, the romantic poet Lamartine was elected to lead the new democracy. There was good reason for hope. His passion for social justice rivaled the passion of the most ardent lover. Mixing egalitarian and agrarian ideals, he compared his work as a poet to the labor of a peasant. "Every proud man can sell his sweat," he wrote. "I sell my grapes like you sell your flowers!"

Poetry is a good medium for revolutionary hope. A parade of images, the music of the language expressing what is almost evanescent. A sense akin to the bodily sense you have when you are vaguely ill, even if health has always eluded you, that there is another way of feeling. You can feel the possibility of social change in your body. An almost physical longing for a shared life with greater dimensions than your own. Embodied in a poem, the possibility becomes palpable; you can taste the life you desire.

But the public trust would soon be broken again. In the practice of politics, Lamartine was naive. It was his eloquent voice that convinced the National Assembly to give the presidency large powers. "It is in the nature of democracy to find personification in a man," he argued, little realizing that in 1852, the year *La dame aux camélias* opened, the elected president, Louis Napoleon, a dubious nephew of Bonaparte, would use these powers to dissolve the National Assembly and declare *himself* emperor.

■ ■ ■

That the revolution was disappointing did not, however, erase the habit of hope altogether. *La dame aux camélias* does include a kind of utopian vision, though the purview of it is small: one rented house in a village called Bougival, just outside Paris, nestled along the Seine, where for a brief period a man and a woman find happiness in their forbidden love. Believing their love will last forever, despite the seriousness of Marguerite's illness, they live in a medium of hope as thick and as warm as the sunlight of their spring idyll.

The hope you feel when you are in love is not necessarily for anything in particular. Love brings something inside you to life. Perhaps it is just the full dimensionality of your own capacity to feel that returns. In this state you think no impediment can be large enough to interrupt your passion. The feeling spills beyond the object of your love to color the whole world. The mood is not unlike the mood of revolutionaries in the first blush of victory, at the dawn of hope. Anything seems possible. And in the event of failure, it will be this taste of possibility that makes disillusion bitter.

The pastoral setting that sequestered the lovers is no longer so idyllic as it once was. I can imagine what the journey there from Paris would have been like. The presence of the Seine, luminous in the evening light, growing larger, the sounds of the city diminishing, quiet descending as the couple made their way to a safe haven. But the route to Bougival has changed. Between this small settlement and Paris, an eerie city has arisen with faceless buildings made of glass and steel. There are almost no people evident, except in the cars that stream by in a lattice of freeways. Instead, the place looks as if it were inhabited by ghosts of an unpleasant future. It is called La Defense, and the name seems appropriate not only because, lacking any apparent doorways, the buildings appear as if they were uninhabited, but also because they create the illusion of being almost supernaturally invulnerable; they are strange structures, oddly impervious to the ravages of time, aloof from season and siege alike, glacial monuments to order.

After La Defense, the road is lined with the international attributes of any large business center, gas stations and sad-looking modern apartment buildings. If the fresh air there once helped Marguerite Gautier to regain her health, she would not come today for that purpose. A busy highway runs alongside the Seine.

Even so, romance could blossom here today. An important aspect of the idyll remains. If you are Parisian, you can still come here for a brief respite from daily cares. Restaurants near the river serve long lunches during which the pace of city life can be forgotten. Even today the Seine, released from its beautiful architecture, has a stronger presence here than in the city. You will feel it even through a stream of cars if you dine at one of the more modest restaurants across the highway from the river. The continuous flow of the water seems to shape your thoughts.

In America, the birthplace of Thoreau, so many meetings and conferences are held in natural places, in woods, parks, mountains, by lakes, the sea. Perhaps the hope is that such a location will awaken a deeper, more authentic knowledge in the discourse and that, though it is not usually put this way, the knowledge of the body will be awakened. Just as I was beginning to recover from the worst symptoms of illness, I attended a conference held on an idyllic plot of land in the mountains near Santa Barbara. The effect of my stay was stimulating, though it was speech more than the land that roused me. The subject we addressed, all that was said and argued, struck a nerve with me. I made a small descent, revisiting unhealed wounds, and it was here, in this place, that for the first time in years unwittingly my attention would be turned to *Camille*.

■ ■ ■

Whether the setting is rural or urban, in our own age such conferences are probably the closest event we have to the café meetings of the eighteenth and nineteenth centuries, where the ideas of the French Revolution were formulated and discussed. It was in a café at the Palais Royal that Camille Desmoulins gave his famous speech, inciting action. Though in fact a kind of revolution had already occurred in these cafés, way before rebellion reached the streets. To talk, to listen, to be heard, to respond, to question, reflect and criticize. To think as a social body. This is certainly a means to power, but it is also an experience of power.

Among my first cogent memories are those of evenings when three generations of my family would be seated around the table speaking, at times heatedly, about some current controversy. It was as if the meal had another course, one served after dessert, and perhaps with a second cup of coffee, or, on holidays, crème de menthe, and this was conversation. The family was not intellectually accomplished. But we talked with intensity about the larger world around us. Integration. Civil rights. Whether Red China, as we called it then, should be recognized. In this way I learned, among many other things, to place myself in a particular scale relative to political and social events. They were large, larger than myself, larger than my family, but somehow they also fit on our dinner table and miraculously could also exist inside the mouths of my parents, my grandparents, my sister, myself. We were not so much diminished by the grandeur of social events as enlarged by ingesting them. Through our discussions we made the body politic part of ourselves.

The conference I attended was held in Ojai, on land that still belongs to a Native American tribe. For an American, this place has a symbolic significance not unlike the one Europe gave to Italy in the nineteenth century. European settlers imagined that a state of nature existed among Native Americans, who were supposed to be free of cultural constraint. The reverie is built on a prejudice: the failure to recognize that Indians, just like Europeans, have diverse cultural traditions. But there is a seed of truth in the dream. Most Native American cultures did exist in a manner far more harmonious with nature than do European cultures. The difference is not just philosophical. A popular joke among Native Americans suggests that the best way to kill a white man would be to steal his watch, because then, not knowing when to eat, he would starve to death.

Neither democracy nor nature nor the body was irrelevant to the subjects we were discussing at this conference. A group of scientists and social thinkers had been assembled to talk about planetary immunity, including the effect of pollution on human, plant, and animal health. On the first night two scientists, both also practicing doctors, presented their work. One was an American man known for his pioneering work in psychoneuroimmunology. The other was a Russian woman who had been part of a team that had studied the immune system for several years. The evening was revelatory for me. Something I had felt in my body for years was finally being put into words.

What fascinated me most was what the Russian doctor had to say. She had been part of a team of scientists who had observed such a close and interwoven relationship among immunity, the nervous system, and the endocrine system that they had come to think of all three as comprising just one system in the body. This was a description that mirrored my experience as never before. Of course, the merging of these systems can be felt by anyone. But when you are ill, bodily events are magnified. What is subtle and therefore almost imperceptible to a healthy person can take up all your attention then.

The illness I have affects immunity, yet there are many experiences—spasms, pain, memory lapses, even partial paralysis—that are considered symptoms of the nervous system and others that seem to belong to the hormonal system. Unlike many with the same illness, I was never told I was not ill or that "it was all in my head." Yet, though I sensed that most of the minor and serious symptoms I had were connected to one another, no doctor could corroborate this or explain it. I was excited by this new map of the body. In a strange way this knowledge felt like intimacy to me. Finally, in the realm of common understandings, I could know and be known. And with this knowing, a part of myself that had seemed banished, as if to a voiceless limbo, was returned to me.

The mood that night was both confirming and revelatory. It was an anticipatory atmosphere, almost joyful. We knew we were participating in a revolution, a radical change in consciousness. The reigning concept, an idea at least two thousand years old, that body and mind are separate, was being challenged. The scientists here had not been put on the rack, but they were embattled by institutional rigidities and the dogma of old paradigms. Among them, you could feel the pleasure of being in like-minded company. It was cold outside, raining off and on, yet inside the air was crackling with an ephemeral warmth. It seemed almost as if a utopian vision were being born. After millennia of dividedness, the hope was for the mind to be reunited with flesh, and perhaps also, spirit returned to nature.

As with the revolutions of the eighteenth century, the vision had been growing over time. One thinks of Sigmund Freud and his theory that repression causes hysteria. Of Wilhelm Reich observing the body of fascism. Of Isadora Duncan displaying softer, more fluid movements in her dance, forever changing our image of the body. I was a child of this revolution too. But every revolution has its own blind spots, though it is precisely from these that new insights grow. Now, questioning what I believed had become a dogma of alternative medicine, I would shift the direction of the discourse to include what I had learned about the failure of this dogma when I was ill. I was preparing to speak not just as a philosopher but as someone who had recently experienced medicine from the other side, as a patient.

For the ill, the promise of a reconciliation between body and mind in the practice of medicine has more than a philosophical meaning. The hope is not just for the healing of the body but for an empathetic understanding. To be seen. To be known. The sufferings of the body, as hard as they are to describe, make for epic experiences. Shaken, left without any way to articulate the nightmare, and therefore isolated not only by bodily trauma but by its incommunicability, I have felt an overriding desire for recognition.

But though the new psychosomatic approach has yielded insight and healing, it also has had the opposite effect. Instead of weaving mind and body together, the approach has been used to deny illness and even the force of physical experience. There are many reasons for this denial, among them, the weight of a culture that for millennia has been eager to claim ascendancy over earthly existence. Even when asserting the connectedness of mind and body, the tendency always is to drift away from the potency of material life toward a belief in the power of the spiritual, the psychological, the mental. Mind over matter is the strategy. It is one that, even if only through denial, can give remarkable hope to some patients. But for others the effect is cruel. Repeatedly, the psychosomatic understanding of illness has been used to blame the ill for their suffering. As Susan Sontag writes, "Patients who have unwittingly caused their disease are also being made to feel that they have deserved it."

The cruelty is not intended. The motive is more often fear. Even witnessing serious illness in another can assault your belief that you are a stationary substance, stable as granite, and, like stone, bound to last at least several centuries. I have experienced the fear myself. Hearing of the serious illness or impending death of a friend, soon after recovering from the first round of shock and grief, I have found my hands reach for my own body, almost to prove that I am still here. Then, as mortality wags its bleak head, I have watched my mind begin a dance of denial. Why did he or she get sick? One smoked, the other ate terrible food, one had too much anger, the other was mired in some negative pattern, still another repressed her feelings, and so on. Reasonable or not, the question is meant to distance oneself from a similar fate. It is an effort at distance those who are ill can feel. On the other side of the divide between illness and health, you will feel suddenly like an outsider.

In the first decade after CFIDS was identified, a prejudicial and nearly tautological reasoning was applied to the illness, as if its existence could be explained away. The medical establishment drew a profile of the person most likely to come down with the disease. A mature woman, professional, upper middle class, white, and overly ambitious, she did not know how to rest, and this is why she was fatigued. The description recalls those tracts from nineteenth-century medicine warning that higher education could damage a woman's ovaries. Both theories have a subtext, the idea that women ought to stay at home. And I can hear another suggestion in the thought, the subtle warning that feminism undermines the feminine body.

The image of CFIDS as a white middle class woman's disease is hard to live down. It lingers in the public mind, so that people are still surprised to learn that there are children, African American, Hispanic, Asian men and women of all classes and ages who have the disease. The profile turns out to be wrong. The error occurred because of the way the statistics were gathered. Doctors were asked to report the number of patients they had diagnosed with CFIDS. Yet such a diagnosis is available only to those with the financial means to pay for a battery of tests or, encountering the earlier bias of the medical establishment, to go from doctor to doctor, searching for one who accepts the reality of the illness.

But the story takes an even grimmer turn. Instead of searching for a virus, supporting extensive laboratory tests, or even conducting epidemiological studies aimed at finding environmental triggers, the National Institutes of Health focused on a single study, one that searched for psychological causes. Stephen Straus, who initiated the study, announced its results to the media. His data showed, he claimed, that a large number of patients with CFIDS he studied had some history of mental disturbance. His statements made an indelible impression in the press. Even today, after clear and ample evidence of the physical etiology of the illness, every once in a while a celebrity doctor still appears on my local television station and, with his boyish good looks and charming manner, casually tells his audience that the disease I have is largely the effect of neurosis.

Yet just like the profile, the study too was wrong. Violating the most basic procedure of statistical science, Straus had used no control group. When another statistician supplied one, comparing the study of Straus's patients to a corresponding group without the illness, he found the rate of mental illness in both groups to be the same.

It is difficult to describe the effect of being told you are not really ill when you are. The disjuncture between private experience and public image is so severe, you can easily become obsessed with establishing the truth. The degree of discomfort felt so intensely in body and soul at such a fracture could itself be a subject for psychosomatic medicine. As certainly as a kind of epiphany is achieved with naming, a shock of recognition that can be physically felt, so also an equally intense and negative shock is experienced with misnaming. It is a sinking feeling, something like missing a train for a journey that is not at all casual. You are left hanging. Disoriented.

Strangely lonely. Though this will not be a peaceful solitude. You will be followed into your privacy by phantoms of rejection and even ridicule for what your body continues to know. The sound of these phantoms may be inaudible, but it will be distracting enough to erase your own voice, to quell any attempt to articulate even for yourself what it is you experience. And this is a serious loss because it is this voice, the intelligent and observing companion to feeling, that dignifies even the worst misery.

The next morning at the conference I spoke from my own experience. Describing the atmosphere of blame that is inseparable from the current practice of psychosomatic medicine, I pointed out the paralyzing effect this approach has on the politics of ecology. By analyzing each incidence of illness as a separate occurrence, whose etiology exists only in individual minds and bodies, patterns of circumstance, especially environmental causes such as pollution or low-level radiation, have been obscured. Indeed, more than once when a community has alerted the government or a corporation to a pattern of ecological damage that endangers the health of its citizens, the official response has been to accuse the community of hysteria. "It's all in your mind," the residents of Love Canal, downwinders, the veterans of Vietnam exposed to Agent Orange, and soldiers suffering from Gulf War Syndrome were told.

The irony is that though a psychosomatic approach to medicine has the potential to heal not only individual illness but, in its wider implications, our shared alienation from nature, the denial that commonly infuses this perspective blends almost imperceptibly with another unconscious belief, the illusory sense that human beings are neither dependent on nor really part of life on earth. But we are part of the earth, and the effects of ecological damage can be seen in the human body.

While I suffered the derangement of various systems in my body, I began to think of myself as a canary in the mine. The phrase, which has become popular among the afflicted, refers to the way in which the safety of the air in mines was tested in the last century. A canary in a cage would be lowered into the shaft and then, after a time, pulled up again. If the bird looked alive and relatively healthy, the air in the mines was judged safe enough for the miners to breathe. I felt as if the destruction of the environment were occurring in my own cells. And from this feeling over time a question formed, not just in my mind, but in my body too. It is a question I still ask. The appearance of AIDS, CFIDS, the epidemic proportions of cancer, the rapid increase of the incidence of numerous other diseases affecting immunity, MS, lupus, point to a larger cause. Is environmental pollution irreversibly damaging the human immune system?

The strongest realization I had of this danger came to me in a dream. While I was still in Germany, just after my collapse, the newspapers were preoccupied with a mysterious illness that was killing seals in the North Sea. Their bodies, lifeless or nearly dead, were washing up by the hundreds on the beaches of northern Europe. The papers suggested that something was injuring the immune systems of these animals. One photograph run on the front page of a German newspaper showed a pile of dead seals, just at the edge of the sea, rising higher than six feet. It must have been the night after I saw the photograph that I dreamed I was on a beach. In their swimsuits, wearing sunglasses and cotton hats, children beside them digging sand with small shovels, several bathers lay on blankets, taking in the sun. They acted as if they were completely unaware of the dead animals all around them. In my dream, I was the only witness. Standing in front of the stacked-up bodies of seals, I began to plead with them. *Don't you know,* I called out to them, *unless you do something now, what is happening to these seals will happen to you too.*

Now, the dream was repeating itself in another form. The original purpose of the conference was to explore the relationship

between the disturbance of ecological systems and the degradation
of immunity in animals and plants. But already on the second day
of the conference we had lost sight of the fearsome design that
these events taken together seemed to reveal. No one had spoken
about it yet.

In a sense, I had been looking forward to the conference for
validation of what I knew in my own body. I spoke with hope and
anger. I was angry because the ill had been stigmatized. Yet I also
hoped that the dividedness between the sick and the well would
dissolve among us. But I myself was making a division as I spoke.

With my speech, the political tide in the room changed. There
was applause and excitement. Now the revolutionary flag was in the
hands of the patients. But before the group could stop applauding,
the American doctor began a question. It was a long one that started
as interrogatory, went still further in the direction of interrogation,
and eventually rolled on into an extensive diatribe against everything he thought I had said. His monologue, spiked with a slightly
sarcastic but authoritative tone, continued at considerable length
until I interrupted him.

We argued with the intensity of different factions in a political
body when survival is at stake. I am not certain what fueled his
anger. Years of having to defend his work against the formidably
entrenched idea of body and mind as divided lay in the balance for
him, as well as his own physical illness, which he kept hidden and I
learned of only later, a condition that he had to some degree
helped to heal with a psychosomatic approach. For my part, I did
not reveal the way the argument touched on my own survival. It
was, to put it simply, an economic question for me. In the bureau-
cracies of public health, the word *psychosomatic* is often read as
meaning "illusory" or "nonexistent." If the illness I had remained
in this diagnostic category, in the event I might need to seek public
assistance or medical aid, my petition would fall into a void. In this
light, the insistence on the primacy of the psyche seemed like a

Brahmin philosophy to me, the kind of idealism that is easy to believe in when the material needs of your life are well met.

The prodigious onslaught of words between us continued, bearing all the drama of a congress or assembly convened to decide who would rule or what laws would be enacted. But of course, none of us present had any such power. We were all equally powerless against the two tragedies we had met to confront, the increase of illness among our own kind and the increase of disease in the creatures, the trees, the life around us.

As we argued back and forth like stubborn dogs hanging onto the bare bones of ideas, we were scarcely aware any longer of the others in the room or of the way the mountains cradled the plateau on which our encampment rested. I had become engaged on another level of my psyche, insulted, defensive, proving my worth. In the course of our conflict, several remarks that the doctor made infuriated me. But one in particular stung my pride. I could hardly forgive him for making it. He referred to a story I had not thought about in years. The ill, he pointed out, are not always stigmatized. They are also celebrated and sentimentalized. "Think of *Camille,*" he said.

I was stunned. For the first time in the afternoon, I could not respond to his remark. I took it into an inner region where it sounded the depths of an old reproach. Here she was staring me in the face, the melodramatic Camille. A mocking reference to this heroine had continued even into my daughter's generation. Whenever she was very upset, my daughter would be called Sarah Heartburn by her father's parents. In her grandparents' childhood, the name of Sarah Bernhardt had become practically synonymous with the role she played in *Camille*.

I can't recall having been called Camille by my mother or my grandparents, though the accusation was in the air. I had a flair for the dramatic. My chief talent was rhetorical. Going to sleep, I would compose what I thought to be moving speeches on my own behalf or in the defense of a larger cause. I was helped along in this tendency. At an early age my grandmother used to read me poetry. Her favorite recitation, and mine too for a while, was "The Highwayman," a lushly romantic ballad about a doomed affair between a passionate young woman with a long black braid and an athletically inclined robber who would climb in her window. My grandmother studied drama before she was married. She wanted to be an actor, but her father would not allow her to go with the traveling troupe that invited her to join them. Even so, she did amateur acting. And she struck poses at home, sometimes in fun and sometimes in all seriousness. I still have photographs of her, with her chin up high and her eyes cast toward heaven, in which she bears a remarkable resemblance to Bernhardt as she posed for Nadar in her great role as Phaedre.

There is no clear demarcation between acting and life. A friend who is an actor once reported to me that the spiritual teacher Muktananda loved actors because he felt that they understand that everyone is always to some degree playing a role. As I get older and learn better how to be amused at myself, I see the wisdom of this insight. Indeed, a kind of theater proceeded at the conference in the southern California mountains. There were even sets and costumes. We met in large tents resembling Indian tepees. There were all sorts of drums and feathers among the props, some clothing evoking Native American traditions, and other outfits inspired by Buddhism, a kind of modified monk's apparel, a blend of St. Francis and the studied minimalism of Japan. Even the learned doctors were playing the role of experts. And for my part, the fact that my illness was real—I was constantly in pain, having to shift my weight or lie closer to the floor to recover my strength—did not stop me from being aware of a certain image of courage through adversity that I might be projecting.

■ ■ ■

But I was not ready yet to laugh at myself. Even after I returned home from the conference, I continued to argue with the doctor, scribbling pages and pages of a letter I never sent to him. Yet as I wrote, another mood began to take hold of me. Exploring what I could remember of *Camille,* I began to sense how, in many uncanny ways, this tale echoed my own. If a story is good enough, everyone will see their own lives reflected in it. But the resonance between this story and mine began to haunt me. The threat of financial ruin. The shame of Camille's profession, the stigma of her disease. That she was abandoned as she grew more ill. As I thought about the concordance of our tales, I could sense a promise of something greater in the mix.

Since seeing the film as a child, I had always thought of *Camille* as just a romantic story. But now that impression was changing. Alongside the love story lay another theme, I was beginning to discover, a veritable discourse on the private life of nineteenth-century capitalism. In this narrative, as in my own life, pain and pleasure, illness and sexuality intersect continually with the realities of money and class. Dumas *fils* had restricted his canvas to intimate scenes, but within these scenes he also depicted a larger social drama.

Over the next several years I began to piece together a larger picture of my own. I wanted to know more about the playwright and how the story came to be written. Then once I learned that it was based on an affair Dumas *fils* had with a real woman, I wanted to learn everything I could about her. And finally as I entered these lives, I was drawn into the period in which they lived. Did I sense then that it would be there, in the history of events that occurred a hundred years before my birth, that I might discover a larger meaning in my own story?

Behind every great legend there are countless other stories to be found. There is, for instance, the medical history of tuberculosis. Dumas *fils* wrote his play thirty years before the discovery of the

bacillus that causes the disease. Robert Koch, the man who discovered the germ, would only publish his famous essay, *The Etiology
of Tuberculosis,* in 1882. Before that date, the disease that killed
Marie Duplessis was considered to be fundamentally a spiritual
malaise. As late as 1881, the year before the bacillus was discovered, an important medical textbook listed depressed emotions as a
major cause of tuberculosis.

Not just the medical profession, but priests, social commenta-
tors, novelists agreed that the disease mirrored the soul. Though
what was reflected in this mirror was not always the same; the
tenor and tone of the diagnosis were determined by social position.
In those who were in the upper classes, aristocrats, or rising bourgeoisie, professional men, or occasionally women who turned to
the arts, tuberculosis was interpreted as a sign of a highly sensitive
nature. One who had the disease might be considered high-strung
or delicate, an aesthete or even a genius. The portrait was so flat-
tering that to be pale or very thin in body or flushed, all symptoms
of the illness, became highly fashionable.

The profile of the tubercular soul among the poor, however, was
not so sanguine. In the indigent or working-class man or woman,
TB was taken as a sign of lust and depravity. "Of all the vices . . . ,"
a medical text written just six years after Duplessis's death reads,
"none are so apt to lead to consumption as the unnatural or unre-
strained indulgence of the sensual passions." In still other treatises,
the cause of the disease among the poor, who were more often
afflicted than the rich, was simply linked to poverty itself. In the
nineteenth century poverty was already regarded as a form of spiritual malaise. The poor were poor because they drank too much or
indulged in promiscuous sex or were lazy, shiftless, thieving. And
it was the same moral failures, especially lust, that according to
this argument made the poor more susceptible to illness. Falling in
between the rich and the poor, Marie Duplessis was seen as both
sinful and sensitive.

. . .

The coupling of sin and disease has almost always had a sexual tinge. This can be seen most clearly with sexual diseases such as syphilis or AIDS. Whenever illness settles in or near the sexual organs, disapprobation increases accordingly. As nasty as the moralizing could be about tuberculosis, the intonation reached a far higher pitch as illness moved from lungs to pubis. In 1629, for instance, Jean Baptiste Lilli wrote of syphilis that "the searing droplets of this cruel disease fall on those who are hot with passion and dirtied with lust; it is a punishment ... for their shameful desires." The viciousness of style had not lessened in the nineteenth century when Pope Leo XII forbade the use of condoms because they might prevent sexual contagion and thus interfere with God's efforts to punish sinners by "striking them in the member" that sinned. And though the attitude had softened by Mother Teresa's time, she did instruct her staff to withhold pain medication from men dying of AIDS so that through suffering they might repent.

The attitude is not confined to the Catholic church nor even to traditional religions. Several years ago I attended a conference at a center of new age spirituality in Scotland. On my arrival, a friend who had been studying there took me aside to tell me about an incident that disturbed her. One of the founders of the center, claiming to have received a message from nature spirits, had warned the community that AIDS is a punishment for amoral behavior.

A punitive attitude toward the ill runs through much of our common history. Even in the scientific annals of diagnosis and blame, where no clear cause can be found, sexual transgression is often named as the source of disease. In the West an antagonism toward sexual pleasure might explain this. But the connection between sexuality and disease has a more obsessive quality, as if it were not just a religious doctrine but also the tenet of a common madness, an unexamined nightmare at the edge of shared consciousness.

■   ■   ■

In the more shadowy labyrinths of our culture, sin and sexuality
are often symbolized by a woman's body. The archetype can impair
perception. When I was ill in Germany, I saw a documentary drama
based on the life of the nineteenth-century doctor Ignaz Philipp
Semmelweis, who discovered the true causes of septicemia in child-
birth. Semmelweis noticed that women giving birth in teaching
hospitals had a far higher rate of childbed fever than the wealthier
women who gave birth at home. When Semmelweis confronted the
director of the hospital with his observations, the older man replied
that the women in his hospital contracted the fever more frequently because they felt guilty. Just as today, these were the hospitals
where the poor sought care; many of the women who gave birth
there were unmarried; others were prostitutes. It was immoral
behavior that made them sick, the director argued. But, as we know
now, what Semmelweis suspected was true. Because these were
teaching hospitals, doctors who had just finished dissecting corpses
in anatomy classes would rush into surgery to deliver babies, carrying disease on their hands.

I too have experienced the shame that exists at the nexus between
a woman's body, sexuality, and sin. Over a number of years I have
had several bouts with an illness known as pelvic inflammatory
disease. Because it is a disease that can be sexually transmitted and
that infects the sexual organs, it is difficult to write about even
here. No one doubts its gravity. This is a serious infection, which as
it spreads from uterus and ovaries upward can cause death from
peritonitis or blood poisoning. But because it is associated with
sexuality, the diagnosis carries with it an element of shame. It is
rarely spoken of in what my grandmother would have called mixed
company. One bout occurred two years before I was diagnosed with
CFIDS. But though not yet diagnosed, I was already having symptoms of CFIDS then. One doctor has suggested that the impairment

to my immune system made it difficult for me to resist infection. I know that, in the way ill health has of spiraling downward, one illness aggravating another, the infection worsened the state of my immune system. I nearly died. For several days I had a high fever and intense pain. I was hospitalized twice, once with an IV for antibiotics and later for exploratory surgery. The infection eventually spread into my kidney and liver, causing damage from which I have never fully recovered. And yet, as troubling and definitive as this experience was in my life, until now as I write, except among close women friends, it has still been difficult for me to speak about it openly.

When I was young I thought I had escaped the shadow of sexual shame, a shadow that settles more on women than on men. I came of age just when the double standard of sexual behavior was beginning to shift. My generation shared a utopian dream of still another kind, the hope for a sexual freedom. I had my first lover at the age of fifteen. I was not seduced unwillingly. Though I knew he loved me, it was I who led my lover into the bedroom. My friends and I dismissed the idea of virginity. We decided we did not want it. We modeled ourselves after artists and writers and certain rebellious women who were film stars. From my grandmother's old hats, I had preserved a woman's black fedora. I wore it with the brim turned down over one side of my face like Marlene Dietrich or Greta Garbo did. Like them, I also had a dark trench coat, and to combat fair hair and blue eyes, which made me seem terribly innocent, I developed the habit of swearing.

This was not difficult. Since my earliest years, I had heard this language in the bars my mother habituated. Yet though my mother could swear herself and be frank, she was never crude. On her part, I know she would have preferred the life of French cafés to the one she lived. Once she even told me that this was the life she was living. But, sadly, we both knew it wasn't true. American bars are dark with an air more of degradation than decadence. This is as much the other side of a puritan past as is drunkenness.

I was drinking the night I decided to take a lover. Jacob had written me poems that I liked. It was late on a Saturday night at the end of one of many parties I held when my father was away at his girlfriend's house. Jacob and a friend of his were the last ones there, so in a grand gesture I invited them both to bed. Since all of us were virgins, none of us did anything except to sleep in one another's arms. But the next day Jacob came over with a passion-flower he had found growing in his neighborhood. And then we made love. What I remember most is how beautiful his body was, which I would not have guessed when he was dressed. The sad part of this time in my life is that because I was living alone with my father, who was gone so often at the firehouse or staying with his girlfriend, I was often frightened and lonely at night. Still, I look back on that period as graced with a feeling I would like to have now. I do not particularly long to take casual lovers or stay up late drinking and partying. It is instead a style I miss, linked less with behavior than with courage. Though this is probably connected with carelessness too and naïveté and youth.

As I read about the courtesans of the nineteenth century, I realize that, though I knew almost nothing of their history when I was young, I inherited a certain bravado from these women. A lineage of sexual freedom and independence stretches from Marie Duplessis, Lola Montez, Anna Deslions, Cora Pearl, Paiva, Alice Ozy—to name just a few of the more famous courtesans—into the twentieth century. It winds through the celebrity of Garbo and Dietrich, only to turn up later in the lives of actresses who were famous when I was a child, Elizabeth Taylor, for instance, or Ingrid Bergman, who, despite public disapproval, led less fettered lives, passing the lineage of their freedom on to me.

But though I was more free than my mother had been, my liberation was far from complete. Like the French Revolution, the sexual revolution was shaped along traditional lines. The double standard was alive and well at the end of it. Just as the French Revolution ultimately served one class at the expense of another, regarding both freedom and pleasure, the sexual revolution served men more than women. And this revolution was orthodox in another way too: the fear of homosexuality remained unquestioned.

In my circle of friends, mostly radicals and artists, homosexuality was still the object of nervous laughter. I told very few people that my sister was a lesbian. Then, when I turned twenty-two, a year before I married, I fell intensely in love with a woman my age. Yet though we were living together, no one knew that we were lovers. And, as if confiding to my sister would seal me into an island of shame, I did not even tell her that I had made love to a woman. But I could not prevent isolation so easily. As the story of this love affair disappeared into silence, something of myself vanished for a while.

The most shameful secrets are almost always about the body. And that the cost of keeping them is great can be taken as evidence of a strong desire in the body for the truth to be told. I have often envied Catholics for the rite of confession. What a brilliant solution the church chose! Because every story can be told there, even shameful experience is saved from the mute voids of denial. And yet in the process the experience is changed, while each story is shaped by the priest, who listens, according to a doctrine that casts the tale, even as it is spoken, into a moral fable whose telling seals redemption.

Thinking now of all the popular stories about illness that are shaped to a subtle moral—the one who is ill, for instance, learning to be a better person because of illness or grateful to have been ill because through it the spirit grew stronger—I am beginning to think that this perspective serves the same purpose. Through this frame, the shameful experience of illness is made more acceptable.

Almost any story can be redeemed by the way it is told. Nineteenth-century French literature is replete with stories about courtesans, tales that are preserved in the acceptable gel of morality. Zola's famous *Nana,* Balzac's *The Splendour and Misery of the Courtesan,* Edmond de Goncourt's *La fille Elisa,* to name a few, all have a courtesan at the center. But in these novels, the heroines, gloriously entertaining as they are, come to grief in the end.

Camille is no exception. The story brings the shameful topics of sexuality and disease into one redemptive plot. The novel, which was written first, is more firmly shaped along the outlines of a moral judgment than is the play. The first scene reminds me of a memento mori or a tempis fugit, one of those medieval still lives, drawn as if by the hand of God, cautioning us that all our earthly pleasures will dissolve to dust. First we see the sale of all Marguerite Gautier's treasures, the worldly goods she had sold her body to acquire. And soon after, the narrative takes us to a cemetery where the body of the heroine is exhumed. "The eyes were simply two holes, the lips had gone, and the white teeth were clenched. The long, dry, black hair was stuck over the temples and partly veiled the green hollows of the cheeks and yet in this face I recognized the pink and white, vivacious face I had seen so often."

The sight is suitably chastening. Following the disinterment of his lover's corpse, Armand falls prey to a mysterious but dangerous fever. The fever purges him of his passion, itself portrayed as a kind of disease. And then, as the last stage of his healing, he makes a confession, telling the story of his love affair with the lady of camellias. His story ends in a purification, which mirrors his lover's death, an ordeal that cleansed her of all her sins.

■ ■ ■

Purification was essential to the form. Tuberculosis was so rampant then, it was a popular subject of fiction. Most novelists rendered the disease according to the same profile. In their otherwise naturalistic novel about tuberculosis, *Soeur Philomene*, the Goncourt brothers describe a tubercular death as creating a "state of elevation, tenderness and love . . . a . . . sublimity which seems almost not to be of this earth." And Dickens too, in *Nicholas Nickelby,* speaks of the dread disease as preparing its "victim . . . for death . . ." by, he writes, refining away "the grosser aspect." It was not just a literary convention but a common belief that in the course of the disease, with the wasting of flesh, the spirit of the stricken would grow more pure.

The romantic image would soon change. When the bacillus that causes TB was discovered, what was taken to be a spiritual experience suddenly became more earthy. But the fear of contagion created still another kind of shame. The shame that comes from contagion. Recently a friend told me that when her father was diagnosed with TB, her mother was counseled to keep the name of the disease secret. She kept the secret too, in her own way. Though I have known her since we were at the university together, this was the first time I had heard that her father had this illness. As a girl, I played with a friend next door whose grandmother lived with her. She had TB. My grandmother told me to keep my distance. But the warning, like warnings she gave me about strange men and offers of candy, was whispered in the back room of our house.

My grandmother's voice carried more than the simple worry about infection in it. The attitude was not just hers. Scientific knowledge failed to cleanse the tone of tawdriness the disease carried. Even the sanatoria created to care for patients with TB maintained the same tone. They were notoriously regimental places, with rules to govern every aspect and moment of day and night, as if their inmates were given to misbehavior and had to be strictly governed, if not punished.

But though TB was especially reprehensible to her, I sensed from my grandmother that she felt all illness was bad behavior. I have not escaped the feeling. Whenever I am in pain of any kind, whether consciously or not, the thought almost always occurs to me that I am being punished. I do not always know what I did wrong. Perhaps I deviated from my diet of healthy foods or exercised too much or too little or misbehaved more boldly, drinking a glass of wine, staying up late. On a deeper level of mind, I struggle to resist the feeling that it is through some serious flaw in my character that I have not suc-ceeded in being well. And, by an equally unspoken but insidious chemistry, the shame at having failed, augmented by the misery of my body, mixes with every other form of shame or embarrassment I have ever felt. Every mistake I have ever made, my unruliness as a child, that I have made love to women, and, potent in the mix, something else, which I could not have named as clearly before my research into the background of Camille, a shame that was more openly invoked in the nineteenth century, though it is still with us now, the embarrassment that comes from a financial crisis of any kind.

The experience of economic failure is not unlike illness. You will feel yourself weakened by it. And as your monetary strength diminishes, you will also feel a shame similar to the one you feel when you are ill. Even as I write now, I feel an odd reticence to describe my economic situation. Along with illness, money was once prominent among topics banned from conversation in polite society. Though writers of the late nineteenth century—Dickens, Sand, Balzac, Zola, Hugo—introduced realistic portraits of poverty into literature, allowing the shadow of the subject to cross into the drawing room, even now, those who prosper generally prefer to exclude the subject of money from their thoughts.

Excepting doctor bills, medical practice is silent on the subject of money. I felt this silence myself. Because the illness I have requires long bed rest, doctors, medical advisers, counselors, even authors of advice columns all suggest that it is crucial to avoid stress. You are counseled to accept the new limitations and slow down. But the prescription is generally given as if everyone had the means to work at a slower pace or take several months off to recuperate. And rarely does a doctor ask if you can afford to pay for the domestic care you will need if you are alone.

Very soon after I returned from Germany, I began to worry about money. I belong to a strange class. Writers and artists float in our own world of finance. Like the inhabitants of the demimonde in nineteenth-century Paris, an artist exists between one class and another. One night you may be entertained at the governor's palace in Hanover, another night be driven by limousine through the streets of mid-Manhattan, one evening drink Dom Perignon from hand-cut crystal and then return, as if by a coach that collapses with the harsh light of day, to a stack of unpaid bills, a menacing mortgage, the grueling anxiety of ends that never meet.

Once I was unable to work any longer, my financial situation verged on disaster. Like many others with my line of work, because I have no employer except myself, I lack what is called in contemporary America benefits. When I fell seriously ill in Germany, I was insured through a loosely associated group of therapists and free-lance teachers. Just before I left for Germany, I had applied for disability insurance, but because of the times I was hospitalized, I was denied coverage.

This was the first time I had tried to buy such insurance. Though I might have thought of it sooner. During the five years that preceded my disablement, my financial resources were stretched to the breaking point. I had bought a new house; it needed repairs, and I needed furniture and bookshelves for my books; the taxes and insurance were high. My daughter was still in high school. The book I was writing, which was about, among other things, the history of nuclear weapons, did not earn me a high advance. And probably because I was writing in an unconventional way about things not usually connected, I had trouble raising money from foundations for the writing. I took on lots of small jobs—editing manuscripts, tutoring beginning writers, lecturing and teaching workshops at universities, contributing to anthologies and magazines when and where there was money to be had.

I knew the money was thin and worried about the unforeseen possibilities that plague most people—my car breaking down, the roof needing repair. And how would I be able to put my daughter through college? But despite my constant exhaustion, I did not often put into words the fear that my body would break down, that I would be unable to go on working. Not only were there too many demands, the work on my book required that I travel thousands of miles for research, when even local trips were tiring to me. Looking back now, I can remember calling a man who lived across the bay to ask if I could interview him. When he said yes I was both exultant and apprehensive. The worry I had was not about how I would conduct the interview but if my strength would hold up long enough for me to drive across the bridge, engage in a long afternoon of work, and then drive back.

When I was very tired, I could hear that voice inside me saying, *I can't go on.* But as soon as I climbed out of the latest well of fatigue, I ignored the message. Because I could not afford to listen to my fears, I did not want to dwell on the thought, and this was made easier because, in the solitude of my work, no one was present to witness the many small collapses I experienced.

Writing has both the virtue and the burden of independence. You have no boss to speak of, but you can be lonely in that freedom, especially when fears arise. A certain bravado is necessary, especially in American culture, which regards the actual work of art with a jaundiced eye, as a frivolous labor that at best should be only vaguely supported. Because of this, leading the life of a writer, I have often felt as if I were getting away with something, not a crime exactly, but a transgression. And as with any caper, the thrill of pulling it off has been shadowed with an uneasiness. When and how will I be caught? Somehow I expected to be punished for my choice. An expectation that no doubt folded into my shame at being ill and strapped for money.

And there is this too: when security is not possible, you train yourself not to let your thoughts wander toward thoughts of peril. In this, the writer or the artist may seem closer to the lower than the upper classes. Two years after Alexandre Dumas *père* built his grand château in Marly (not far from Bougival), he had to sell it to pay off his debts. An investment he had made in a theater that was producing his plays failed badly. Bernhardt too regularly lost great fortunes. Her repeated tours of America were made to recoup her losses. It is interesting now to think that the fame of *La dame aux camélias* in America, and perhaps even my own early knowledge of *Camille,* is indebted to these swings of fortune.

Tradition and habit can mute awareness. Like the tiredness that quietly began to take over my body, my constant financial precariousness caught my attention only when I seemed just about to fall over the edge. In those days, though my income was small, no one would call me poor. I traveled, ate well, dressed well enough. But in the months just before I left for Germany, my knowledge of my vulnerability must have sharpened. Was it that my body did not seem as resilient? I seemed never to return to what I used to call normal. Or was it because, with a new diagnosis, I was beginning to understand how likely it was that I would not be well in just a few weeks, or a few months, that I applied for disability insurance?

Later I was to learn that in the scant studies that have been done of CFIDS, it appeared that only about a third of those who are ill recover completely, and these are for the most part people who have had the illness for just a short period. Those, like me, who have had the illness over several years have a very low chance of complete recovery. Though I have never given up the hope that I might be among the rare few to recover completely, the evidence of days and weeks, of months and years of repeated illness, weighed heavily on me then. I felt relieved to write two checks to cover the possibility that my health might decline still further.

It was not until I returned from Germany that I learned my application for insurance had been denied. The knowledge came in the midst of a nightmare of confluent insolvencies, disappointments, and defeats. The first, of course, was the insolvency of my own body. But this weakness seemed to ooze out into the world around me, rendering all my life chaotic. When the body is weary, even the simplest job seems formidable. The thought of answering my mail, for example, seemed impossible. And even more overwhelming was the task of paying bills. Never mind whether or not I had sufficient funds for next few months, how was I going to open the envelopes, write the checks, subtract the appropriate figures from my balance? It was not just that the fatigue I felt made such a chore seem gargantuan, it was also that my mind had lost the deft linearity necessary for such calculations. I had never hired an accountant, but now I had no choice. I paid a young woman who had occasionally assisted me with correspondence to handle my bills. But given my disability and my dwindling resources, her bill seemed staggering.

And there was still one more blow to my sense of viability. In a terrible moment of bad timing, within the first weeks that I was bedridden, the monthly payments for my medical insurance had nearly tripled. But the old adage is still true, the rich get richer and the poor get poorer. Though my need for a lower rate was far greater than ever before, in the tortuous logic of the current medical economy, because I was ill, and hence had a pre-existing condition, I could not seek another insurance company with more competitive rates.

Money operates in the world much like physical energy does in a body. The lack of it undermines every aspect of existence. Now every structure of my life around me seemed to be collapsing. Even the meeting of my most basic needs seemed tenuous. Because I could not afford to pay for the preparation of my meals, one friend had patiently called women and men in our community, arranging dates and times for meals to be brought to me for a month. But at the end of that time I had no one to arrange a new schedule. Friends had to be called. Yet I was wary of calling. When you are forced to ask and ask again for help, the delicate balance of give-and-take among friends can be disturbed. Fearing I would put my friends on the spot, I did not want to make the calls myself. But when I paid the same assistant to arrange a new schedule of care, she performed the task perfunctorily and unsuccessfully. And given her bill, I knew I could not afford to hire her, or anyone else, again. Eventually a friend was found who could arrange a new schedule; in the meantime, I was caught between a Scylla and Charybdis of my imagination, the idea of going without care or losing my friends, and this was where my panic usually began.

At the turn of the century, almost four decades after the death of the courtesan Marie Duplessis, the author Charles Péguy wrote that "short of genius, a rich man cannot imagine poverty." He was not thinking of the capacity to imagine the conditions of poverty, many of which, in his time, were plain to the public eye. Nor, as I read his words now, do I think he meant to say that the rich never have to endure physical hardship. Then, as now, a young scion of wealth or a rising professional, like Dumas *père* had once been,

would sometimes experience a temporary period of relative simplicity, during student days or a voluntary bohemianism. For a period,
Alexandre Dumas, the father of Dumas *fils*, lived in a very humble
apartment, but soon he moved to wider worlds. In order to know
poverty, you must understand it as an impassable boundary.

From the time that I was a single mother, working two or three
jobs, renting rooms in my house, using food stamps, I thought I
had some idea of what it is to be poor. But I had not grasped the
heart of the circumstance. Exhausted by too much work and the
intensity of the changes taking place in my life, I had more than
one moment of fear that I would not be able to make my way and
provide for my daughter. Yet fear did not predominate. It would be
only later in my life, and because I was so ill, that a raw terror of
an economic collapse would come to me, one from which I have
still not entirely recovered.

As each day passed and I did not regain the strength to work,
and as I watched the date of reckoning grow closer, terror worked
its way into every moment. It would not leave me. Waking with me
at three in the morning, casting a cold shadow over the first morning light, intractable in the slow stretch of midafternoon. If it came
to it, all my resources spent, what would I do?

A door into the quagmire of public assistance, which had once
opened slightly, now stood ajar. I knew from receiving food stamps
that the story bureaucracy requires you to tell has to be fiction.
You have to have a place to live and yet be earning an income too
low to afford rent or utilities or any reasonable expense, bus fare,
or, God forbid, the occasional movie. Going over the list of require-
ments for aid to the disabled, I realized I would have to lose all my
assets to qualify for help. And without my house, my situation,
even with public assistance, would worsen, not improve.

One must add to this, of course, the fact that I did not want to
lose my home. Just beyond the wild and increasingly strange terrain
of my body, here was familiar ground. With my body failing, the

best sense of safety I had was in the outer walls of my house. And it was a house I loved. Ringed with plum trees, it was surrounded by white blossoms in the spring, green leaves in the summer. And to my surprise, outside the window over my bed, there was a pine tree that turned bright orange in the fall. I learned that the tree was a rare species, a deciduous conifer, that had become extinct until, seeds rescued from ice, it had revived and grown. From then on the tree took on an almost mythic presence for me, like the house itself, that, built around the turn of the century, had survived the great fire of the Berkeley hills, which roared through town in 1926. When I had the roof replaced, I saw the marks of fire still on the beams. I loved the way that it clung to the hillside, bravely careening over a view of the bay, the blue of the water and sky turbulent with change.

In the same way that the house seemed tenacious in its struggle for life, in the six years I had lived there I struggled not only to maintain it, but also to revive its beauty. An architect had designed it with a glass sunburst pattern over the front door and built-in cabinets, a graceful staircase, and sloping, atticlike ceilings upstairs. Bit by bit, with small amounts of money I saved and with my own efforts, rooms were painted and papered, shelves were built for books, doors were installed in the back wall of the kitchen, a small wooden deck added outside, a window added in a passageway. I wanted to stay there.

But even if, in desperation, I had decided to give up my house, there was the matter of my diagnosis. Yes, chronic fatigue immune dysfunction syndrome did qualify for aid, but a bureaucracy that habitually makes it difficult for quadriplegics to receive what they need was especially unfriendly to this diagnosis. Jan, who from her work as an organizer of patients with CFIDS knew well the bureau-cratic trials and tribulations of public assistance, discouraged me from trying to apply. The effort, she said, took years, with costly legal battles along the way. And finally the mathematics simply did not work out. After selling the house, my assets would go to taxes and rent for a new place, and though I would probably break even, I would not be ahead.

Studiously, I tried to keep my thoughts away from my uncertain fate. Sleep was precarious. Even a restful state was hard to achieve. I knew that to get well I needed to discipline my mind away from anxiety. But in unguarded moments I found my eyes surveying everything around me, estimating the unthinkable labor it would take to move. By a circular process, this anxiety was as much born of my body as affecting it. The feeling of wellness has a particular chemistry of which, until it is disturbed, one is seldom aware. But those with CFIDS cannot help but be conscious of it. From one hour to the next we will feel as if we have taken some form of speed and then a kind of depressant affecting the mind as well as the body. In the first state, to put it simply, I could not stop my mind from racing. And once my racing mind fixed on impending poverty, I knew I was on a course that would spiral swiftly downward, toward panic. Then, as toward night I grew physically weaker, the panic grew stronger, washing over me like a tidal wave, less liquid than force. Gripped by fear and an utterly stark sense of having been abandoned, I could neither sleep nor rest but instead thrashed about fruitlessly in my thoughts, panic and desperation strengthening with every effort.

What I feared so much never happened to me. I remained in my house, in a warm bed, and, with only minor lapses, was fed and cared for. The real trauma that I suffered was only to imagine what might have happened to me. And though, in my weakened state, even to imagine what might have been was terrible, unholy as my mood became, I am grateful for what I learned. Unlike the popular conversion stories of our times in which someone who is ill becomes well because of spiritual insight, what I learned did not alleviate my illness. Instead, with a ruthlessly uncompromising clarity, this mood brought home to me the dimensions of our current economy, how being sick can impoverish, how poverty increases the misery of sickness, and how the implicit violence of this process wounds the soul as well as the body.

Though I had not read the study suggesting that many people disabled by CFIDS for over six years, having lost their jobs, their spouses, their homes, and their savings, end up on the street, I could have guessed at the scenario. I knew there were people with AIDS out there. I had seen more than one man, thin, with open sores sitting on the pavement. And I had seen women there too, mentally or physically ill. The idea of such injustice troubled me. But now I would shudder with a more intimate knowledge at the thought of anyone spending a night outdoors or in a shelter, subject to chills and pain and disturbed sleep, without the comfort of a familiar bed.

And there were other thoughts, less extreme perhaps, but dreadful too, of someone ill, cold in an unheated apartment or hungry because no one is there to help with shopping or cooking. These were states so close to my own it was as if I could reach out and touch them. My friends for the most part were kind and generous beyond measure. But they could not continue to sustain the care they were giving. I could see the strain. There were those who were irritated and frightened by illness and others who, helping at first, simply could not afford to continue. They seemed like harbingers of the grim future awaiting me. I descended into a fear of abandonment, one that must be felt by anyone who is ill and dependent on others for help when no secure avenue of care exists.

But through this fearsome episode I also experienced a revelation. It came to me as a rude awakening. Though the sense of abandonment I felt echoed my childhood, I realized it mirrored a larger world too. Night after night, thinking about how I would survive, as fear dissolved into anguish only to become panic again, I was afforded a vision beyond my private history into the nature of society itself. Over time these were the words that formed in my mind: *They would have let me die.*

As I write it on the page, this utterance has the oddly paradoxical quality of seeming both self-evident and melodramatic. Everyone knows that for want of resources—a house, medical insurance, food—people perish, even in America. Many of us are aware that here in this society the incidence of these casualties increases daily. And yet, here the mind does a kind of dance, skipping over or away from the full force of knowledge. Even the phrase *everyone knows* deadens the impact. There is that distance you believe you can place between misfortune and yourself. Unaware and in the most inaudible of whispers, you will quickly tell yourself that you are exempt, that you will never fall into the category of the neglected.

The distance can be achieved, of course, by still other means. There are different neighborhoods, different styles. Acting as buffers against cataclysm, there are all kinds of insurance policies. Still, while paying the bill for such policies, we are able to keep these crises in a strangely separate region of the mind, a foreign place, as removed from our awareness as the broken-down neighborhoods and slums riddling our cities.

And yet, as foreign as it may seem, this is a place that exists in the body. I have located the region from a passage in a book by Daniel Goleman, called *Emotional Intelligence,* that describes the way the brain functions. At the base of the skull, in a territory known as limbic, there is a small but essential structure called, because it resembles a cluster of almonds, the *amygdalae.* It is a part of the brain that knows the world independently from the conscious thought that arises from the cerebral cortex. A hand reaches for fruit on a plate before the mind has registered the presence of food or called up the words *peaches, grapes, apricots.* The body jumps away from an oncoming car before the mind has brought into awareness any sign of danger. A man leaps into water and finds himself swimming toward a drowning child, unaware that from the bank he saw her drowning. Though he will not recall seeing her drowning, his body has no doubt of the situation. His body knows.

They would have let me die. The sentence seems like the first line of a longer work I am just beginning to read. Like a volume found in a dream, it has many authors, and the cover, heavy in the hand and seemingly hard to open, will suddenly, from time to time, open itself, while the substance of the pages seeps into my fingers as if by osmosis. This book fills me with a distrust that is also an urgent knowledge. All at once I am poised on the bank, seeing nothing yet ready to jump; I am swimming, and I am the child who is drowning. But I am also that more anonymous figure, the one who is too far away to rescue the child or who is afraid the current of the water is too strong or who, driving by in a car, only glances sideways and, sensing danger, moves quickly on because she is in a hurry. Yet as she drives by there is a sinking feeling, as if a part of herself were drowning.

In my own way I am attempting what could be called a rescue. Or, to put it more modestly, I am trying to express a longing that, though it is not often articulated in contemporary life, I can sense at the margins of desire. An almost hidden desire, as if to speak it would be naive or sentimental: the wish for a less brutal, more caring world.

That modern history is not without attempts to make such a world is perhaps one reason why the question falters. In my stay in Italy, one of the artists in our small and temporary community was from Romania. I knew some of the perils of communism in that country, but I learned more from him. I asked him in particular about medical care. The system was bad, he told me. Not money enough for equipment. Hypodermic needles used and washed and used again. No generators, so that during a power shortage, patients undergoing open heart surgery or babies in incubators simply died. Because of these conditions and low salaries, whenever they could, the best doctors would leave the country. But, I said hopefully, at least medical care was free. Well, he explained, officially, yes, but to receive decent care, everyone—doctors, nurses, even orderlies—had to be paid under the table by the patients' families.

One night after dinner, the larger group began to discuss Marxism. Given the record of communist countries, was Marx's work still relevant? We broke into several camps along the lines of this question. Two men defended Marxism with the old argument that the·theory had been misapplied. The Romanian artist who had been force-fed Marx's work all through his schooling was ready to throw out the whole socialist canon. Though from his recent experiences with venture capitalism, he was not happy with this system either. The same corrupt men who ruled under communism, and who were the only ones with enough capital to invest in the new order, had risen to positions of power again.

Among the rest of us, one woman, who was from Canada, had no strong opinion, except she quietly said that the systems for social supports, including socialized medical care, were very good where she lived. Another woman believed we should ignore Marx altogether and move into the future with an open mind. For my part, sometimes agreeing with one side and sometimes with the other, I argued that it was not just the practice of Marxism but the theory itself that had serious flaws, and I added some phrases about a blind faith in industrial development into the fray.

While the evening wore on, though we shared a camaraderie and the discussion for the most part was good-natured, we kept on drinking the light, new wine that was so abundantly offered us and as we drank our voices grew louder and louder. Somewhere near

two in the morning I found myself shouting into the din, "Central-
ization is the problem!" but of course no one heard me. Like the
discussion between the American doctor and me, but for happier
reasons, we had reached that stage of solipsistic debate when
everyone talks and no one listens. Then I began to laugh. Since I
rarely drink more than one glass with dinner, my perception was
colored with a certain warmth and generosity. Suddenly I could see
us all as if we were in a film, one to be shown, in the distant
future, to an audience filled with our great-grandchildren's children, who would watch us as we engaged in mental struggle within
the imaginary boundaries of our time.

And then, as if everyone had seen this moment at the same
time, we all began to laugh. And in our laughter was a deep regard
for one another. Drinking and talking together, we had grown closer. Perhaps it was the subject matter we addressed—how a society
meets the needs of the body—that made it seem almost as if we had
poured this new wine in a chalice, blessed it, and shared it among
ourselves. We were celebrants and, like all celebrants, had ritually
shared our sorrow too, the weight of a common sadness behind all
our talk, a longing for that seemingly untouchable world toward
which Marx had aimed his utopian ideas.

Aiming myself in the same direction now, in my attempt to rescue
that mysterious quality of human nature still folded in myself and
others, I find myself poised and ready to leap into the waters of this
past. I am once again bending into time, not precisely toward
Marx's ideas, but toward the conditions from which they sprang.
There is little heroism in my attempt. I am simply trying to tell a
story, to watch it as it winds out past familiarity. Though given my
post-traumatic obsession with cleanliness, it was a minor act of
courage for me, during my tenure in Paris, to wander through the
grimier parts of the ninth arrondissement, home to streetwalkers,
and to spend so much time in bookstores smelling of dust and mold,

bringing home with me volumes whose pages had grown gray and yellow with soot and age. I was looking for bits of history, odd fragments that, pieced together, would give me a picture of the conditions of poverty in the middle of the nineteenth century, the years during which Marie Duplessis, the real courtesan who was the model for the heroine of *La dame aux camélias,* raised herself from a poor working girl to the splendorous life of a famous courtesan. I wanted to learn more about her life before she was a courtesan, where she was born, who her parents were, what her childhood had been. This is what I discovered.

The woman who inspired the legend was born and raised in a small rural village, called Nonant-le-Pin, in Normandy. The countryside there is beautiful now, with deep pine forests and rolling, lushly green fields, though at the time of her birth, in 1824, the forests were deeper still, and to one coming from a city, the countryside would have seemed almost untouched. But this would not have been true even then. Industrial development had already effected great and rapid changes in society. Times were difficult. Though the wealth of France had doubled, this new wealth went into just a few hands. Peasant economies everywhere were collapsing, and, as today, poverty grew by leaps and bounds. Both destitution and the threat of destitution formed the background for her early years.

"Marie Duplessis," as she was known after she became a famous figure in Paris, was not the name she was given at birth. Her parents, Marie Louise Deshayes and Marin Plessis, named her Alphonsine. The *du* before *Plessis* was also her invention. Her father's family was far from aristocratic. Marin's mother, Louise Renée Plessis, was a beggar and sometime prostitute. It was she who gave him his family name. His father, a wayward priest, neither supported nor acknowledged him.

When Marin met his future wife, Marie Louise Deshayes, he plied a trade at the very bottom of the Norman economy. He was an itinerant salesman, a *colporteur,* who wandered from village to village selling small items. He made barely enough money to stay alive. The Deshayes, Marie Louise's family, were opposed to the marriage. Though peasants, they were somewhat better off and far more respectable than Marin Plessis.

Marie Louise's father, Louis Deshayes, had descended from aristocracy. The large imposing estate where his mother was born still stands, not far from Nonant-le-Pin. It must have been an impressive monument in Alphonsine's mind, a sign of her noble heritage. Alphonsine's great-grandmother, her grandfather Louis's mother, Anne du Mesnil, belonged to a noble family prosperous from the sixteenth century. But by the time Anne came of age, her family had squandered their money. She had no inheritance. Still, led more by love than practicality, instead of seeking a prosperous marriage, at the age of twenty she married one of her family's domestic servants, Etienne Deshayes. Between them they had six children, among them Louis.

When he came of age, Louis Deshayes fell in love with and married a good-looking peasant woman, known to be somewhat wild, named Marie-Madeleine Marre. In turn, she gave birth to two beautiful daughters, the first named Julie and the second named Marie Louise. Given the hardship of the times, Marie Louise had a relatively happy childhood. But by the time she reached her twenties, her mother, still wild and not known to be faithful, abandoned her family. She died a short time later. Marie Louise was left to manage the house.

Six years later, when Marie Louise met Marin, she had little hope of marriage. Though uneducated and poor, Marin had an extraordinary gift for storytelling and beautiful, hypnotic eyes, eyes his daughter would one day inherit. He charmed Marie Louise with tales of exotic journeys filled with romantic adventure and resplendent pleasures. Though the stories proved untrue, they must have evoked her grandmother's memories, a grand estate, coaches, balls. She was mesmerized by the worlds he painted.

■ ■ ■

Stories can be even more seductive than beauty. As I retell this tale, I am aware that I have lost myself to it. I am for a while far less interested in my own fate. Though I have faith that somewhere in the details of this history I will understand my own story more deeply, I find myself surrendering entirely to this drama of peasants and aristocrats, wealth and poverty, truth and fiction. I am fascinated by subtle patterns as they unfold before my eyes. A pattern, for instance, passed from one generation to the next. For to the mix of noble and peasant progenitors in Alphonsine's blood, something else belonged to Alphonsine's inheritance, a lineage of wildness. But such is the grounding where the noble and the low-born, the rich and the poor, often meet, a wild and forbidden territory, charged with adventure and eros.

Marie Louise was warned against the marriage by her father and her sister. The man was disreputable. He had no respectable family. How could he possibly support her? But Marie Louise was in love with him. On the first of March 1821, she married Marin nevertheless.

The Deshayes family set up Marin and Marie Louise in a stable business, a small general store. Outwardly, according to reports that even now are in the memory of the village and the family, the couple looked happy. They had two daughters in rapid succession, Delphine in 1822 and Alphonsine in 1824. She was a remarkably beautiful child who had her father's eyes, as more than one of her biographers describes them, eyes made of velvet. Her youngest years must have formed a kind of idyll in her memory. She was still with her mother, who was gentle and kind and liked to dress her with small touches of luxury, a ribbon here, a ruffle there. With the other children of this countryside, Alphonsine and her sister played often outdoors, picking cherries in midsummer, playing at sauté-mouton, a kind of leapfrog.

But if she trusted her small world, a betrayal was soon to come. The shadow of it had been present since before her birth. Her parents quarreled continually. Marin returned to his old ways, leaving home for extended periods, drinking, womanizing. Marie Louise complained that he worked too little and used too much of the family finances for his exploits. He in turn accused her of having pretensions, of thinking herself better than he, and of wanting too much luxury. She had inherited a taste for fine things from her mother, which she passed on to her daughter.

Their quarrels reached a climax one morning when, while Delphine and Alphonsine both watched, Marin dragged his wife by her hair into the fireplace, where he set a fire. Only the chance arrival of a delivery man saved her life. Seeing smoke, hearing screams, he burst in, knocked Marin down, and pulled Marie Louise free of the flames.

Fearing for her life, she left the house with her daughters and did not return. She took refuge for a brief period in her sister Julie's house. But everyone feared Marin's violence. Mary Wollstonecraft, shielding her mother from her father's violence as a child, had already argued eloquently for the rights of married women to be protected by law from the violence of their husbands. Margaret Fuller and Flora Tristan would make similar pleas. But there would be no avenue of protection until over a century had passed. Leaving Delphine and Alphonsine with Julie, Marie Louise accepted a position as a maid with an English lady. She departed with her employer almost immediately for Paris. Alphonsine was eight years old. It was the last time she would see her mother.

Two years later, just after traveling to Switzerland with her employer, Marie Louise died. Here body and mind must have conspired. The trauma. The loss. The endless grief and worry for her daughters. She was worn down by it. Despair must have wasted her away. And perhaps she was also unlucky enough to have the same bacillus in her system that would one day strike her daughter.

How soon after her death did the letter arrive? It would have had to come thousands of miles by coach. Three weeks at least would have passed by, if not a month. Only then would Julie know her sister had died. Did she tell her nieces what she knew, or did she let them continue awhile with the comforting illusion that their mother might return one day?

I know what it is to lose a mother and to wait for years for her return. Hope keeps your spirits up. But the end of every day brings disappointment. An arc of expectation and despair enters your body, as every day you are strengthened with hope only to be weakened again with defeat.

The girls would stay in their aunt's household for two more years. The rations at home were meager. Julie had two children of her own. Alphonsine roamed the countryside, occasionally asking for food from the parents of a friend. Wild herself now, unruly, like a tomboy, she played with the boys. Then, wearied by the extra burden of her care, Julie summoned Marin. Delphine was apprenticed at a dairy. And, reluctantly, Marin took his younger daughter with him.

Alphonsine was twelve years old when she began to travel with her father on his route, buying and selling. According to Delphine's testimony, passed down through generations of her descendants, Marin treated his younger daughter like a servant. What was it she did for him? Cook, do his wash, polish his boots. Whatever he asked. Finally, she herself became the ware.

In his account of the incident, a friend from her childhood wrote that she bragged about it. Going to bed with an old man who gave her gold. Now she could buy beautiful things, she boasted. Since at the time this boy had a crush on her, his version of events could be distorted. Still, I remember Garbo's brilliant depiction, her shame covered by bravado and mockery. Though the real Marie Duplessis gave herself more brilliant lines: "If society condemns me," she said, "I accuse society—and I have the right to do so—of never having protected me."

There would have been so many feelings. How old was she by then. Still twelve? Or had she turned thirteen? She had made love only once before. This was after a harvest, in the fields, with a peasant. The word *love* was probably never used. Nor was he a constant lover. Could he have been tender at all with her? This was her first time.

Unless an earlier time occurred, when, sharing a room with her father, who, after he returned from a long night of drinking in the bar below, might reach for her and, if she turned away, remind her that her only other choice was an orphanage or the workhouse, both of which were often death sentences. Taking her, he would have taken something intangible too. Not virginity so much as a sense of inviolability.

But this is only speculation. On this score, one can only guess at what did or did not happen between them. There are just bits and pieces of remembrance, a few documents, and the circumstances of the times to judge by. All that is known for certain is that Marin sold her repeatedly to one wealthy man. And this alone would have made its mark. That she was sold by her own father.

As I try to imagine the sale, a kind of effacement occurs. The truth of bodily desire and response, so close to the core of my self, become an object of trade, a commodity in my father's hands. My life no longer the value but instead commanding value. The fondling, kisses, penetration of the man who bought me setting me steadily at a distance from the authority of my own being. Later, I would have to think I chose this fate.

Whenever an economy fails to feed its population, the prostitution of children becomes more common. According to de Maupassant, in the countryside of Normandy the practice of selling a daughter was common, even accepted. "It is a paying trade," he imagines a peasant saying. But even if he heard these words spoken, I do not entirely trust his reading of them; he lived in different circumstances, and this was not his daughter. The practice still occurs throughout Southeast Asia today. Fathers will sell their daughters, sometimes to brokers who promise jobs or marriage but instead take the girls to brothels, where they are virtually beaten into submission until economic dependence and shame imprison them. And one more process entraps them, that slow habituation by which a young woman will become used to what is done to her and, just as in illness, confuse her affliction with who she is.

In Gacé, a village near Nonant-le-Pin (where Alphonsine worked for a period, making umbrellas), a small museum has been established in her honor by one of her descendants. The village takes a certain pride in her history. The museum adjoins city hall. Here the legend is corrected by the true facts of her life. The artifacts are carefully displayed. There are photographs of the church where her sister, Delphine, later was married. Of her great-grandmother Anne de Mesnil's home. A drawing of the home where she had lived with her mother and father, smoke coming from the chimney. A pair of andirons from her Paris apartment. A faded list of her belongings that were auctioned after her death. I was touched to see her story is being preserved by those who live on the same land where the story began and who know this early history in another dimension. The taste and touch and even ache of it familiar.

Marin must have beaten his daughter, as he beat her mother and as he himself was beaten as a child. It would have become part of Alphonsine, her bodily memory. Overworked, ill fed, exposed to the very cold winters of this part of Normandy, abandoned by her mother, mistreated by her father. One can easily see how she might have contracted tuberculosis during these years, the illness invisibly beginning its destruction.

But she was not so miserable as this description would lead you to think. Whenever injustice has been suffered in childhood, other qualities rise to meet the injury. Marin himself, the perpetrator, once perpetrated against, had an extraordinary resilience. A spirit-edness. Cast down into the lowest life, disliked, even reviled, he kept coming back, with laughter, charm, more stories, and a beauty that despite all he had done remained in his eyes. And though she succumbed in the end, Alphonsine's mother, Marie Louise, must have had an extraordinary will too, fighting with her husband, leaving him to save her life. The same will to survive was to be found in Alphonsine. The journalists and dandies who encountered her in Paris before her stellar climb wrote of her high spirits. Her pluck. She did not bend easily to fate.

Why did Marin eventually take her to Paris? She must have been a handful. Less easy to dominate than her mother. More trouble than she was worth to him. Or was there a moment of fatherly love? Though he had never been there, he had told her so many seductive tales about this city. She must have wanted to see it. And, of course, there is this too: her mother had disappeared from her sight in that direction.

I know what it is to long for this city. From an early age I remember wanting to see the famous lights, the bridges, the river. My mother, who had never been there, loved Paris even so, and she taught me to love it too. I wanted to immerse myself in this city, which existed at the periphery of my consciousness as promise, the sparkling life, intelligent and sensual at once, that I might live if only I could get there.

As Marin and Alphonsine traveled toward the great city, she must have begun to think of her destination as a kind of salvation. Along the way she met a Bohemian woman, who, grasping Alphonsine's hand, turned over her palm to read a future filled with success, abundance, elegance, and many lovers. She left Alphonsine with a talisman, a dried lizard. I saw the lizard displayed in a glass case in the museum in Gace. She had kept it with her all of her life.

I am trying to imagine what this day would have been like for her. Coming from Normandy, the coach would have entered the great city from the northeast. Did they pass through the Arc de Triomphe, which had just been completed the year before? Was she able to glimpse the Champs Elysées, still green like a field, before they came to the monumental heart of the city? The vast Place de la Concorde, where Louis XVI had been executed, would have been on their route as they made their way toward the entrance to Les Halles, the old marketplace, looking for the rue des Deux-Écus. This was where the family of a distant cousin to Alphonsine's mother lived. The Vitals were strangers, really, but Marin, using his formidable skills as a salesman, urged his daughter on them. When he left he promised to return, but he did not. Alphonsine would never see him again.

Later she said that she knew he would not return. The mix of her feelings must have been intense. The exhilaration that anyone feels first coming to Paris—the beauty of the place, all the stories she had heard, she just a country girl who had never seen any large city before. The relief she must have felt to be free of Marin's tyranny. But still she was only fourteen years old. And she had just lost the man who, after all, was her father.

Every connection to her family had been severed. Her sister was not told where she was. When Marin returned without Alphonsine, Delphine asked him where her sister was. "Paris is such a big city," he replied, "so big, it is not easy to find a lost object there."

The Vital family was not particularly welcoming to her. They had a small store that sold fruits and vegetables, above which they lived. Space, time, money were not easily had. She did not work hard or well. Her presence with them was burdensome. Still, something in

her was irrepressible. Following the same wild ways she had
learned in the country, she would leave the house to roam the
streets for hours. Slowly she discovered the ways of the city.

And soon she began her rise. Making a delivery for a laundress
who did business with the Vitals, she discovered a shop where lingerie was made and sold. She worked there for awhile, until less
than a year later, in 1839, when she found a place as a couturier's
assistant. She had always been drawn to beautiful clothing. Even
to stitch other women's garments must have given her pleasure.
And in the fine fabrics, the lace, the fashionable cuts, there would
have been the scent of her mother. Not only did Marie Louise love
fine things, she took them as a sign of her aristocratic lineage.

Romain Vienne, one of the boys Alphonsine played with in Normandy, tells us this story from her childhood. His father owned the
coach house in St. Germaine à Nonant where wealthy men and
women would stop to rest and water their horses. One day when
Alphonsine wandered over to visit Romain, he took her inside to
where the coaches would stop so she could see the splendid visitors
as they stepped from their coaches. Nearly invisible at the sidelines,
she watched as beautiful women in velvet and silk stepped into her
view.

Lace and feathers and beads and brocades, ribbons, taffeta, tulle,
gloves, hats, stockings and garters and shoes, veils, capes, and
crinolines and corsets, panniers and bustiers, the all-important
Kashmir shawl, pearls, diamonds of varying carats and cuts, especially the canary, rubies, emeralds, the traffic of so many avenues
of desire would meet in a luminescent whole, fashionable dress, the
mix of sensations like a busy boulevard at night, light from the
cafés spilling into darkness, sweeping away every thought of loss,
electrifying her mood and lifting her spirits, the force of desire in
her body inextricable from another force, strong like water breaking through a hard surface, the desire to live.

■ ■ ■

Now, she was making the clothes she had admired from a distance. She was a *grisette,* a figure at least as important to the history of the times as a dandy or a *flâneur.* A translation of the term requires some knowledge of nineteenth-century society, its fashions, its morals, its economies. A recent dictionary defines the *grisette* as a milliner's assistant. But the definition in common usage then included all the girls and young women who worked anywhere in the garment trade, as couturier's assistants, sewing or selling lingerie or hats, weaving silk. And loosely applied, as it was, it also came to stand for working women in general. But it also had another meaning. In the dictionary I have owned since I was a university student, this definition survived the passage of time: "a young woman of easy virtue."

Here is linguistic evidence of a history not usually told in polite society. And yet frank as the phrase is, "easy virtue" hides the grueling circumstances that led to this kind of easyness. As a *grisette,* Alphonsine would have worked thirteen hours a day, from seven in the morning to eight at night, and still not have earned enough money to keep life and limb together. Since this was piecework, to make ends meet she would have had to work at a merciless pace, taking meals at her workstation. And doing this, she could earn one or perhaps one and a half francs a day, barely enough to subsist, sharing a room with others, eating meagerly, bread and water, perhaps on good days affording what was called "a working girl's cutlet," a slice of Camembert. But the work was seasonal. A *grisette* might work several seventy-two-hour shifts during one month, which was not uncommon, and then be unemployed for weeks. Nor would she be paid for Sundays or holidays. Yet with the small salary she earned, there would be no way to save anything to sustain her through these days, much less the inevitable periods of unemployment.

This was why a *grisette* so often took on lovers, sometimes for one-night stands, sometimes living with young men on the rise, students or apprenticed professionals, or occasionally walked the streets in search of casual prostitution. She did it to survive.

Alphonsine followed the pattern. Before she moved in with a student, she lived in a kind of dormitory room over the couturier's shop where, on rising, she would be given a bowl of milk before she began her work. In this way she was fortunate. Housing in Paris was hard to find and, once found, for the poor, mostly terrible. Peasant families, who had lost their land or who could not make a living from the small holdings they had, migrated to the cities. There was massive unemployment; the poor flocked to Paris searching for work. Because in this period the population of Paris more than doubled, a shortage of housing caused the rents to soar. The situation has a contemporary ring. Many were homeless, living in the streets.

Those among the working poor who could afford a roof over their heads were only marginally better off. It was not uncommon to find six, seven, or more people living in one room. Everything would have gone on here—the preparation of food, eating, sleeping, washing, and sometimes piecework, sewing or weaving. Most often brackish water was carried into these neighborhoods by hand (one of the tasks Alphonsine was given by the Vitals to do). There was little ventilation or light; most likely the room would have had no window. Though, since the doors in these places were not built to keep out drafts, it would be damp and cold and full of the smell of the street. It was not just cold that came in through the cracks. The streets of the city were filled with garbage, including carrion and the occasional human corpse, and rivers of slop and human waste flowed down them, permeating the air with foul odors.

Perhaps this is how Alphonsine contracted her disease. Not surprisingly, given the overcrowding and unsanitary conditions, these neighborhoods in which it was estimated each citizen had only

seven square meters of space in which to live had the highest con-
centrations of tuberculosis. A woman, for instance, who shared a
room with someone else who had TB, overtired, worn down by too
much work and too little food, not dressed warmly enough, continuing to work despite her cough—because how else would she
live?—might sit at the same table as Alphonsine while they completed a garment. Tuberculosis, as most everyone knows by now, is
caught by breathing contaminated air. The bacillus thrives in a
damp and close environment. The workroom dark and unventilat-
ed, Alphonsine would be exposed.

And her body would provide an excellent host. The journalist
and dandy Nestor Roqueplan recalls his first meeting with her.
Standing on the Pont Neuf, near the Vert Galant, the breathtaking-
ly handsome statue of Henry IV astride his fine horse, she was ill
kempt, unwashed, and clearly covetous of the *pommes frites* sold
at an outdoor stand there. He bought some for her, and by his
account she devoured it, unceremoniously. Stunned only by the
roughness of her manners, he did not grasp the depth of her
hunger.

Several years after 1847, the year of her death, when France fell
under the regime of Napoleon III, Paris would be besieged by a massive effort at redevelopment. The effort was not made for improving
the lives of the poor. Already the shortage of housing had led to
desperate settlements at the periphery of the city. Shanties appeared
among garbage dumps, crude dwellings pieced together from discarded boards, boxes, and bits of tin. Now these shantytowns were
to grow substantially. This decade was later known as the age of
Hausmann, the architect and city planner who created the wide
boulevards for which Paris is now famous. Because of the volumi-
nous and speeding traffic that occupies them, I have never found
them particularly spacious. But Baron Hausmann was a child of
this grandiloquent age, and he wanted a grand effect. That he had

to destroy block upon block of buildings in neighborhoods where the poor lived was considered an added virtue of his plans. And since it is difficult to build a barricade over a boulevard, redevelopment would also impede rebellion. To make the city a theater of national pride. To banish the ill and wipe out rebellion. The three ideas fit together as well as a jacket over a waistcoat over a shirt. Increasingly, the men who had finally taken on the mantle of leadership and who were busy creating a new sense of order thought of rebellion as a species of disease.

Revolution as disease. There is a fear and loathing in the metaphor that moves in two directions. The fear of a change in the social order is expressed here. But so is the fear of death. The reasoning may seem irrational, but this is the way the mind works. Reason is often sacrificed to create an illusion of safety. If rebellion can be contained, so might illness, the unconscious argument goes. That anyone can fall ill, that sickness and death are the great levelers, would have been obvious to the conscious mind, of course. In the last century even the Dauphin lost a lung to tuberculosis. He did not live long enough to rule. Yet in the more shadowy quarters of conviction, picturing illness as a form of revolution, one could easily imagine winning a victory over mortality itself.

The subject of illness is a breeding ground for unconscious desires, prejudices, and projections. Though in the nineteenth-century mind the real nature of contagion was not yet understood, according to one popular theory a cloud of illness, called a miasma, would emanate from neighborhoods largely inhabited by the poor. This idea led to an attempted solution, the *cordon sanitaire,* a kind of quarantine by which neighborhoods that harbored large numbers of men, women, and children ill or dying from cholera or tuberculosis would be cordoned off from the rest of Paris. But the plan was not practical. One in ten of the city's citizens was unemployed, indigent, or a beggar. One of three died from a struggle for subsistence. By some estimates more than three-quarters of the people of Paris lived in poverty, sometimes in the same neighborhoods, even the same buildings as the rich. Buildings were graded like reverse hierarchies, the poorest living in garrets at the top, luxury increasing by descent, greatest on the first floor. Under these conditions the *cordon sanitaire* could not protect you. You might meet disease on your own stairway.

A later generation saw clearly that it was poverty and the eroding effects of poverty on the bodies of the poor that fostered disease. And just as environmental destruction can be sensed now almost as a form of bodily knowledge, there must have been an inward knowing even then, an intuitive grasp of the real causes of tuberculosis. But bodily knowledge of this kind is easily denied. And for the wealthy, while the poor died by the thousands of tuberculosis, there was reason enough for denial. The argument that the poor had made themselves ill would have relieved guilt. As with those who blame homelessness today on dereliction and the use of drugs (with no attempt to understand how poverty itself can create addiction), any thought of responsibility would fade into indignation. And the knowledge that the lives of the poor had been sacrificed to create luxury for the rich would sink to the most obscure regions of consciousness.

What would Alphonsine's death have been like had she remained a working girl? Certainly she would have died sooner. Though as a courtesan she often worked all night, once she left the close air of the sweatshop, she had servants, comfort, more than enough food. She could go to the country for a rest. She went on several different excursions to Europe's fashionable spas, to immerse herself in the healing waters. It was on one such trip, to Baden, that she met the count who would support her in grand style for years. Had she remained where she was, she would have had to continue working until she could no longer rise out of bed. As she died, no one would have been able to attend to her needs. And where would she have lived if she could no longer earn her rent? Would she die on the street? Or perhaps she would be taken to a hospital.

Though to a modern ear the last suggestion may sound merciful, it would have had a terrifying ring to anyone in that period. In my research into the background of Alphonsine's life, I learned this too: hospitals, or hotels of God, as they were earlier called in France, since they were established by the church in the Middle Ages as charitable efforts, existed mainly for the poor, who went to them only in extreme illness or in the process of dying. After the revolution the administration of these institutions passed to the state. Because the church regarded illness as a judgment, before this transfer a patient, once in a hospital, became a kind of ward, disciplined, ruled, chastised, ceding all individual rights. The revolutionaries wished to restore liberty to the patient, and, in the letter of the law, they did. But the atmosphere of hospitals remained punitive, the care harsh, rooms so overcrowded beds filled the hallways, sanitation poor. They were places to die and not places for dying well.

Still, a hospital, if she could find one, might be a better place to die than the street. Though even that was not always possible. While the Goncourt brothers were conducting research for their novel on tuberculosis, they saw a man "with a bony and emaciated face, sunken eyes ... shaken like an old dead tree blown by a winter wind" begging for admittance to one hospital. The intern who turned the man away explained that were the hospital to admit all those with TB, there would be no room for anyone else.

And no doubt this was part of the reasoning too: because the hospitals were also institutions for teaching and research, the doctors needed a variety of cases to study. Those who applied for admittance were valued as the raw material of science. In this way, the practice of science fit hand in glove with the hierarchies of class.

Falling into poverty, one fell into a kind of invisibility. Despite the utopian dream that the combined efforts of science and industry would eradicate hunger and hard labor, in the development of both, the lives of working people were considered expendable. The institutions that conducted medical research treated the bodies of the poor accordingly. If sometimes patients were asked to take part in experiments, at other times they were required to agree. And often they were not told at all but instead simply used. What was tried on their bodies was largely unregulated. The result could lead to a horrifying death.

But the use of these bodies did not end here. In order to pay for what they or their families needed, for a small sum the poor would often sign away the rights to their bodies after death. Burial for the poor, who could not afford a cemetery plot, was already an indignity. More often than not they would be consigned to an unmarked, common grave. Yet another, even less dignified fate was offered them in exchange for cash. Their bodies would be dissected in anatomy classes or used, after death, still again for experiments.

I have heard similar stories from the twentieth century. I am thinking of the Tuskegee experiments. African American men, ill with syphilis, were allowed a slow disablement and death during experiments conducted in the American South. Then there were the experiments carried out by doctors and scientists on prisoners in concentration camps. And later the high doses of radiation given to unknowing patients in the fifties.

The permission lies in the philosophy. Though fair inquiry is the goal, science places itself above the material world. In this philosophy, the knowledge and experience of the subject of study are deemed irrelevant. Disenfranchised by poverty, the patient would be disenfranchised still again by medical science, robbed of intelligence, will, spirit.

■   ■   ■

The effect remains. I experienced it in the period of my own worst illness. Having lost the strength of my body, and watching my financial capacity also drain away, I felt still another realm of my power to be under assault, the force of consciousness. My ability to know and articulate what I felt, to question, reason, think about why I was ill and know the nature of my affliction was undermined. All my intelligence was focused then on what seemed to be most crucial in my life, my health, and yet the philosophy of medicine excludes this intelligence. The realities of my body were exiled from the realms of meaning that society shares.

It was from another banished reality that Alphonsine Plessis made her ascension toward visibility. A ladder existed that working girls and women could try to climb. The *grisette* was at the lowest level. Just above her on the ladder of success was the *lorette,* whose amorous labors would earn her a humble roof over her head, enough to eat, and pretty if not grand dresses.

And there was something less tangible she would have gained. Society may have accused the *lorette* of compromising her soul. But in another way, she would have freed it from the numbing effect of long hours at work, work that was dismally repetitive. As Simone Weil has written of the "unbroken succession of ever identical movements" that comprise factory work, such labor robs one not only of spirit but of consciousness itself.

Named after the church Notre Dame des Lorettes in the neighborhood where they lived in cheap apartments, *lorettes* were supported but not in high style. Though the end of this story was not always happy. Unless she climbed to the next level, a *lorette* would most likely run out of funds by the time she became too old to sell her body. Then she might end up in Salpêtrière, which in the nineteenth century was half madhouse, half prison, the place where anyone considered a nuisance, mad, or politically out of favor was taken.

A *cocodette* shared the same status as a courtesan. Splendidly attired, refined more by birth than by tutelage, she had fallen from society because of scandal, divorce, adultery, and the broad category of licentiousness. But from the larger pool of *lorettes,* who were not born to refinement, few were lucky enough to realize the ultimate achievement. To become a courtesan was the dream of many poor girls. *The Grandes Horizontales,* as they were also called, were symbols of hope, just as basketball players are today for many inner city children. Like sports heroes or movie stars now, courtesans were gossiped about in the press, recognized on the street, their glamour the mirror of a million transitory wishes hovering like angels of hope around misery and disappointment.

Alphonsine's elevation to the rank of *lorette* began when she was taken up by the portly owner of a restaurant along the Galerie Montpensier of the Palais Royal. She was sixteen years old. He housed her in a small room on the rue de L'Arcade. Before that she had lived for a while with a student. At night she would go to one of the many balls on the Left Bank, public dances where working girls could meet bourgeois gentlemen or even aristocrats. Crossing over to the other side of the river Seine, a wealthy man could easily pick up a lover here for a night or find a woman to keep.

But Alphonsine's career as a *lorette* would be short. Within a matter of months, while she was attending the Bal Prado, a fashionable dance hall just across the street from the Closerie des Lilas (where a century later Hemingway would drink with his friends), she met the young aristocrat and playboy who would change her life dramatically, Agénor de Guiche.

Though according to one of her biographers, Micheline Boudet, this was not the first time Alphonsine laid eyes on Agénor. They had not met, but she saw him from a distance once when she was still a child. If she was unknowingly witnessing her own future, she was also a chance witness to history. This was a liminal time;

the social body still fluctuated between one order and another, regency and democracy. For a while the Bourbon king, Charles X, was restored to the throne. But he would be the last man with royal blood to rule France. Revolution returned. In July of 1830, following a bad harvest, with hunger and suffering in its wake, barricades appeared in Paris again, and the king abdicated. On August 8, 1830, parading into exile, Charles passed through Nonant-le-Pin. His retinue was large, including the queen, who brought along a carriage filled with her clothing, his servants, and several noble families, still loyal to his cause, among them the duc du Gramont and his family. So Agénor de Guiche, the son of a duke, rode by on a horse, whose saddle and bridle, according to aristocratic custom, must have been splendidly ornamented. The crowds of Norman peasants, having been told not to express their sentiments, whether for or against the end of Bourbon power, watched silently. De Guiche was just ten years old at the time. He did not remember the small girl, just six, who stood with a starstruck expression at the side of the road. That night, as royalty passed out of history, her dreams were peopled with celebrated figures.

Guiche became her Pygmalion, transforming Alphonsine from a peasant girl into a sophisticated woman, one who could pass as a lady. It was only after his efforts that Alphonsine was considered to have arrived. At least this is how Henri Lyonnet described it in 1929. But in French the verb he uses is more revealing. Of the famous courtesan at this pivotal moment in her life he writes, "Alphonsine Plessis *a vécu*," meaning, if you translate it literally, that she had become *real*.

For the higher circles of society, the poor did not really exist. And so complete was the change as she moved from *grisette* to courtesan that in a sense Alphonsine Plessis did perish. Guiche taught the young woman he loved all the manners of polite society.

He arranged for singing and dancing lessons and taught her the skill, so meaningful to the French, of speaking with correct grammar. Her accent changed. She learned to read and write, assembling and annotating over two hundred volumes during her short life, in the process gaining the education in literature, theater, opera she needed to become what is called cultivated. And of course, augmenting the talent she already had in this direction, Guiche also taught her how to dress and wear her hair. The results were famous. Graceful and elegant at the peak of her fame she would become known as one of the best-dressed women in Paris. And finally, as if in recognition of her transformation, at the age of eighteen she took a new name. The common Alphonsine Plessis yielded to the aristocratic Marie Duplessis.

To many observers, it seemed as if Marie had inherited her manners. Writing in 1892, the English traveler Albert Vandam declared that she had "an instinctive refinement no education could enhance." Where did the real woman end and the tutored one begin? But that is a question almost anyone can ask of herself. Even beauty can be learned. Still, she was born with many extraordinary qualities. An exquisite beauty, her black hair framing a pale and rosy face, blushed no doubt with fever, long, narrow, and vivid, very dark eyes, white teeth, of which she was also famous for saying, "Lying keeps them white."

Her legendary charm must have been part of her character even as a child. And to learn all she did so quickly she would have needed an extraordinary intelligence, along with quick-wittedness. To be always on her toes, though she did not lie about her past, always acting as if she were to the manor born. And she was famous for possessing that elusive capacity to recognize what is found beautiful, especially by the powerful, that is called good taste.

In a less-than-perfect society, learning and accomplishment of every kind provide an escape from closed worlds. I am thinking of the

French term for a house of prostitution, *maison close.* The term evokes the other kinds of enclosure class creates. Occasions that cannot be entered. Larger worlds of meaning of which you will remain ignorant. When I was a child, the first language I learned was the working-class grammar my father spoke. Then, when I was six years old, my grandmother began a slow and painful process of correction until my speech was more widely acceptable. She also schooled me in the dicta of etiquette, and though I rebelled from all her lessons, the effort to pass unnoticed into a world of my betters became as if second nature to me.

Even before I entered college, though I was politically opposed to such distinctions, I had unwittingly outdistanced my grandmother's sophistication. If in my childhood my clothing was often the cheaper, less refined version of what was fashionable, later I learned to have a good eye, creating the illusion of wearing finer clothing than I could afford. I learned the vocabulary of haute cuisine from the men I dated or had as lovers. One, a married man several years my senior, took me to the private rooms of a French restaurant to sample classic dishes I had never eaten, *boeuf bourguignon, coq au vin, sole meunière,* words as crucial to my education as any I learned in schoolrooms. Yet, despite my learning, I had many moments of secret shame.

Though in France, shaped as the culture is by an elaborate *politesse,* the signs designed to elevate or diminish are infinitely more numerous and more complex than in America, America is not without the means to make withering distinctions. Even among children, clothing is a sure sign of social position. I was forced to the painful recognition of this as a child. I never had the right clothes. Either what I wore was not stylish or my clothes were visibly cheap imitations of the real thing. I remember vividly the feeling of being wrong in my clothes. The shoddiness of my dress seemed to penetrate my skin and mingle with my body or, conversely, to bring to the surface and make recognizable a fact that was clear to me, namely, that I was not *suitable.*

By the time I was a young woman in college, I learned to cope with my sense of inferiority. I was fortunate because my father, who was a working-class man, had left me just enough money to pay for the costs of an education. But there was hardly any margin. My clothes were often secondhand or bought on sale and not of the best quality. Silk blouses were in fashion then but out of my reach. Yet, my radical politics did not prevent me from the recurrent fantasy of opening a closet in which not one but several silk blouses hung. Now, looking back, I see that in my estimation of myself I had made some progress. As a younger child, I never even imagined myself as having better clothes. Neither did I tell myself that others were better dressed simply because they had more money. Instead I believed that the low quality of my clothing confirmed an indelible quality that was *in* me.

The loss of my mother, which I had experienced as rejection, no doubt folded neatly in with any intimation of inferiority I received from economics or class. And this may be why, though over time I've shed the sense of being less acceptable than others, it never goes away entirely. Dormant, the old feeling will come to life when the right events trigger it. Illness is one of those events. Like a shoddily made, ill-fitting piece of clothing, illness strengthens any idea you may have that you are unworthy. All your waking hours, every feeling, sensation, thought, is filtered through a body that feels wrong to you. Cold to the bone or sweating, a razorlike pain as you rise, your gait thrown off as you walk, your balance affected, your memory slower, your face swollen, your eyesight slightly blurred, you walk as in a second skin, one that marks you, at least in your own mind, as less than others, damaged material.

The loss of her mother, her aunt's rejection, her father's violence, his use of her and then his rejection, her hunger, the cold and fatigue she had suffered as working girl, delivered almost like a punishment, the coarseness of her ways before she was taught how to behave properly—all these memories would have blended perfectly into what she felt in her body when she was ill, feverish, then chilled, coughing violently blood and sputum. No wonder she preferred to hide the signs of her illness. And to surround herself with another skin, layer upon layer of luxury.

Each object that Marie Duplessis possessed was a sign that she belonged. Her prized shawl made of Indian cashmere alone had the power to dazzle and impress. In *Villette,* Charlotte Brontë creates a character living in a boardinghouse who is able to strike "a certain awe through the household" simply because she owns such a shawl. As she pulled it around her shoulders, the superior quality obvious, well made, soft to the touch, the feeling would have brought her back to herself in a way. The child who was loved once by her mother. But the accoutrement was also necessary to her trade. Though it would have cost her thousands of francs, far more than she had earned over several years as a *grisette,* the investment was crucial in the life of a courtesan. Without one, like the women of Lyon, who wove the satin she sat upon and the silk she wore, or the women of Millau, who made the gloves she drew on her hands when she went out, or the women of Picardy, who made the stockings she pulled over her legs, or of Dieppe, not far from where she was raised, who stitched the lace at the edges of her lingerie, she might have faded into obscurity once more.

The shawl and all that she needed—the rest of her elegant clothing, jewelry, the box she held at the opera, her furniture, china, crystal glasses, linen, servants—were paid for by her benefactors. Not just Guiche and his circle of friends (a group of young dandies called "The Lions," who were wealthy members of the exclusive Jockey Club), but also the comte Édouard de Perregaux, who loved her deeply, and a Russian diplomat in his eighties, the wealthy comte de Stackelberg, all joined the ranks of her supporters. Though Dumas *fils* maintained that this count was her lover just like the rest, about Stackelberg the story was told that when he met Marie at a spa, she reminded him of his daughter who had recently died of TB and that was why he gave her such lavish support. It was this man who gave her a coach to take her to the theater or on a promenade in the Bois de Boulogne, where everyone went to see and be seen.

Her coach, made by the famous house of Doldrigen and drawn by thoroughbred horses, was said to be particularly magnificent. Her most munificent benefactor, Stackelberg, also bought her the splendid apartment where she was to live until her death, once number 11, now 15 boulevard de la Madeleine. This was the site of many lavish dinner parties. Extravagant fare served on hand-painted porcelain plates. Fine wine poured into crystal glasses. The guests, Alfred de Musset, Franz Liszt, and Eugène Sue among them, celebrated.

The apartment was legendary for its beauty. Furniture of rosewood and birch. Not only Sèvres but also rare Chinese vases, statues from Saxony, porcelain shepherds and shepherdesses, Venetian glass, an eighteenth-century gold pendulum clock, two chests from the regime of Henry II, gleaming plates of silver and vermilion, chairs upholstered with cherry red satin, a grand piano, a four-poster bed, designed by Boule, sporting caryatids fashioned after fawns, Bacchus grinning from each corner, columns carved with grapevines encircling two lovers. And in her grand salon there was a gold lacquered trellis on which blossoms of camellias grew.

Even after her death the glamour continued. To pay her remaining bills, her belongings were sold by her creditors. The auction was a grand public event in its time, rivaling the sale of the Jacqueline Onassis estate. Everyone was there; even Charles Dickens crossed the channel to attend. And scores of society ladies, curious to see inside this bastion of the demimonde from which they were supposed to be protected, crowded the once forbidden rooms.

■ ■ ■

Prohibition almost always creates curiosity. But something else can be detected here in the sway of attraction. Everyone has a tendency to want to cross the boundaries that divide us. Perhaps we are all part of one creature, and for this reason, like Ouroboros, the Greek god of wholeness, who was a serpent, we want to bend back into ourselves. (Though in the modern age, when every effort, even the effort toward wholeness, has accelerated, we seem more like frenetic dogs chasing our tails.) In chasing courtesans, even if unwittingly, wealthy men were forging a certain kind of bond with the lower classes while the courtesans themselves were bending in the opposite direction, toward union with the upper classes. The effects rippled through society. Making every attempt to pass as ladies, courtesans demanded more and more currency from their benefactors so they could dress to the nines. Whereupon, seeing the splendor of these gowns in the theater, ladies of society began to emulate courtesans.

Versace, who in the late twentieth century made a sensation by copying the clothes of streetwalkers, was actually following a tradition. What courtesans and *cocottes* chose to wear would determine the next season. Describing the appeal of the courtesan in the middle of the nineteenth century, H. d'Orvalle wrote that "people gathered around her, not only to look at her but also to copy her dress or her hat or to study the way she draped her shawl." Courtesans were more daring with their clothing, perhaps because, since they were fallen women already, they could take more risks. But the opposite also would be true, that through the rough circumstances they had braved they had become more bold than ladies.

Providing, as Philippe Perrot writes, "the testing ground" for new styles, courtesans became the reigning queens of fashion. Appearing at balls or the opera or in the Bois de Boulogne, they were studied carefully by the wives of the elite. But the most crucial show occurred at the beginning of the spring season, during the first week of the horse races at Longchamp. This event, almost as important to clothing designers as horsemen, inspired competition among the women as fierce as in the races themselves. Though courtesans were not allowed to sit in the section reserved for high society, as they appeared at the entrance near the weighing enclosure (conveniently close to where the gentlemen in the Jockey Club sat), every lady would train her eyes on them. Wearing brilliant colors of cherry or purple, sea green, azure blue dresses, beaded or ornamented with silver, ribbons streaming, taffeta shimmering, with feathered hats or perhaps a hat resembling a jockey's toque, each one would make her grand entrance and then walk around the track, modeling the latest look.

Studying this history, I am struck by the intricate connections between one life and another. The lives of women placed in different categories of virtue, dwelling in different classes and hence supposedly different worlds, are firmly connected. Even by the manner of her dress, the very symbol of a lady's high position in society, the respectable, upper-class woman forged her fate with whores and working women.

I am beginning to believe that if you search long enough you will find that each story contains every other story within it. My story has a new chiaroscuro now. I am seeing my experience in a broader light. Along with one courtesan, peasants, working men and women, prostitutes, dressmakers, fashion designers, upper-class ladies and even aristocrats and bourgeois gentlemen have crowded their way into my picture of myself.

And thus it was on a search for more of my own history that one rainy afternoon while I was in Paris I made a visit to the Jockey Club. The address has changed, and since women stay there now as hotel guests, the club is not what it once was. But I hoped at least some evidence of the old atmosphere it had when Agénor de

Guiche was a member remained. It did. The place is still *gentille* and aristocratic. I was not, as it turned out, allowed beyond a small room near the entrance. The club protects its guests from such disturbances. But the director had kindly arranged for me to meet one of the members, the Baron du Cassagne, who knew something of the history.

Wearing the kind of green uniform adorned with gold braid that might have been designed in the roaring twenties, the bellboy, who spoke better English than the baron and better French than I, acted as our translator. The baron sent him into the inner sanctum of the club to retrieve paintings and photographs of what the club once looked like. Elegant, simple rooms, lots of wood, bookshelves, deep leather chairs. The kind of rooms men retire to after dinner to smoke cigars. All in the English style, which was the fashion then.

Through the course of the afternoon, as the baron spoke, the atmosphere of the old Jockey Club came alive for me. The same men who owned racehorses and gambled away fortunes inherited from great families or newly earned in the rapid markets of the Second Empire, would place high stakes on a young woman. She could never be brought to the club. It was a male preserve. Even when wives would come they had to go to a special dining room reserved for female guests. But one woman was always there. This was the vendor who sold flowers near the door, sending bouquets to various discreet addresses. She knew *everything*, the baron told me, which woman each man would spend his night with, all the intrigues. The baron and I and the bellboy laughed together at the knowledge she must have had. Each of us no doubt would have liked to know what she knew.

I asked the baron what he thought was the great appeal of the courtesans. So much money was spent in procuring them. More than one man was financially ruined by the extravagance. Marriages in that time were not usually made for love, he answered. We nodded. I was familiar with this history in my own country.

The novels of James and Wharton I read when I was young portrayed the same dilemma over and over, the terrible choice one was forced to make between money and love.

I remember this wonderful description from *The House of Mirth,* when a woman turns her face "like an empty plate held up to be filled" toward her suitor, a man who must have seen his own emptiness reflected there too. He is courting her for her fortune. When the void proves too much for him, he begins to betray signs of an "encroaching boredom which would presently crack the thin veneer of his smile."

Still, there would have been some drama here. The stakes were high. If a man or a woman did not inherit enough money, the need to marry could be desperate. But even those with inherited wealth sought good financial matches. Like royal marriages made as alliances between kingdoms, bourgeois marriages were made to increase the wealth of two families by adding together the greatest possible financial resources. Thus, a young man from the Rockefeller family might marry a young woman from the Payne Whitney family, their union creating a formidable stronghold.

But the economic drama would not have made the necessary courtships less tedious. And the marriages that resulted would have been more tedious still. It was not amorous attraction that drew these couples together. And what would they talk about? They could not discuss what had really brought them together. According to the rules of polite society, money, the *sine qua non* of these unions, could not be spoken of openly.

Silence of this kind can mortify an atmosphere. I am imagining a young wife, for instance, who might have faced ruin had she not made a good marriage. She would have had to apply herself as seriously to the art of seduction as a courtesan. And just as a courtesan needed accoutrements, so did a young society woman being presented. The same novel that gives us the image of a woman's face as an empty plate reveals another, more compelling tale, a common one that was hidden under the vacuousness of high society. In this story, a woman is rejected by her suitor because her fortune is too small, and thus having spent her money on apparel, she stumbles by degrees down a ladder that leads her from her station as an eligible debutante to a position as a ladies' secretary and finally to the place where Alphonsine Plessis started, a wage earner, working for just a pittance, making hats. Though the young wife I have imagined would have escaped this fate, the rush of the effort she had made to escape would still be in her blood. But in the atmosphere she had risen to, the story could not have been told. She would have to silence the bright flush and energy of it.

This would provide one answer to the question why wealthy men were so attracted to courtesans. Proper marriages were so boring. And courtesans were so exciting. This kind of woman could not be silenced. She spoke openly about both money and sex, satisfying for a night the same thirst for honesty that would also lead these men into music halls, to hear the lustily frank songs of Yvette Guilbert spelling out every naughty, forbidden fact of their lives. Truth has a way of asserting itself in the end. Thus in the nineteenth century, a time of euphemism and mannered pretension, directness became a form of art.

What transpired in the world of courtesans, *cocottes, lorettes,* and the realm of music halls, Left Bank dance halls, and salons were small revolutions of a kind. Here all the orders of class could be escaped for a night. And sexuality would seem to be liberated as, for a few hours, the constricting rules of proper behavior were broken. The atmosphere must have been heady, not just wild but giddy. The women in this world were called "gay" (a word that in my lifetime would slide over to a different group), and that was the mood of these rebellions.

As the afternoon continued, the baron, the bellboy, and I were in the same mood too. Together in a small anteroom of the Jockey Club, we had wandered outside the boundaries of class ourselves. We were giddy with the subject of our conversation. The baron described the way one famous courtesan, La Belle Otero, entered a cafe. He saw her do it once when he was with his parents in Monte Carlo. He demonstrated her walk for us. The elegant carriage she had. She was well past her prime, he said, and no longer beautiful, but still as she came in, every head turned. Then he told another story about her that touched us all. She got lucky one night at Monte Carlo. Poor, she gambled what she had and carried away enough money to buy all the necessary gear—the all-important coach, the necessary Kashmir shawl, several elegant gowns, shoes, hats, gloves. Over her many years as a celebrated courtesan she garnered several fortunes, returning each year to Monte Carlo to gamble some of it away again. Finally, too old to attract benefactors any longer, she gambled it all away. And it was then, the baron told us, that the proprietors of Monte Carlo, having known her for so many years, and not wishing her to die in poverty, gave her a pension for the rest of her life.

The charm of this story is that it breaks the mold. At least regarding money, these were mock revolutions. Some courtesans flourished through old age, some wealthy men were ruined. But in general the social order remained intact. And even these temporary idylls became occasions for the competition that increasingly determined who would hold power. "There is one more explanation for the vast fortunes men spent on courtesans," the baron said, answering my question in still another way. During the Second Empire, when the baron's grandfather was young, a gentleman had to have a courtesan to maintain his social standing. Even men who preferred other men as lovers would keep a woman for the appearance. Possessing a woman was an indication of his status among other wealthy men.

The more rich and powerful the lovers a courtesan had had in her past, the more she was sought after by other men, who competed among one another for her favor.

A similar rivalry existed between courtesans. In one of her famous letters from Paris, Janet Flanner tells a story about Liane de Pougy. Describing the appeal of the great courtesan, Flanner writes, "Every Parisian who could afford it fell in love with her." Since, for a courtesan, both her value and her prowess were measured by the gems she had been given, to humble one of her rivals, Pougy once entered the opera wearing no jewelry at all, but her maid trailed behind her carrying everything she owned—diamond tiaras, ruby rings, sapphire bracelets—piled high on a red pillow. I told the baron this story. But he knew a slightly different version. In his story, the rivalry was set at Maxims.

Marie Duplessis was known to be less competitive than the others. In his film, Cukor portrays her as generous to the other women in her trade. And apparently this was true. But in other ways the portrait of her in *Camille* is far too sentimental. She made no sacrifice for Dumas *fils*. His father, the elder Dumas, profligate as he was himself, did not disapprove of their tryst. And it was Dumas *fils* who made the decision to leave, not she. The disapproval was his. Because he could not afford to support her, she took other lovers to pay her bills. And this made him jealous. After he left her, she fell in love with the romantic composer Liszt for a period. And near the end of her life, she even married Count Edouard Perregaux, though because she married him in England without the consent of his family, the union was annulled in France. Nevertheless, she had his crest emblazoned on her china.

She did not deny herself life. She wanted everything quickly. Her style was lavish to the end. "It's not me who is dancing too fast but the violins which play too slowly," she is remembered as saying. She let the money flow.

Had she not been dying, perhaps she would have been more frugal, less intense. But she was dying. She knew this in her flesh. Rising to stand, she would feel the warmth that was part of constant fever turn to heat. Pulling harder for air, she would strain to stay in motion and by motion be distracted from what otherwise might become an endless descent.

She was seen a few weeks before her death at the theater, drawn, pale, even thinner than before, in the words of one eyewitness, looking more like a ghost than herself. That night, dressing carefully, glad for the aid of her servants, shakily descending a flight of stairs, but still able to rise into her coach, sinking into her seat for a brief rest, then passing through the crowd that waited to watch all the entrances, settling in her private box, exhaustion and pain pursuing her, she could sustain herself with the comfort and beauty that surrounded her. Her silk dress, the delicate embroidery of her petticoat, the flowers she wore, camellias instead of roses because the scent of roses made her sick, the glittering bracelets on her wrists, the satin ribbons she used to fashion her hair, the gold-rimmed tiers of the theater, the soft chairs in her private box lined with red velvet, the dazzling sight of the well-dressed crowd providing as if still another skin, not the miserable miasma surrounding her when she was poor, but one that shimmered with all the pleasures of the body.

All the signs of ascent. They stayed with her even after her death. She was not buried in an unmarked grave. What remains of her body lies in the Cimitière Montmartre. Though the name on the gravestone, the name you will have to ask for if you visit, is Alphonsine Plessis, her grave has two elegant markers. Stone camellias trail over one, and a woman's ethereally beautiful face emerges from another. The site has many visitors. Some leave flowers, among them the great-grandson of Agénor de Guiche. Out of respect, the baron told me, for the love they had.

■   ■   ■

Time has passed. Morality has changed. In the intervening century, life for a great many working people has improved. The working day has been shortened and salaries increased. Even the landscape of fashion provides signs of the social change. There are department stores now, the first founded a few years after Alphonsine died, where common people can dress respectably, even stylishly. And in the first decade of this century a young *grisette,* a milliner's assistant with a great talent for decorating hats, was given the means to start her own hat shop by her aristocratic lover. But Coco Chanel was not a courtesan. And she was never excluded from society.

A great shift has taken place. And still I find myself reading this history with a growing intensity. In an odd way it feels more contemporary than many narratives written over the past decades, which are suffused with an unstated quality of security, as if the question of how to survive never occurs to anyone any longer. Though no one can claim this question is irrelevant now. The homeless wander the streets, camp out in doorways and parks. Men and women work two and three jobs just to make ends meet. The victories once made by labor movements are rapidly eroding. The daily fear of devastation so closely braided with that almost ineradicable sense of being less has continued, not only in the working class, but in anyone who shares that history.

I can find it in my family. Both my father and my stepfather earned enough money to pay for decent housing and food by working no more than eight hours a day. Yet entering this past, I find the mood familiar. I recognize it as a mute current of emotion in both my childhood and my life now, faded, more subtle, harder to recognize, yet undeniably present. *It was indeed miserable to be poor,* Edith Wharton wrote of the descent of her heroine from one class to another, *to look forward to a shabby, anxious middle age, leading by dreary degrees of economy and self-denial to gradual absorption in the dingy communal existence of the boarding-house.*

This is, after all, a fate that I feared too, being sick and unable to work, that I would descend not only to the greater physical sufferings of penury but to a place outside society, into the exile of poverty, where I would be consumed by *the feeling of being something rootless and ephemeral, mere spindrift of the whirling surface of existence.*

Forced as I was to the edge of descent, I had looked into an abyss. Far more frightening than the thought of dying was the experience of erasure already occurring in my life. My fear of becoming someone who did not count. Not simply the thought of going hungry, but being *allowed* to starve, not just the thought of waiting in uncomfortable, crowded rooms for indifferent medical care, but being *allowed* to suffer this way. Yet this is what Camille's story brought to me. Through this tale my perspective went back in time. It was there in that past that the ground of the modern world, my world, had been laid. An economy built on the principle that while some will flourish, others will not even survive.

This was as revelatory a vision as I can imagine. Such insights are bound to transform your understanding. Suddenly you notice new pockets of meaning in stories told many times before. As I began to move back from the brink of this abyss, when I heard or told stories of smaller anxieties about earnings and expenditures, I sensed in these reports the upswelling of a desolation that, though it may seem to belong only to the desperate, is really all our inheritance. For in the glowing accomplishments of American success, the fate of being uncounted can be felt nearly all the time; it remains subtly palpable, a stubbornly fearsome and cold backdrop for all of our lives.

And there is this too that I saw in the vision. Not just the whirling surface of disparate destinies, but the rootedness of our connections. How the wound of being allowed to suffer points to our need to meet one another at the deepest level, to make an exchange at the nadir of life and death, the giving and taking that will weave a more spacious fabric of existence, *communitas,* community. Thinking again of the crucibles formed in flowers on the ancient streets of Italy, the women, men, children who live nearby making these shapes from baskets of petals they have collected together, I find in myself a longing to drink from these vessels, to take in and give nourishment and meaning at once, to see, taste, touch the corpus of communion, to partake in the whole body.

The Social Body

O to realize space!
The plenteousness of all, that there are no bounds,
To emerge and be of the sky, of the sun and moon and
   flying clouds, as one with them.

WALT WHITMAN, "A Song of Joys"

LAP

I am not supposed to leave my bed. But a nightmare has frightened me. Emerging from the hallway, I can feel their eyes on me. And I am relieved. They are glad to see me. No one is angry. A sweet light flows from their eyes as they laugh. My body is coated with sugar. Momma takes me onto her lap. As she listens to my nightmare, her smile wraps around me. Looking up, I take them all in, their happiness. Then they offer me something sweet to eat.

CLOUD

Here I am part of the dark, part of the sheets, part of my sister's breathing. In our breath, the tangle of sheets seems endless, floating out like a great cloud. The window shade flaps against the open window, steady music in my ears by which I calibrate my flight as I dream, her body and mine navigating the dark sky.

VOICES

We arrange ourselves around it. My sister sits closer than I. I do not understand everything the voices say. But I like to be with the others as they listen. Later I will ask my sister to imitate the sound of the creaking door that starts the show. Their eyes are fixed downward as they listen. When something bad happens, everyone looks afraid. But they are not really afraid. My mother says something funny. I don't understand the joke, but when I see her smile I smile too. The others tell her to be quiet. They are listening hard. I can hear them listening.

EYES

They are like one body with countless arms and legs. The force of all those eyes looking at me is too much to bear. My shoulders and knees curve inward, my head bends down to my chest, I move behind my mother. But soon she is gone, leaving me exposed. I stand near the teacher and do my best not to look at them. Finally they stop looking at me. Now they are an excited blur, a whirring rush of energy beckoning just at the edge of what I will allow myself to see.

SMILES

You can feel it in the room though you can't name it. You don't say anything. And the others are all smiling. Years later, looking at the photographs, you will see what was underneath. This one angry, that one on the verge of tears. You have a smile too, confused. But all you saw that day was the impenetrability of their smiles. And you felt alone in your body with what you knew.

SPACE

My sister is not there any longer, breathing the same air. It is just empty space that is left here at night. Violent. Amputated. Figures arise from it. Full of stealth and menace. Ready to capture me as I fall asleep.

ROSES

He is in the chair, and I sit next to his feet when he tells the story. It is about the dog he once had. The fields where they played. The moist afternoon heat of a Midwestern farm town. Thorns on the rosebushes near the front gate. I can smell the roses now, thick and pungent.

PAPER

It is like all the others. On thin blue paper. For two days after it comes I keep it on the top of my dresser drawer so I will see it every morning. Sometimes I just touch my hand to it; at other times I open the envelope again. Her handwriting—my sister is left-handed—is distinctive. I try to write that way but I can't. Staring at the ink on the paper, I can slide into the letter, feel her in the room with me.

THE PLACE

Everyone wanted to see it, and so did you. The place where she put her hands. They had shown her putting them there in a news-reel. She was wearing a fur stole. Lighter than the one hanging in your grandmother's closet. A man standing next to her helped her get down on her knees. She turned to him briefly to smile before she sank her hand into the cement. It was a small hand. Though I was so much younger, my hand covered the place where she had put hers. Doing this, I felt an exhilaration shoot through me, to touch the place that she had touched.

WAVE

You are at the crest of a wave. You can feel their laughter. It is buoying you higher and higher. You know you are not supposed to, but the laugh is inside you now, and it bursts out all by itself. Then the words come to you. If you say them Mrs. Siegal will take your gold star off the chart, you know it, but you cannot help yourself. The laughter of the whole room is in you, and you say it, and the laugh gets bigger and grows in you too, shaking you until you are bending over, with that ache in your side that always comes, then you are gulping for air, limp with laughter, tears running down your face, as you try to be still.

HOUSES

As I enter the block where they live, I can feel the grandness of the houses, the long pathways, the stately lawns, the tall trees, the stone statues, the massive doors made of dark wood older than I am. I feel smaller, and a shock, part fear, part delight, runs up my spine when I step through the leaf-dappled light.

HARMONY

The smell is indescribable. High glass windows. Murmuring voices. When it reaches your nostrils, you know immediately where you are. The cool stone walls. Wooden pews. Choir books with the crisp gold edges. When everyone stands, no one has to tell you. You will stand with them. There is a soft rustle as you all rise. They reach for the book. You reach. Then there is that moment of silence, as if you are taking in the same breath. Later, when you are older, you will be the first to turn to the right page. And you sound the note just as the organ does. You have learned harmony. As your ears lean into the melody, you resist the strong pull of the voices next to you, focusing your eyes straight ahead, hearing your own voice now, traveling across the room, finding the other high voices, the altos like low grass around the soprano trees, and one wind rushing all of it through you.

SPEECH

A cold fear rises in me, and my heart beats faster until I can hardly keep quiet. Words are assembling in my mind as a clear thought blazes through me, making me stand. Despite my fear, a force is making me speak, the same force I can feel in the room, propelling all the others too.

MAP

Here, alone with your things still in boxes, you are sad, confused. You wanted to come here, but now you feel alone and a little bit lost. Then you read the map. There is north. Across the campus. West is toward the ocean. In the east you can see the hills. You follow the map, taking the shortest route to the edge of the university. Then you walk under the trees, around the library, up to the creek that runs under a bridge, and to the other side. As you walk back again, the map becomes part of your body.

BIRTH

This body, wet, still swimming from the womb, lying against my breasts. The cord cut, the room swarming, tumbling together around one point, bright face looking at me, dark eyes visible now, arms, legs, skin still unbroken from me, daughter, one undivided body.

LINENS

It is Tuesday night, and the sheets have been changed. As I turn my face into the clean smell of the pillowcase, my skin remembers my grandmother and her sheets. More than a decade since her death, what she did every day part of my memory. The spoons she used to stir batter in my kitchen drawer now. Worn and smooth to the touch of the thumb. Soft silver, she told me, from Brazil. When she washed the sheets, passing them through the wringer, I liked to watch. Her body hot with the effort, she must have thought of her mother, as her mother would have thought of her own, only her mother's sheets were probably made of linen, as they were then, which is why we call them that now, especially when they are handed down.

MEETING

She has said what I have thought myself but never dared to say, and now despite my weariness at the end of the day, I am wide awake. There is quick vibration in the room, as we tell one story after another, the timing perfect, no missed beats.

TIME

Crossing the square, you can feel time under your feet. The stones worn. The shadows of the arcade sheltering the faded signs of shops long gone. New signs like the youngest children. Water as fresh as rain and old as the sea pours from the fountain. In the corner the café has become a restaurant. But the walls and ceilings are the same. Now and then the current owner has them restored. The ornamental curves and flowers no one sees anymore except in the old places. The words of the illustrious ones who dined here still in the air. Hugo's table by the window. The view from here and from the apartment upstairs where Colette used to live much the same. Though the costumes have changed and, in general, the children don't have hoops anymore. And every season different flowers are planted. But as you walk in the center now, hearing the steady rhythm of your footfall on the fine gravel, all of it is with you. You feel it almost as a wind blowing you back as you advance. Be slow. Attend.

Three

All the world's a stage . . .

WILLIAM SHAKESPEARE

I am Emma Bovary.

GUSTAVE FLAUBERT

Bless me that I can exchange myself with others.

Tibetan sacred text

AUGUST

As you begin you are alone, making notes, placing a line here, a piece of dialogue there. And then perhaps when you have a moment of doubt, because for instance the scene you have described is not quite right or strikes a false note, you shudder as you become aware of the others. A sea, an obdurate mass, a jeering crowd, disappointed with your feeble efforts. But you keep your nerve. You adjust the language. Shift the focus. Add complexity to the order of events. Until slowly, by almost imperceptible degrees, the gaze of the others no longer troubles you. Not because you are pleased with your efforts—you are still erasing, adding, altering— but because you have joined the audience yourself. Curious and attentive, you too are watching, eager to see how the plot proceeds.

Theater

Though the glittering nightlife and the elegant cafés have vanished along the boulevard over the last century, one relic remains, standing almost unseen in the frenzied commercial world that surrounds it now, a famous site in the history of French culture, Théâtre des Variétés. Many celebrated plays have opened or been performed here, including *La dame aux camélias*. Sarah Bernhardt played the role of Marguerite in this theater in 1899. And just as the younger Dumas describes the meeting in his novel, this was the place where he first encountered Marie Duplessis. She came here often, attending light operas by Offenbach or variety shows.

To the modern eye the building does not seem like a theater. In the nineteenth century the style was more common, but today the look, with its stone columns supporting a classic triangle beneath which you must pass as if into a temple, is startling. It seems more sacred than profane. The architecture reminds you that the earliest theaters were also temples. It was here that through the movements of the actors or hearing their voices and the songs of the chorus, the world of the divine would be revealed. Even now in the most modern of theaters, there is a way you are elevated toward a divine perspective. Beholding any plot unfold, a story of love, for instance, or of war, tragic as the outcome may be, you are able to accept the twists and turns of fate with grace.

■   ■   ■

The body is the first theater. The startling drama of birth. One body coming from another. That cry signaling a first intake of breath. All eyes on the small new being. The infant groping eagerly over the mother's body for the breast and finding there not only nourishment but the familiar music of a heartbeat. Then like an ancient ritual, preserved and repeated in its fundamental form, after the narrative line of maturation and age, and including years of waking and sleeping (even sleep captivated by the strange and shadowy dramas of dreams), majestic in its finality, without exception there will be an end.

Like theater, the body will eventually teach you to let go of expectation and attachment. And there are other similarities. Along with diurnal rhythms that begin and end, hunger, thirst, sexual desire, the need for heat or shade or rest constantly give daily existence the arc of a plot. There is a protagonist, a motive, sometimes a mystery, suspense, and resolution. And there is this too in common with what we call art: delineated by skin, bones, musculature, height, and weight, a form, one that not only contributes to identity but also shapes bodily experience. And tradition is also present. Events will be reenacted as they have for centuries. Like sacred texts kept in a sanctuary, templates are encoded at the heart of every cell, inscribed on the thin filaments of matter called DNA.

In turn, every drama mimics the span of a life, if only by beginning and ending. Even in a comedy, when the suggestion is that the characters we love will live happily ever after, you can sense mortality as the curtain falls. This is a moment I cherish, in the dark of the theater, that quiet, a palpable hush blanketing the audience. At this instant, in an aftershock of perception, the whole play, both form and meaning, seems to enter you more deeply. It is a moment remarkably like the one that follows a real death.

■   ■   ■

A few years ago I was present in the room when an old friend died. She was my former husband's mother and thus my daughter's grandmother. During her last days there was a constant vigil at her apartment. She had fallen into a coma from the morphine. Visitors would come and go; though she was unconscious by then, they would stand near her for a few moments, perhaps touching her hand or face, and then say good-bye. But those of us who were close friends or family lingered, moving from the bedroom where, quiet as it was, the air was charged to the living room, which now became a kind of lobby where we would go to rest and speak to one another, out of kindness, of other, lighter subjects.

As it happened, I was sitting with her nephew reading passages to her from the Song of Songs, which she had requested while she was still conscious, when the day nurse noticed that her troubled breathing, the sound that both electrified and held the room, had grown distinctly more shallow. Noah and I were sent to assemble the others, and without prearrangement, a circle quickly formed around her bed. Someone kept on talking, but soon he responded to the general quiet, as we all leaned into her subtle breath, listening for the last. The moment was hardly detectable; bit by bit one could no longer hear her lungs work, except that I could have sworn some invisible element in the atmosphere plummeted. As Auden wrote of Yeats's death, "the mercury sank in the mouth of the dying day."

Still silent, we bent toward her body with full focus as the nurse felt her pulses and then turned to us, nodding, as if to say, yes, you sensed the moment, she is gone. Yet, even after the clarity of this news reached us, the silence held for a full minute or even two, before the first of us, her daughter, began to weep. In the quiet we had all taken in absence, and now all of us could weep.

The sudden absence of a life, the body quickly hardening, then eroding, leaking back into earth, has been taken as evidence in some minds that the body is really inconsequential in some way, a dumb vessel for the soul, unthinking. But witnessing a death, I have had a different experience, believing I saw, even in the final moments of a life, the eloquent ability of the body to impart, even by the most subtle of gestures, an almost unutterable wisdom.

What took place in ancient theaters was taken to be as auspicious as death or birth. Supposed to be symbolic, these events were also portentous in themselves. As with lifting the sheaf of grain for an initiate to see, in the old rites at Eleusis, or with the ritual gestures that are still with us, passing a wafer into the mouth, taking the Torah from the ark, a knowledge that cannot be expressed in language was transmitted there.

The sun rising over the edge of a dark mountain, a river washing over rocks, grass as high as the hips waving in the wind. The world of mute substance seems even so to hold a mysterious significance. And the body shares this strange eloquence. Many popular and professional accounts of the connection between body and mind portray the body as being like a kind of puppet of the mind or like an unskilled actor, blunt and amateur, a player of charades, making crude attempts to communicate what would be so much easier to say in words—sore shoulders, for instance, taken as a sign of "shouldering" too much responsibility, stomachache described as the result of "stomaching" anger. But physical experience preceded the language that uses the body as a metaphor. And the life of the body transmits a knowledge that, like the gestures of a mime, bespeaks a world significant unto itself, a parallel world of meaning, its signs as revelatory as those in ancient dramas that bring one to wonder at the texture and complexity of existence.

More and more, as the workings of the nervous system are understood, medicine is coming to acknowledge that the body has an intricate intelligence. Various modes of communication take place inside the body almost continually. Signs, calls for attention or for help, which vary in pitch and call up different audiences, different responses from among the body's vast collection of cells. Here, there are many simultaneous actions as if occurring on several stages and performed to many different audiences. The focus shifts. Now food is entering the mouth, then there is a finger nicked while cutting vegetables and bleeding, then there is the grumbling of a stomach overfilled, a heart pounding, a slight chill, or just the silent process of chemicals, moving along their pathways, agents of the alchemy of flesh and at the same time message bearers.

Perhaps because I have an illness that affects the nervous system I am fascinated by this process. For whatever reason, it pleases me that the body survives by self-reflection. And that this single being is also a couple, the knower and the known, acting at once as both performer and audience, existence and the witness to existence.

The desire for self-knowledge can be felt in the body. As I write, it is almost with a physical longing that I seek to understand the earlier history of my illness. Mixed in with a host of causes—viruses, damp weather, overwork, bad luck—I can quickly name loss as one of the circumstances. Even now I feel the effects of this sorrow in my body. My childhood was not as catastrophic as Alphonsine's was, but still there are similarities. Like her legendary counterpart, Camille, I knew what it was to be abandoned. I lost my mother several times over, first at the age of six and then after I was twice returned to her and taken away again at eight and, for the last time, at fourteen. Each in their own ways, my father and my grandmother left me too. The story is so familiar to me I would not be eager to tell it here except that now I am studying it in a new light. I want to know how my body responded, to trace more precisely how loss made me more susceptible to illness. And there is this too: the sense that in some mysterious way, this search might be redemptive to my soul.

■ ■ ■

My earliest memories come from my second year of life, a time when I could walk easily and feel some independence but was still largely subject to the needs of infancy. The youngest in the family, I had the sway of a small world. My sister was six years older. I adored her, and since she had asked for a brother or sister, in those years she did not act as a rival. My grandparents, who doted on me, lived next door in the other half of a duplex they owned. As is common in southern California, there were front and back yards, small but large enough for grass and play. I can remember pedaling the little metal car I had been given for Christmas on the sloping concrete that led to the double garage in back. I would talk to myself or call out to my grandfather, who had a workshop under the house just across from the garages, where he sawed and planed and shaped and sanded the little drawers of a beautiful desk that now, in the way of time, I have given to my daughter.

My mother was beautiful, with a wild side and a witty laugh. My father was a good-looking man, slightly shy, who liked to play with us. They were both, as my sister and I have often said to each other, like children themselves. Yet then, since we had the security of our very grown-up grandparents nearby, we loved this about them. Since I was the youngest in our extended family, my memory from these years is of seeing knees and legs as much as faces and of always looking upward toward the larger figures who protected me.

Still, there were frightening moments. There is only one I remember with any clarity. It was just before Easter. Two friends were visiting. My father had organized an egg-painting contest. Because he was kind, everyone got to win. But my sense of accomplishment was interrupted by a dramatic scene in the hallway. My mother, who only in hindsight do I realize had been drinking, kept reeling out of the back bedroom, shouting in a frightening voice, fighting off the efforts of my grandparents to keep her confined there. I must have run to the kitchen door to watch for a moment because my mind still holds an image of her struggling to be free, except that in this image she looks more like a great dark bird, its wide wings flapping wildly, than my mother. They were able to quiet her finally, and we continued, subdued, my father fending off questions, but the mood was broken.

Despite my mother's alcoholism, I was a somewhat confident child. Trouble and misery are more balanced in an extended family by the presence of many. When I try to remember my body during these years, it is the feeling of a body in health, sturdy, sustaining. Photographs of me from this time bear witness to this feeling.

The other memories I have from the period before I turned six seem relatively benign and, as vivid as they are, almost trivial. I remember that I loved school. I made a best friend quickly. Because Philip was a boy, my family called him my boyfriend. His light brown hair fell across his brow like the drawings of Prince Valiant I admired in cartoons. We placed our mats next to each other to take naps until the afternoon when, because we talked and laughed too much, we were separated. Then one day he betrayed me.

It was our last day of school that year. My mother came to pick us both up to walk us home, and because this was a special day we all stopped at a market on the way, where she bought us each a bunch of lollipops, brightly wrapped, tied with ribbon. But as she leaned over to hand Philip his, he grabbed them both and went running, and that was the last I saw of him. Distraught as I was by the theft, over time what disturbed me more was that since this was the last day of school, there was no way to make our friendship right, to repair the connection that would have remained even if we were never to see each other again.

And we did not meet again. The separation was not temporary. That fall, my family moved to the valley, a place just over a low-lying range of hills, outside Los Angeles proper. I don't remember being aware of our plans until the day when, our car loaded up with boxes and suitcases, we drove toward those hills. What I remember most about that day is that my father made a brief stop at my kindergarten. Perhaps expecting to see my old friends, I followed him out of the car as he carried a big box into the room filled now with children I did not know. Then, as he lowered the carton into the arms of the teacher, I could see the long neck of my stuffed giraffe hanging over the side. The box was filled with toys that were mine. The things that my mother and father must have decided I had outgrown were being given away. But I was not prepared for this loss. Outraged, I clamored and pleaded and cried, all the while feeling humiliated in front of the teacher and the other children, whom I hated equally for not being the same ones I knew and for witnessing my shame.

I have always thought my earliest memories to be haphazard. Until describing them here, I begin to see that they form a structure, one that reflects a real history yet altered with hindsight, as if to make the plot more logical. Like the overture to an opera, which contains all the themes the audience is about to hear and which the composer writes only after he has completed the entire score, I suspect I chose these incidents because they echo and frame major themes to come.

My motive in choosing them was not aesthetic. Instead, these reminiscences formed the illusion of a buffer between myself and unpredictable disaster, a system of imagined warnings that, looking back, I decided had prepared the way for what would come, lessening, at least in memory, the eventual shock of a far greater loss.

In the year that my mother and father moved to the San Fernando Valley, my mother began an affair with a man who lived at the far end of our block. The man and his wife were friends of our family. My sister would sometimes baby-sit for their children. It is odd to me now to realize that I don't remember anyone in this family as well as I remember Philip and his theft of sweets. But then again, the story of the lollipops could be told openly in our own family, and this story could not. My sister whispered the details to me one night many years later. How my mother was often absent when our father, a fireman, would be working on one of his overnight or weekend shifts. How when she did not come back to feed us, my sister, who was twelve, did not know what to do. She must have felt overwhelmed. Once, she said, she held slices of roast beef under the hot water to warm them up for us, but I complained and would not eat the soggy results. I don't remember this. And I remember only vaguely going next door with her on some holiday to ask the neighbors for something to eat. Apparently there were many times during our mother's extended absences that I would be so upset, asking for her over and over again, that in desperation my sister would pick up the phone and pretend to talk to her, responding as if she were hearing her voice on the other end of the line. She would, she said, give me counterfeit messages, *Momma says she'll be home soon* or *Momma sends her love.*

It bothers me that I don't remember this. The memories from this time are all minor. Or at least at first glance they seem so. Because as I look more closely, the pattern is there. A correspondence of signs, not unlike the various alphabets found on the Rosetta stone, which allowed a translation not only of that text, but of a whole language.

There was the Christmas, for instance, when my grandparents came to visit. During their visit I went outside to play, and by the time I returned they had gone. I was disconsolate that I missed them. Another clear recollection is that one morning after breakfast when I asked my father where my sister had gone, he said she was in the orchard with her friends and didn't want me to tag along, that sometimes she liked to go places without me. Because my sister was more than six years older than I this made sense, but it was a reality I was not prepared to accept, and so I was furious with my father for telling me.

The theme, of course, is absence and loss. And there is another story, a sequel to the one I have already told. It is about my toys and how I sold them. My sister and I had been told that we were moving again. Though it wasn't entirely clear to me yet, my parents were divorcing. What I remember is sitting in our open garage behind the small table my sister and I used as a tea table, having set up a sign, as I had learned to do to sell lemonade, negotiating prices with the neighborhood children for all of my toys. It was solely my idea, one that horrified my mother and father especially because, having no idea of value, I had sold everything for pennies. That night my father went from house to house retrieving what he could. Did he ever relocate our splendid model of a fire truck, the one on wheels, just big enough for a small child to ride? I know I felt remorse, but still, as far as my toys were concerned, the strategy worked. I did not fear for their loss.

But I could not stem the loss that followed. One night just after I turned six I found myself in the backseat of a car with my sister. We were driving down Olympic Boulevard in Los Angeles, and as we passed the low brick buildings of Wilshire Crest, my sister said, pointing out the window, *Look, Susie, it's your old school. You'll be able to go back there again.* I was confused. How could I go there? Would my father drive me from the valley every day? *No,* my father, who was driving the car, said. And then he explained. Whether I was told before, I cannot say, but in any case, it was at this moment when I understood. I was to live with my grandparents. My mother was not with us in the car. And she would not be coming. Did I know yet that I alone was to be left with my grandparents? That the same night my father and sister would continue their drive down to San Pedro, where my sister was to live, at least for a few months, with my father's grandmother? I must not have taken this in yet, because my grief was concentrated on my mother. I remember this. I cried and could not be comforted, and when I could speak at all, the only words that would come out were that I had not said good-bye to her.

I can recall little else that happened that night. From what was told to me later, I have reconstructed what followed. My father took me to my grandmother's house. It was already dark. Did we eat dinner together, all of us? My sense of events, which is just that, a bodily feeling without imagery, is that we did not. For my father and my sister, there would have been a three-hour drive still to come. My father would have wanted to settle my sister before it got too late and, knowing him and his tendency to denial, he would have wanted to have the pain of the partings all behind him as soon as possible.

Did they lie to me? From their perspective, the word is too harsh. There would have been the desire to soften the experience. They would not have wanted to say as they left me behind, *This is forever; this is for good*. They would have said instead, *We'll see you soon; it won't be long*. Somehow I know that the first night at my grandparents' was terrible, and on one level of consciousness I must have known how complete my loss was. But I also know that I lied to myself too. That I told myself this was just a short episode, a brief story. I know this for a certainty because I waited, for weeks, months, years, half-consciously and then as time progressed unconsciously expecting each reunion to be final, the return that would at last put an end to leave-takings. This is how waiting became part of my body.

For a time my father, my sister, and I were frequently together at my great-grandmother's house in San Pedro. When I remember these gatherings it is as if in them I were a different child than the one who waited at my grandmother's house for the next visit. Left there, it was not just bereavement I felt but a kind of wrongness that began at the unseen core of myself and radiated outward, through my flesh into the atmosphere. Yet the movement was not only outward, nor was the origin of the wrongness clear. When I felt abandoned, it simply seemed to exist everywhere and could assault me in many forms. So one of my strongest memories from this time is the afternoon I was stung by a bee. The sharp needle of pain seemed to well out around me, fusing with the calamity of my family's departure, the sensation high pitched, maddening in its insistence, another proof that I was trapped in a torturous and hellish world whose miseries would only increase.

By contrast, the meetings at my great-grandmother's house seemed to float in their own aura, a world apart from the ferocious pain of loss. Sometimes I would stay overnight. We would all have dinner together and then go to the living room, where my sister and I would sit on the floor playing Pick-Up Sticks or Chinese checkers or Parcheesi. These were the days before television. Unlike my great-grandmother, Nanny, my father's father, Hal, who lived in this house with his mother, was preternaturally quiet. We were hardly aware of his presence. But the rest of us were animated and together measured as if to the same tempo, rounded to a kind of sweet normalcy. I remember being happy.

Except for the absence of my mother (and my father's mother), we easily could have been mistaken for the idealized family that was soon to be televised into so many homes. But like the eye of successive storms, one whose calm seems all the more untroubled because of its placement in time, this was a brief and transitory tranquillity. My great-grandmother was very old. As she grew more and more frail, my father could see that she was dying. So one morning before dawn, he asked my sister to pack her belongings and, with no more warning than that, put her in the car and drove ten hours north to where my great-aunt lived. She had been designated as my sister's eventual guardian, but no date had been set, and she too had not been warned. Years later, when my sister told me about the night she arrived, you could still hear the shock and hurt of it in her voice. How our aunt, who was shy and lived alone for years, was startled, how no welcome had been prepared, how a shyness that often seemed like sternness felt like sandpaper on the wound of my sister's sudden dislocation, how all of us seemed so far away, how my father nearly left her on the doorstep.

I too was unprepared, left ignorant of this, the last loss. Like the survivor of a disaster who wakes to find the world different, I was bewildered to find my sister absent. Standing in the hallway outside my great-grandmother's room, I heard my father argue with her. She was refusing to eat. Soon after, she died. My mother, my sister, my great-grandmother gone, and gradually my father's visiting twice a month: the ground beneath my feet had shifted, leaving my life shorn of all its reason.

The loss became part of my body. The other body, the body connected to my family, a lighter, quicker body, disappeared. I was pale and thin now. It wasn't lack of appetite so much as a subtle nausea I felt. Like that drop in the mercury one feels at a death, a nearly dizzy nausea had invaded me. Yet I was alert. Because the coma of my sadness was met with the opposite feeling, quickness again, but now a quickness of another sort, springing from my body not as natural expression but as effort. Like a weary explorer, cut off from her fellows, battling the elements alone, I was afraid of resting. I had to keep a vigil. I was looking for the return.

This vigilance became a habit, which, practiced for years, no doubt took a heavy toll on my body. And something else too made its way into my flesh, a subtle but always present sense of guilt, which drove me to another form of constant alertness. The wrongness I felt in my circumstances shaped itself into a story, a logic that afforded some order to the chaos of events as I remembered them. According to this plot, I was the one who had caused the diaspora of my family. Something in my character, something I did, had driven them all away. And now I was alert for causes in myself, errors and faults that might prevent them from ever returning.

Both kinds of vigilance blended easily with my grandmother's regimens. She had her eye on improving me. Only later have I understood that most everything that needed adjusting in me was a sign of being from an inferior class. The subtle snobbery that existed in America in the fifties, so proud of its growing middle classes, existed inside our family too, my father from a more working-class family, my maternal grandparents just over the line of status.

My speech, which was my father's speech, had to be corrected. Whenever I said, *He don't,* my grandmother would be fast to trill a sharp *He doesn't,* making me repeat the phrase. Constant corrections in posture, grooming, manners followed suit. No doubt these corrections contributed to the shyness I felt after my parents' divorce. Convinced of my general unacceptability, I worried constantly about making the wrong move. Slowly, sorrow and the sense of being rejected mixed with the sense that I too was from an underclass, a feeling that affected the way I held myself, becoming part of my posture, the shape of my spine.

Yet, though shyness made me appear quiet, that was not the weather of my internal condition. Where the body is concerned, being shy is not the same as being withdrawn. Withdrawal places a curtain between yourself and the rest of the world; you can be quiet in your isolation. But shyness will place you on an edge between society and solitude. Tense with watching, I was eager to decipher the rules, to catch signs of disapproval before they would explode into more rejection.

Years later an older lover took me for a picnic, and as we lay under pine trees he pointed out the small birds flying around the branches. They spend most of their lives, he told me, like this. Wings fluttering, moving rapidly from place to place, alert for predators, searching for food for themselves and their young. The description moved me. It was as if my own life were reflected in these creatures, rarely at rest, always working the air.

I held onto the image for years, longing to see the birds again, speaking with fascination about them to others, even before I understood what they evoked in me.

■ ■ ■

History left its mark. Grief's migration into my body could be seen
by anyone with a perceptive eye. That slumping posture of sorrow,
hunched shoulders anticipating rejection and the shame of being
rejected. A posture that is continually held will begin to shape the
spine. The attrition can be read now in X rays of the three cervical
disks that, like the uppermost branches of a tree, fan out at the top
of the spine, where there is evidence of a slow arthritic deterioration.

Aggravated by whiplash, this damage would have made me
more susceptible to a virus that attacks the nervous system. And
then there is the question of immunity. It is not just that fear and
anxiety create adrenaline, which suppresses the body's ability to
heal infection, but severe trauma in early childhood is known to
injure the developing immune system itself. Though exactly how, I
do not know. Is something altered in the blood? Or rather, the
intelligence of the blood? It is not just the brain that thinks. By
recent physiologies, what is called mind—the capacity for thought,
learning, response, memory, emotion—is spread by chemistry and
molecular structure throughout the body. The liver thinks and feels,
as does the heart, the kidney, and even blood cells.

Does trauma alter this intelligence, stunt it, the way abuse will
foreshorten a child's creativity? Perhaps the cell's ability to gener-
ate new antibodies, that creative activity of the immune system, is
affected. I am speculating now, of course, but the metaphor is
compelling. A state of shock for instance, the extended shock that
accompanies emotional trauma. You are bewildered by it. And not
just in your mind but in your flesh and bone. The hands with
which you pick up crayons and try to draw the letters of the
alphabet are leaden, numb. And deep inside, under your skin, the
cells coursing in your veins are blunted in their intelligence too,
narrowing their focus on survival, stupefied with exhaustion,
stopped in the beautiful spinning out of life, the intricacies of possibility. Swift to react to danger, the body tightens, limiting its

range, and the play of that vast and complex system of responses known as immunity is stunted.

This description gives me a certain sense of peace. Not from justification but through the satisfaction of exactitude, as if I had reached that place of rest in consciousness that can only be had after an experience has been named. Why is it then that the pronouncements of psychosomatic theory so often produce the opposite effect? They are disturbing. And in an undeniable way, humiliating. The description of your experience from this angle of perception is like an ill-fitting suit of clothes, unacceptably wrong, askew.

Dressed in this theoretical fabric, you will feel as if the fault lies with you, not with the garments given you. But no wonder this clothing does not fit. The cut too vague, the tailoring imprecise, these ideas are shaped not to bodily history so much as to a tradition afraid of the body. Like earlier philosophies that elevated the spirit above the material world, these theories hover above flesh, afraid to penetrate deeper, fearful of entering the dense and bloody realm of nature, afraid, above all, of the signature matter inscribes on the soul and thus, in a subtle but certain way, preserving the divide between mind and body.

Is this why I experience the suggestion that my mind has made my body sick with a dense, almost viscous shame? For me the embarrassment has a feminine feel, as if my slip were showing or I had bled onto the back of a skirt. The source is slippery, hard to define. But sex is somehow central to the prejudice.

The habit of associating women with mentally induced, imagined disease goes back at least in modern times to the first days of psychoanalysis. The bare beginnings can be found in the late nineteenth century, in the Salpêtrière hospital, where a group of women called hysterics were studied by Charcot. Some of these women seemed to have physical maladies, but no organic causes could be found, and in many ways, from their extravagant, irrational, and sometimes sexually provocative behavior, these women appeared to be mad. Then starting about 1888, working both separately and together Josef Breuer and Sigmund Freud claimed to have found both the cause and the cure of hysteria. Repression of memories and what Freud called "pathogenic ideas," among them improperly sexual desires, had caused the maladies, the doctors said, and the cure was to tell the real story.

But since a culture too has an unconscious life—assumptions, dreams, fears, prejudices that distort apprehension—I am looking now at certain pathogenic ideas that are part of the history of medicine. I am struck by the role women were given to play in this history. Depicted in the annals of medicine as inappropriate and mad, these women behave appropriately for their sex in one way: they are the passive recipients of healing. I can almost see the patient now, sitting on the half-round stage of the medical theater, an audience of doctors and students banked in tiers above her, the doctors who know her mind better than she does explaining her to them.

The passivity heightens the shame somehow. And the anonymity of subjects who seem to have no other story except madness. Miss Lucy R, Fräulein Elizabeth von R, Frau Emmy von N, Anna O. The bare initial was meant to protect reputations. But over time the disguise, like a mask worn in public by one who makes a shameful confession, lends to the embarrassment.

The discourse has changed over the last century. Details omitted or hardly emphasized in the history have come to light, altering the impression that these women were passive. The fact, for instance, that the "talking cure" was invented by a patient, one of the first whose illness was studied by Breuer, known as Anna O. She discovered that describing the first incidence of a symptom seemed to help her. And we know who Anna O was now. Hardly a passive woman, Bertha Pappenheim was the first social worker in Germany, a feminist organizer who founded the German Jewish feminist movement, translated Mary Wollstonecraft, worked for women's education.

Still, I can feel the dead weight of an earlier impression even now. Women depicted as ignorant of our own bodies, our own desires, prey to our own thoughts. Women's illnesses unreal and shrouding forbidden fantasies with an almost pornographic tone. It was not just psychoanalysis that was affected. All of medicine has inherited the mood.

And even apart from this mood, an emphasis on repression has narrowed the meaning of physical illness. More than once in my life I have found the insight liberating: whatever remains unspoken or buried will find a way to the surface. Even unconscious lies cause suffering in body and mind. But liberating as the insight is, regarding the psychology of illness, it has limited the field of understanding. Because, though undoubtedly repression is expressed as physical symptoms in some lives, what is far more common is the reverse. Conscious memory causes illness. Exploring the causes of my own sickness, I found I did not bury my childhood feelings. Though in the inner landscape of painful memory there will always be more to learn, I remembered what I suffered as a child. My problem was not repression but memory itself. I could not forget what I endured. It was not denial but vigilance that made me ill.

And there is this too. My illness was not the affect of a mute attempt by my body to express pain that my mind alone held. In its own way, my body thought, felt, and expressed everything that my mind did. Regarding the coherence of mind and body, ironically, the idea that the body expresses thoughts and feelings hidden in the mind preserves an odd duality, as if the body did not think and feel. Yet the mind does not inscribe the body with disease. Histories of sorrow enter flesh and bone at the same time as they enter the mind. Grief and fear move directly into flesh.

Of course in the beginning, Freud's insights into repression were not meant to apply to physical illness. He believed the symptoms he observed had no physical etiology. Though the categorization seems too simple now. Whether an illness is labeled as mental or physical, one can hardly ever isolate illness in either mind or body alone. Thinking of Anna O again I learned recently that, despite Breuer's claims, the talking cure did not heal her. She was hospitalized after she left his care, recovering only later when she moved to Frankfurt. And since no one has ever been able to say for certain how she recovered or why, both Freud's cure and his diagnosis are left in doubt. Perhaps among the other causes for her illness, there was also an organic reason for her hallucinatory states, one that, in the last century, would have been imperceptible to medical science. I can easily imagine coming across her case in a book by Oliver Sacks, the doctor who in our own times bears witness to the strange terrain of physical illness in the nervous system that we are just beginning to discover now.

Scientists are continually discovering that reality is far more interesting than science had supposed it to be before. Older systems of healing, ones we call superstitious now, recognized the limits of human knowledge. And this seems wise. Considering the causes of illness, one layered on another—a frightened thought, a cellular structure altered by environmental pollution, a virus, a social condition such as long hours of work—each intensifying the others, the complexity is infinite. As with consciousness itself, all of existence comes into play.

■ ■ ■

Time, for instance, is crucial. Though single dramatic events, repressed or remembered, can do terrible damage, what is far more common is a pattern of events, a repetition through which abuse or suffering is both evident and habitual. The effect is like geological erosion, as if history were inscribed in flesh.

Because of habit, though you may remember the original injuries, you may not be aware of the effect they have had on the body. Conscious awareness is like a theater, which, though it has a long repertoire in its archives, stages only one play at a time. Though an endless number of names, events, senses, feelings exist in memory all the time, very few of these memories are noticed at any given time. And given the neurological structure of awareness, which is tuned to notice what is new, the very abundance and familiarity of evidence can obscure significance. Repeated events, be they abusive or saddening, wounding or confusing, do not command attention. Unremarkable and quotidian, they are hardly noticeable. Like a proscenium arch or a curtain at the edge of the stage, what is habitual fades into the background.

By the repeated conditions of my childhood, I was made fearful and anxious in my body. But because fear and distrust had become the medium of my existence, until recently I never thought of myself as afraid. Yet over time the constant vigilance that once had helped me to survive became a source of danger, putting me on edge, making me fearful and worn out with worry. Though I do not seem like an anxious person, and the worry is hardly visible. Only now am I able to see that I have become accustomed to living as if perpetually on the edge of loss. If for much of my life I was unaware of feeling on the edge, it was because the feeling seemed normal to me.

The vigilance is not just in my mind. My body has learned the response. Whether the design be in the minuscule fragments of DNA inside the cell that create inheritance or in habitual responses to unpredictable events, the intelligence of the body is coded and expressed by pattern. And in the body, embedded in chemistry and nerve, pattern becomes substance. Though I am aware of the causes of my vigilance, my body remains vigilant without conscious will or desire.

But as a child, after my parents' divorce, I did not understand my frailty as the unwilled consequence of loss. Eventually I did provide a theoretical frame for my tendency toward illness, a logic that in its own way mirrors the shadowy blame of psychosomatic theory. I believed I was ill as a punishment for being ill. The reasoning is tautological. Such logic, itself nearly repressed, is never fully analyzed, and from this obscurity it derives a considerable power. Thus I could believe with an almost unshakable certainty that I was ill as a punishment for being ill.

I did have some evidence for my thinking. There was my mother's seeming indifference to my illness—when at eleven, for instance, I had my appendix taken out or when at an earlier age, a year after the family divorce, I had my tonsils surgically removed, and she did not come to the hospital. She said to me what she probably said to herself, that she could not come because she did not know how to drive a car. I remember waking up in the dark of a hospital room, a freakish pain in my throat from surgery that had gone badly, still nauseous from gas, the room nightmarishly unfamiliar, and she was not there. Nor did she come the next day when I was released to go home with my grandparents. Her absence continued. I can remember the radio by my bed and eating ice cream for supper but never a visit from her.

Even after she remarried when I lived with her again, I could not rely on her care. She might be there for two days, as once she was when I had a high fever, but if my illness continued past that her perseverance did not. On the third afternoon she would be gone again. And I would call my father or my grandmother to help me.

The pattern of neglect was clear. I could feel it in my flesh, as I could when my mother would draw away as we embraced. Her love for me was tenuous. Such a message migrates directly into bone, blood, marrow, tissue. When one is left alone, vulnerable, weak, filled with trepidation and pain, a process of reasoning begins. Neglect creates a physical sense of being bad that will be seared into the memory of flesh. And from this memory the body asks a question: *Why?* The answer, of course, is inevitable. The sense I had in my body was of a fundamental wrongness, an essential, unalterable part of the crystalline structure of my being, inseparable from any illness I had, a vortex condemning me to pain and rejection, suffering the cause of suffering.

I rarely expressed these feelings in words. Except, after my parents' divorce, during the first year with my grandmother, when I was chastened or found at fault, I would run down the long hallway in the back of the house, curl myself into a corner, and cry. And when my grandmother or father coaxed me out of the corner, I would say that nobody loved me, speaking not as recrimination against others but as an expression of my own failure.

Yet that is not the whole story. Like Alphonsine Plessis, I was spirited. Looking at photographs of myself from this time, I am struck by how different I appeared from how I thought I looked. I would have expected a forlorn face, slumped body. But along with frailty there is a bright energy in these pictures, even humor. No history is simple. Even tragedy has laughter in it. For any character to be true to life and in any way compelling, the author must capture not only the wound but resistance to the wound, the vast and complex creativity of human response to pain and difficulty.

All the complexity of human intelligence is evident in the body. This is one of the reasons why *Camille* is still so compelling on the stage. The novel seems outdated. But if in his prose, Dumas *fils* overburdened his telling with an antiquated morality, on the stage, his lines are spoken by a real woman. We can see and feel and hear her. Her body is present. I saw a production of *Traviata* recently at the Metropolitan Opera, and its last act had me at the edge of my seat. Violetta's poignancy was terrifying, the white folds of her lacy dressing gown swooping now upward with exhilaration, hope, now downward with a failing life force, her body shuddering with sobs, then calm and quietly balanced, her voice floating on the thinnest strand of existence.

That the life of the body has a meaning all its own is made evident in death. All the meaning of bodily existence is transfixed by this moment. And if there is a meaning that is intrinsic to each death, at the same time each death is symbolic of every death. Such is the case with all the events in the life of the body; to eat, to sleep, to make love, to be born, to die are not only meaningful in themselves, they also evoke every meal, every kind of rest or union, every beginning and every end.

To make one thing stand for another is the fundamental activity of consciousness. Neither thought nor feeling as we know them could exist without metaphor. The idea moves me as I write in the direction of a subtle hope. To understand that metaphor is part of the structure of body and mind. Because in the deepest sense, metaphor is itself symbolic. It both signifies and proves connection. Whenever you say a child's cheeks are apple red or you call an actor a star, you are weaving all existence—human character, culture, the cosmos—into one fabric. Can it be that in this way consciousness mirrors nature? How everything has a common origin, how the atoms and molecules and the cells that make up our bodies once belonged to other bodies, bodies of animals or plants or to the soil, the sunlight, the air, stars, how in death the stuff of ourselves will slowly return to the common supply of matter.

■　■　■

Metaphor is at the heart of all sacred rituals too; the cross, the wafer, the Torah, the ark, all holy in themselves, also stand for larger realms of meaning. The same is true of what occurs on any stage, whether sacred or profane. Even the most realistic play is also symbolic. As you watch the story of a child with AIDS prevented from attending school, you know that the plot is not unique. The drama is meant to reveal a pattern. In this way the theater is like so many holy sacraments through which the body of a god is symbolically eaten. Consuming this body, you take all existence into yourself.

The magic occurs in the reflection. The same events that are revelatory in the theater can have another effect when they are experienced directly. In real life any of the great and tragic emotions—grief, sorrow, fear, desire, loss—can as easily foreshorten as enlarge the life of your soul. This is especially so with the fear that accompanies poverty. As Lar Eighner writes about his homelessness, "Your perspective on the street shrinks to the next five minutes and the last five minutes." Only by surviving to tell the tale was he able to gain wisdom from his suffering.

Even now as I write about my own life, I can feel that curious separation from myself that occurs from self-reflection. The usual way of thinking of this divide is that the mind removes itself from the body. But if you believe, as I do, that body and mind are one, the mystery of the separation deepens.

Dumas *fils* must have felt a slight but enlightening distance from his own life as he wrote first the novel and then the play, *La dame aux camélias*. Everyone who attended the first performances would have known the play was based on a real story. And the story of his love affair with Marie Duplessis stood for many other stories too. Stories of other courtesans and lovers, rich and poor. By a common miracle of art, as he wrote, the story ceased to be his own any longer. Yet distance has a paradoxical effect. Though I have experienced it countless times, the process is always astonishing. As you distance yourself from your story, you are moved by the telling toward still deeper levels of yourself.

Was Dumas *fils* aware of all the ways that the story he told reflected his own history? Much of his family history, including the author's grief over the loss of his mother, can be found there. Though, of course, all this history is told between the lines.

Like Alphonsine Plessis, Marie-Catherine Labay, who was the mother of Dumas *fils,* started as a *grisette.* She met Alexandre's father, the elder Dumas, when he arrived in Paris to work as a secretary for the duc d'Orleans. He took a room in number one Place des Italiens, a building where students or clerks on the rise lived alongside the working people. This is where Catherine lived too. Soon they were lovers and soon after sharing rooms. Their son Alexandre was born two years later. But he was listed in the registry as *father unknown.* The elder Dumas left before he was born.

That fathers sometimes abandon their children is an old story. But here the plot turns. When his son was almost eight years old, the elder Alexandre decided to claim custody of him. His mother fought the decision, but the usual charges were brought against her. *She had conceived her son out of wedlock. She was a fallen woman.* And then there was this. While Dumas had risen in the world, she remained poor. Catherine would not be able to give her son the same advantages of education, culture, station. The court gave her son to his father.

The boy was grief-stricken. He adored his mother and never forgave his father for the loss. Neither could he forget that his father took him from her only to send him away to a boarding school. Here he had his first taste of humiliation. His illegitimate birth, his mother's poverty, that he was not schooled in the manners of upper-class boys made him the object of merciless teasing.

And this is where an even earlier history enters. Still another fact from his heritage drew the ridicule of his fellow students. When he was at school, the younger Dumas was also teased for being black. His great-grandmother, Marie-Cessette Dumas, was of African descent. Sometime in the third decade of the eighteenth century, Antoine-Alexandre, the future marquis de la Pailleterie, seeking to make his fortune, arrived in Haiti. There, paying an "exorbitant price" because she was so beautiful, he bought Marie-Cessette. Whether she wished it or not is unknown, but they lived together as lovers for twenty years. And in that time she bore him four children, one of whom was named Thomas-Alexandre.

Many themes in *Camille* must have migrated onto the stage from this history filled with abandonment and loss, the sad effects of a rigid class system and the sale of human bodies. In 1772 after the death of Marie-Cessette, Antoine-Alexandre, now a marquis, returned to France to reclaim his estate. The new marquis left three of his children in Haiti, arranging a fictitious sale of them to a friend whom he believed would "treat them well." He planned to take Thomas-Alexandre with him. But first, because he did not have the means to pay the captain even for his own passage home, the marquis traded his son for the price of his own passage, with the understanding that as soon as he sent the necessary funds, the captain would put Thomas-Alexandre on a ship for France.

The transaction went as planned, but I cannot help but wonder what it was like for Thomas-Alexandre in the meantime. He had never really been treated as a slave. He could not know for certain that his father would return to him. That his temporary condition was a practical necessity would not have erased the terror.

When Thomas arrived in France to live with his father, he was openly received into aristocratic society. But Antoine failed to provide the support his son would need to become financially independent. He gave his son money on request yet refused to give him any support for professional training. Thomas had no career, no means to earn his own living. Thus when Antoine married his housekeeper, placing his son's inheritance in doubt, Thomas decided to join the army as a foot soldier. Opposing the decision, Antoine forbade his son to use the family's aristocratic name. Thomas's rank was so low that Antoine felt the family name would be dishonored. But Thomas would not obey his father. Instead he angrily relinquished his aristocratic heritage. It was at this point that he took his mother's name, Dumas.

His rebellion was not just against his father. He questioned the whole social order, including the power of aristocrats. As Thomas's famous son would do one day, the young soldier cast his lot with the Republican cause. Many times decorated for his heroism, Thomas became a general in Napoleon's army. Eventually he commanded all the cavalry in Napoleon's Italian campaign. It was perhaps these exploits that inspired the heroism in his son's famous novel, *The Three Musketeers*. Thomas-Alexandre Dumas was a legendary warrior. According to one story, though wounded three times, his coat pierced by seven balls, he single-handedly defended the Bridge of Bixen in Austria, fending off dozens of men, two or three at a time, with only his saber.

In 1772, the general married a French woman named Marie-Louise. They rented a castle in Villers-Cotterêts, not far from Paris, and began a family. But his fortune was soon to fall. Brave in his speech as well as deed, Thomas openly protested when Napoleon's ambitions began to exceed his democratic ideals. For this, in a long and lonely sojourn reminiscent again of a novel by his son, he was to spend several years in prison. Napoleon jailed his general. When in 1801 he was released, he was a broken man. Alexandre, born just over a year after his father's return, was only four when his father died. Yet as Dumas writes of a young character in *The Count of Monte Cristo,* he was not too young to suffer and recall an event of "great significance."

Thomas-Alexandre was ashamed of dying in bed, "like a coward," abandoning his wife and children. Shame is rarely just. I doubt Napoleon felt ashamed over what he had done to his general or for his treatment, a few years later, of another man, the Haitian insurrectionist Toussaint L'Ouverture, whom he also imprisoned. Dumas worshiped his father as a hero. But he must have inherited his shame too. Without a public acknowledgment of justice, shame has a long half-life. It will be silently transmitted from one generation to the next.

In the first decades of the nineteenth century, when first Alexandre Dumas and then his son were born, slavery was still legal in the United States. The moral tide, however, was turning. By the time I was born, over a hundred years later, slavery had become an unthinkable evil. But shame still fell more heavily on those who came from the families of former slaves than on those from families that had engaged in slavery. I remember seeing a film when I was about ten years old about the shame of having any African heritage. The heroine's mother was considered black, but she could pass as white. She tried to keep her secret. Yet secrets cause their own grief.

Moving from one class to another, you retain more than your share of secrets. At the Château de Monte Cristo, his father's country house, which has recently been restored, I saw a painting of Alexandre as a boy. It must have been painted around the time his father took him from his mother. He is dressed luxuriously in lace and velvet. But the posture of his slight body and the expression on his small, almost ethereal face suggest he is not entirely comfortable in this costume.

I can sense the eros of their union, the real lovers, Marie and
Alexandre. These two histories intersect in so many places. A lover
who shares an experience with you is like a mirror, a metaphor
connecting you to larger worlds, different and yet the same,
expanding the boundaries of your own past. Both were in mourn-
ing for a lost world, which nevertheless they were happy to leave
behind. On the deepest unspoken levels of the body, they must
have shared an ambivalence, reflecting the divisions of class within
them. That Alexandre's father was celebrated, his mother poor, his
great-grandfather an aristocrat, his great-grandmother a slave was
echoed in Marie's history, her mother's father from an aristocratic
family, her father illegitimate and poor. And in still another way of
understanding the tale, her story mirrored his too, her father a
charming and duplicitous survivor, her mother, the victim of his
brutality, gone.

Alexandre was furious at his father for abandoning his mother.
Eventually he took up the cause of single, unmarried mothers, yet,
perhaps because he still wished to be accepted by conventional
society, he did so in a conventional fashion. As he aged, though he
had extramarital affairs himself, he was known to be something of
a prude. At the end of his life he grudgingly supported women's
rights but never their sexual freedom. His morality bore the tincture of a convert. He liked to compare himself with Augustine. The
simile held. Because in his younger years he had imitated his
father's style of life, gambling, womanizing, dressing as a dandy,
spending more money than he had, like the saint, he saw himself
as a repentant sinner.

That he had acquired a highly cultivated taste for luxury would
be an understatement. In this perhaps he had the manner of a convert too. The story goes that one night his father stopped at an inn
for dinner, and seeing several chickens roasting on the fire, asked
for one. But the waiter said they had no chickens left, since all the

chickens roasting on the fire had been ordered by one man dining alone upstairs. This man had ordered six of a part known as *le sot-ly-laisse,* the treasured tenderloin, a small morsel to be found on the back of the breast, favored by gourmets. From the sophistication and extravagance of the order, Dumas knew immediately that his son was the man who was dining upstairs.

Thinking of the near-starvation diet consigned to so many who worked with their hands, the contrast is appalling. But sitting at the tavern, Alexandre would be experiencing the contrast in another way. Like the shimmering velvet that had shined from his legs as a boy, the dish was a sign of his refinement. Along with Marie Duplessis, he was drawn to aristocracy. For years he had an affair with the wife of a Russian prince who bore him a daughter before they married.

At age sixty-three Dumas *fils* left his wife for a woman who was just thirty-six years old. Many powerful men marry young women late in life. It is almost as if they were trying to buy back a youthful body for themselves. But it must be something more than physical youthfulness they want too. After the getting of money, which requires the loss of innocence, the desire would be to possess innocence again.

Much of what we consider refined, if not innocent, is delicate, tender, or soft. I understand the desire for luxury. Surrounded by it, you become alive again to subtle gradations in taste, scent, texture. Immersed in it, you can easily enter a blissful state, not unlike enlightenment. Having been poor and deprived once would only heighten the feeling. It must have been what Marie Duplessis felt, emerging from the miseries of *grisette*'s life into a world of sheen and delight. And because she was ill, this feeling would only have been redoubled. To move from a darkened bedroom out into the world, in a body newly freed of pain, is a dazzling experience.

■ ■ ■

In her lifetime, Marie Duplessis was a living symbol of refinement. The composer Franz Liszt described her as the most feminine woman he had ever known. Of course, he was describing a femininity she was able to achieve only after her rise, the product of many goods and services. But he must have loved her also because she was the child of Norman peasants and had grown up wandering the fields. Through all her refinement, she still had a wild side, a seemingly uncontrollable nature. She delighted in irreverent humor. And she would dismiss men who bored her, whatever their station in life. She must have shared this side of herself too with Liszt. Despite the astonishing technical polish of his music, you can hear a rawness in the temper of it. I can sense the connection between them in the crashing force.

He spoke of her as the first great love of his life. As she lay dying, it was Liszt and not Dumas whom she hoped to see again. "I will not live; I am an odd girl and I will not be able to hold on to this life which I have no idea how to lead," she wrote him, "and which I can't stand anymore." She wanted to go with Liszt on his tour. "Take me, lead me wherever you like; I will be no trouble to you," she said. "I sleep all day, go to the theater in the evening and at night you may do what you will to me." Even though Liszt was a lover and not a customer, she was still trading sex for what she wanted. He promised to return and take her with him into warmer weather, but he never did.

Dumas did not include this interlude in his story of her death. The plot was so much more romantic with just one lover, just one loss. Though in a sense, traces of Liszt were present in Armand's father, who worries about his son's future, his career. Ambition was something Liszt shared with Marie Duplessis. Both were pushed too early into hard work. First as her father's servant, then as a *grisette,* Alphonsine had had to work long hours as a child, and if she was freed from this labor at the age of sixteen, she made great and rapid efforts to transform herself, body and soul, into the cultivated woman Liszt celebrated. For his part, talented as a child, Franz was pushed by his father, who sensed his value as a prodigy and drove him demonically to practice at every available hour. He was still very young when he began to meet a grueling schedule of performances and tours. They were of course not alone in the passion for success. Then as now, it defined the age.

If you are worked to the edge or beyond your capacity every day, strain becomes habitual. You do not stop when others would but continue until continuing further seems impossible. Even idle, your body will hurry; it will keep laboring at nothing. You can hear a certain haste in the great composer's music. It has a pounding urgency, almost like heavy metal. He was famous for writing compositions that required such a quick agility that only he could play them.

But there is something else present too, a kind of rebellion that the lovers must have shared. The mood is evident in Liszt's tone poems, a dreaminess along with floating moments of sweetness. But strangely, though the tempo is slower, the propelling force remains, as if the music were searching desperately for what was always just out of reach. And wouldn't this also have been the case with Marie, who kept long nights after the gentlemen who supported her had gone home, desperately trying to find, in these early hours, a life of her own?

She was famous for her restless activity. *If I slow down,* she told a friend, *I might die.* Though her pace contradicted the needs of the body, her words echo a modern logic that is familiar. Among all the other appeals of this legend, one must include the fact that the frenzied pace of her life was a harbinger of things to come. Trains. Steamboats. Airplanes. Cars. More speed lay in the future. Technology mirrors intent. Speed is the modality of ambition. Clerks hoping to rise in the bureaucracy of government, lawyers wanting to make a name for themselves, businessmen seeking to stay ahead of inflation, the economy growing daily. In this atmosphere, every minute counts.

Franz never forgave his father for pushing him so violently. But I wonder what drove his father. A memory of poverty? The fear of falling back is the cost of ascension. Did he fear that his son would be swallowed up by circumstances, lost in the stream of men and women whose years were used up like coal or timber for the profits of others? Or had the memory of want faded in the family tradition, become just a bodily response, a reaction whose original cause no one could name any longer?

The consequences of social history are often disguised when they enter family history. Thinking of the ambitions of the last century, I have been able to trace a lineage of uneasiness in my family history. The effects came into my own life in a form that was hardly recognizable. Delivered to me by my mother through drunken invectives, this inheritance encased my soul in judgment. By daylight when my mother was sober, she would praise me. I was good, intelligent, talented, good looking, she said. She lavished her greatest praise on my early accomplishments. But late at night, if she had had enough to drink, her attitude toward me would change. Settling the intensity of her gaze on me again, she would begin a litany of my sins. She began with what I can see clearly now is a projection. I was too critical of her, she said. Then she complained that I was prudish. I didn't know what it was to have fun. But soon she accelerated her censure. I was not capable of loving anyone, she said. Or her remarks would take a more direct focus; my laugh was too loud, my hair wrong. I knew she was drunk and unjust in what she said. But the sting of her words entered me all the same, mixing with her drunkenness, the bad smell of liquor and cigarettes, the disheveled state of the room, as if everything there reflected me and I was someone secretly worthy of assault.

In the daytime, I would work to redeem myself with the perfection of my accomplishments, my behavior, my appearance. My ambition was tied irrevocably with shame and, as I have come to understand over time, my family's lineage. I was able to trace the pattern of the cycle from what my mother told me years later. She was shy, she said, listing this as among the reasons why she drank. Linking her shyness to my own, I remembered how critical my grandmother could be. Everything and everyone in her purview fell under a scrutinizing gaze. She was looking for flaws. Evidence of being ill mannered, ill bred, common. But of course I can see now that she must have been constantly anxious herself. As if she also was never quite good enough. And from a remark repeated frequently to me by my sister, I have located the source of her anxiety. My great-grandfather, her father, an exacting man, was a farmer. *But he had pretensions,* my sister said, *he wanted to be a gentleman farmer.* He wanted, in other words, to assume a station in society higher than the one to which he had been born.

Some version of this history must exist in every family, whether rich or poor. On my mother's side I know that more than once fortunes rose and fell. There was one revolutionary general. There were the more prosperous relatives in Virginia. But as with Alphonsine's great-grandmother, not everyone born to wealth inherits it. Fear of falling rings all our lives.

As I write about my grandmother another story returns to me. It is a tale of almost military glory, recalling knights in shining armor. Here the goal of the effort is not wealth but nobility. The story is about a particularly virulent illness she survived. Was it scarlet fever? Influenza? I can't say. I only know that her fever was very high and that her mother was worried. It was a time when children more often died of passing disease. There were no antibiotics then. When the doctor came, he prescribed a shot of whiskey. But the week before when she was in church, my grandmother had taken a pledge not to drink alcohol. And so, despite the intensity of her illness, she declined the medicine.

Even though my mother was an alcoholic, a fact that caused much misery to the family, this was not a cautionary story about the evils of liquor. Our home was not dry. Curtailed in his habits, my grandfather who himself had been an alcoholic before I was born, was allowed just one shot of whiskey daily, which he drank every night at six in the evening, and occasionally my grandmother, no longer particularly religious, had a frozen daiquiri with him. The real point of the story was not drink. My grandmother wanted us to know that she had stared down her fever and won. She never broke her resolve. Her body and its own desire to survive were clearly subsidiary to the main line of the plot, a drama that showed her gallantry.

Her story belongs to a popular genre, one that can only be described as heroic. In it the ill are courageous or uncomplaining or spiritually transformed as they rise above staggering odds to get well. Braving the battleground of disease, mind conquers body. Though he has collapsed into sleep, the stalwart soldier stays in his saddle. Believing she is suffering for the sins of the world, a saint refuses medical treatment. Against medical advice, an athlete pushes his ailing body to run. Asserting mind over matter, a woman imagines herself well and recovers. A man changes his profession, moves to another country; a grumpy old woman begins to get well as she becomes loving toward others; a young man says he is determined not to let his illness defeat him and, despite the virus in his blood, seems healthy.

I could easily have fashioned my story along these lines. Certainly suffering winnows the grain of the soul. And although I am still ill, I am far less ill. Able to work, to shop for my own groceries, to take care of myself, to the uneducated eye I appear well. But I decided to tell the story of my recovery less as a heroic triumph than as good fortune. As reassuring as stories of triumph are, bringing with them the sense that the challenge of illness can be met by courage and conversion, there is an aftereffect to this drama. A second plot begins to echo even as the curtain is falling. Subtly but surely, a scripture of shame has been etched into ailing flesh. In the shadow of triumph, those who remain ill, who succumb to chronic suffering, or who die in too much pain or deprivation to die well have lost a battle.

My loyalty to those who are ill now is too great to cast my narrative in this mode. And I am thinking too of the frailer self I leave at home when I am well enough to go out. Despite the shame I feel when I am ill, I have also wished that someone would simply bear witness to my experience. I know I am not alone in this wish. I suspect even the heroic share the desire to be known in this way.

As I navigate my memory of my grandmother, I am beginning to sense the silence of a frightened child underneath the story of her heroism. Vain and charming, seemingly confident, my grandmother exuded a social power that was only augmented by an abiding sense that she was morally superior to the rest of the family. Up at dawn, she worked hard at her domestic tasks, letting us all feel the sacrifice. When her feelings were hurt or she was offended, she expressed herself grandly with superb dramatic timing. She was so formidable one never thought of her as fearful. And yet, though the feeling would have been buried deep and covered by several protective layers, she must have been afraid.

It was hidden from me at the time, but as an adult I learned that she had an operation for cancer. No one spoke of it openly in our household. The silence was not just for my benefit. I doubt many of her friends knew. In the light of this disclosure, I find my mind rereading the barely concealed resentment with which she cared for me whenever I was ill.

■ ■ ■

And I am beginning to see the delineations of a larger narrative too in these private memories. A story that does not belong to my family exclusively but to a shared body. Born of a specific time and place, modern European and American history, I have named it the mercantile body. A body, still familiar to us today, that frantically consumes more than it needs. But this body is also being consumed and in the process made meaningless, a thing.

In the process of destruction, the mercantile body might be compared to a soldier's body, trained to be fodder for the battlefield. In many ways, living in our current economy is like being engaged in warfare. The battles here may be less visibly violent, but survival is still at stake and death, though often slower and more subtle, a product of the attrition of work that is too demanding, harsh conditions, or the constant stress, which belongs even to the successful, may well be the price of both defeat and victory. Answering the question, *What has made me ill,* I know the mercantile body is also mine.

Any illness can be read as a metaphor of the soul. But it is not just one soul that lies in the balance. Illness of every kind holds up a mirror to society. Considering my own history—the psychological antecedents to my illness, all the specificities of my childhood, the loss of those I loved, the continual moves, a surfeit of anxiety as well as grief—though this would appear to be just a personal history of casualty occurring from the private disasters of one family alone, it is not. For my generation, divorce and alcoholism have been twin hallmarks of family life in America.

Even regarding abandonment, my history is less unique than exemplary. I was fortunate in one sense. Though I was abandoned at every turn, someone took me in—my grandparents, my father, and finally the adoptive family who sheltered me after my father's death. This is not always the case with children whose parents cannot care for them or who leave them. And then, of course, even with parents who seem to be present, there are many ways to abandon a child. Perhaps those of us who have suffered abandonment in a more visible way are like canaries in the mine too. The state of grief, loss, and disorientation we have felt are just an exaggeration of the mood many share.

The cycle of cause and effect folds back on itself. The hope is that success will heal the grief. And thus the mood of loss only provides fuel for the mercantile body. Yet, in the great effort to succeed, something inside must be continually abandoned. A larger range of emotion, love, need, desire, bodily knowledge, which is irrelevant to ambition. Despite the sacrifices we make, whatever we are seeking always eludes us. We are left with that state of urgency, alertness, distrust, anxiety I felt as a child. Hurry, stress, overwork, the constant rush of adrenaline, all features of daily life in America now, compose the tenor and tone of the contemporary zeitgeist.

Still, as chastening as it is, there is something in the insight that I find healing. I am able to see my illness now as both consequence and measure of a common history. This larger vision transforms the alienation I have felt being ill into a kind of kinship. There is poetic justice here. Damaged as a child in body and soul by separation, I am weaving a fabric of union from the threads of isolation.

And there is something else too that I am experiencing now from this new angle of vision. The sense I have is of an almost transparent presence. I am thinking of the light Corot saw, first gracing the landscape of Italy, then everywhere, a light so warm you feel it. When I understand how my story is not just my own but belongs to a larger one, I can feel a distinct bodily pleasure. It is like being held, sustained by perception.

Is this what we seek from theater? In Paris, I interrupted my research on *La dame aux camélias* to attend a rare screening of several short films made at the turn of the century, roughly fifty years after the premiere of Dumas's play. Europeans dressed in khaki suits trekking into Africa had shot footage of religious ceremonies. Bodies painted and costumed to resemble the spirits of animals and ancestors moved in resonant chorus. Except for the Europeans, there was no audience. Only men and women dancing as one body.

Communion is at the heart of Greek theater too, the ancestor of drama as I came to know it finally, watching the light body of Garbo's laughter on my grandparents' television. Everyone gathering in one place, in accordance with a shared calendar, the earth's turning, the seasons, moving in syncopation, wondering at the same events, the drama hardly distinguishable from the mystery of existence itself.

Union. Participation. You are at the edge of a circle, a curving force of mystery that will sweep you into its motion and then, as you join its expanding path, enlarge you even as you recognize your own smallness. You will begin to feel yourself dissolve into this that you cannot even name as it touches and then swallows everything you see. The sloping hill, the mountain beyond, the birds that fly over the mountain, the sky, memory, all the dead, and even the unborn.

In the remains of the old Greek theaters, the one at Dodona for instance, one can still see the circle where all things become one. If once there was no separation between actor and audience, the round is still there, audience in a half circle, altar and stage at the center of the diameter, and past the *skene,* the other half of the circle, a circumference that includes everything, the high peaks beyond, the thunderous creation that peaks over these mountains, all that is visible trailing off into invisibility beyond, the infinite.

■　■　■

Though in modern theater the audience may have receded into a darkened rectangle, the pull of the circle can still be felt, gathering every thought and emotion, even the tendrils of each imagination, into a central action. An actor going close to the bone of any experience evokes every experience and in this way seems to capture the most private feelings of the audience as if they were part of the play.

How is it done? Emotion made so palpable that you who are in the audience begin to feel it too. The great French actor Talma, who paved the way for realism in the nineteenth century, believed that actors are born with a larger capacity to feel. Sarah Bernhardt, who came after him, felt the same. "He who is incapable of feeling strong passion," she said, "of being shaken by anger, of living in every sense of the word, will never be a great actor."

Unless they are failing at the art, actors do not pretend to feel. The emotions you see on stage or in a film are real. Watching *Camille*, one senses this reality. As George Cukor once said of Garbo, she lived the parts she played. She would go to great lengths to let herself experience whatever the role required. As preparation for *Camille*, she did all she could to make herself fall in love with Robert Taylor, who was to play Armand. She did not want to meet him until just before the filming began. She asked that their first meeting take place on the set where the lovers meet in the film. Cukor, who directed the film, had built an exact replica of the Théâtre des Variétés. She entered the stage an hour late, wearing silk pajamas, and remained polite but distant. She wanted to retain a romantic image of him, untarnished by familiarity.

But how is it an actor can portray feelings she has not experienced herself? The question intrigues me if only because I suspect it implies an answer that is even more mysterious, that the knowledge of every possible human experience is in everyone. The entire body of human emotions. And just as actors call on this knowledge when they perform, we in the audience call on a similar ability, ferreting out whether or not the acting seems true to the event, even when the event is not one we have experienced ourselves.

And there is still one more kind of alchemy that occurs in the theater. In any one performance, countless lives will people the stage. Along with the life of the playwright, the lives of all those who take part in the production will be present. Since theater is a communal form, in the creative process each expression of insight and emotion multiplies in other hearts and minds only to echo in still other expressions. The story is, for instance, that Giuseppe Verdi began to write the score for *La Traviata* on the same night that he saw *La dame aux camélias*. The love affair between Marguerite and Armand reflected a circumstance in his own life. He attended the play with his mistress, Giuseppina Strepponi, a singer and star in Italian opera. They had sought refuge in Paris to escape the scandal that their liaison had caused in Italy. Seeing the play, he was able to hear the music of his own story.

During any performance, there are always many stories being staged. Actors borrow feelings from their own memories to create a role. Bernhardt would have used her own experience of illness, for instance, performing the role of a sick woman. She claimed she had tuberculosis, which many people had, in that era, in an almost chronic form; at times she coughed up blood or fainted, and despite her prodigious energy she could be frail.

And as she played Marguerite Gautier, dying, abandoned by her lover, hoping against hope for his return, she could also call on her childhood. Sent away as an infant to live with a wet nurse then later to live with her nanny, she was separated from her mother at an even younger age than either Dumas *fils* or Alphonsine Plessis had been. Parting was the most continuous event in her young life.

■ ■ ■

By what strange chemistry do so many disparate events come to exist on one stage? As Sarah performed the part of Marguerite, her early losses would have been there, just as the playwright's grief for his mother was there as he wrote. When a play has had a long life, transmuting to different forms, as *La dame aux camélias* has had, life after life will be burnished into its patina. Just as Verdi's love for his mistress can be heard in the music of *Traviata*, the death of Irving Thalberg, the well-loved producer who suggested Camille to Garbo, is present in the film. As is the death of George Cukor's mother, or the vaguely defined illness that Garbo was fighting. When Callas sang the part of Violetta in *Traviata*, soon after Onassis left her, you would have heard that loss in her voice. And shadowing all the characters, the lives of the men and women the characters represented, those of rising professionals like Armand, of bourgeois men like Armand's father, of playboys like Gaston, of philandering aristocrats like the Count de Giray or Arthur de Varville, or of courtesans like Marguerite, would have been there too.

And by the same wonderful alchemy, as Sarah Bernhardt played Marguerite Gautier, Bernhardt's mother, Youle, would have been on the stage too. She was a courtesan. Well known in her time, she was hostess and lover to many prominent and famous men, among them the elder Dumas. With her amorous labors, she paid for a comfortable, even luxurious, household, including the cost of Sarah's nanny and the privileged Catholic school to which Sarah was sent when she was older.

Youle's intention was to give her daughter an upper-class education. A kept woman had to know how to behave. But Sarah fell in love with the church, the ritual, the incense, the gold robes, the beautiful prayers, the fervent, kneeling postures of her teachers. For a period, though this was not what her mother had planned for her, Sarah was determined to become a nun. The desire was taken as calamitous by Youle, who hoped her daughter would soon be able to add income to the household. Growing older and less beautiful, she knew her income would decrease with age.

Soon after Sarah graduated from school, Youle began to teach the art she practiced to her daughter. In this craft one is expected less to feel than to pretend. To earn her keep she would have to cock her head at a lover, stick out her lower lip, look moved, seem aroused, seductive, lower her eyelids, pout her lips for a kiss, stick her bustle out, not too far, not too crudely, but farther than a lady would, hover over him, showing the dark crease between her breasts, pluck at his beard, pull open his tie, toss her head and laugh as if teasing him, focus on him alone, her eyes adoring, pretending all the while that he was the only man in her thoughts.

Sarah did not like the vocation. On more than one occasion Youle badgered, prodded, and pushed her daughter into the arms of a benefactor. She would grow angry when her daughter was not successful in enticing enough money. In a thinly disguised novel about Bernhardt, a friend, the actress Marie Colombier, recalled an incident when Sarah was urged to sit on the lap of a man who was old enough to have been her grandfather. "Hypnotized by her mother's unwavering stare, Sarah, despite her aversion, allowed Monsieur Regis to fondle her although she shuddered each time his lips touched her lovely neck. . . . Her docility was rewarded with a banknote from Regis and a smile of approval from her mother." But Sarah was even more stubborn than her mother. Her insistence on a religious calling continued unabated.

Sometimes history will present a surprising solution to a conflict. It was the elder Dumas who broke the impasse. He suggested taking Sarah with her mother to a performance at the Comédie-Française. Though Youle was hardly interested in what occurred onstage, Sarah was transfixed. "When the curtain went up," Sarah wrote years later, "I thought I would faint. It was the curtain of my life that rose before me." At the end of the play she broke into wild sobs. Dumas could see the signs of talent in her passionate response. Soon he was teaching her how to read lines from Racine's *Phèdre,* in preparation for her studies at the Conservatoire.

Still, even after she became an actor, she would continue to be a courtesan for at least two more decades. Only after touring America with *Camille,* where she made over a million dollars, could she afford to stop her second profession. She was not alone in her second profession. In the last century, most actresses were paid too little to support themselves. It was understood that their salaries would be supplemented by wealthy admirers.

In the light of this hidden history, I can understand why my great-grandfather so adamantly refused to let my grandmother join the traveling theater that passed through Champaign-Urbana, Illinois, near the end of the century. She was a talented young woman, and extraordinary for the time, studying dramatic arts at the university. The disappointment was devastating. She spoke of it frequently. I have often thought that the frustration of her talent shaped our family, with sad reverberations in my mother's life and in my own.

As I watched *Camille* so many years ago, the circumstances that shaped my grandmother's destiny eluded me. I hardly knew that courtesans were paid for the pleasure of their favors, much less that actresses plied the same profession. But Garbo knew. And her knowledge must have reached me wordlessly, so that, though it was not told openly, my body learned the secret.

Perhaps the necessity for discretion explains why the meeting at the Théâtre des Variétés between Marguerite and Armand, so wonderful in both the novel and the film, does not appear in the play. Of course there is the fact that the play is well made. Requiring only two sets, it is easy to stage. To include this scene, the interior of a theater would have had to have been built. A theater within a theater. The idea appeals to the contemporary mind. The actor playing Armand would have looked up toward a box built on the stage, and stared with ardor at the woman who played the courtesan. But because in the nineteenth century the same event occurring onstage would also have been taking place in the audience, the scene would have been too revealing. The theater was a favored place for liaisons between courtesans and men of means. During almost any performance, as many eyes would be trained on other members of the audience as on the stage.

But the stage held its own attractions. Recently I attended an exhibition of prints drawn by the great social commentator Honoré Daumier. A satiric panorama of nineteenth-century France flowed from his pen. He was especially fond of ridiculing the hypocrisies of the upper classes. I was fascinated by one drawing, *La loge grille,* which depicts an old gentleman salivating behind the screen in his private box while training his opera glasses on a ballet dancer's legs.

After every performance arrangements were made between certain men in the audience and the performers they selected. Dancers were the most popular. The classic and revealing costumes worn in the ballet, a form of dance described by Hippolyte Taine as "an exhibition of girls for sale," made the choice easier. A display of legs was considered obligatory. At the opera, during the Second Empire, if the evening did not include at least one balletic performance, it was considered a failure. In the audience, successful bourgeois men as well as aristocrats and men of the court would focus their eyes on the stage with the intensity of a desire that would soon be met.

The knowledge of these transactions surrounds the august events of history with a different atmosphere. Though I cannot say precisely how, the mood, for instance of international politics, changes as I think of the time that King Victor Emmanuel of Piedmont, while making a state visit to France, asked Louis Napoleon if it were true that French dancers did not wear undergarments, adding, "If that is so, earthly paradise is in store for me." The shift in mood deepens when I learn that later when Victor Emmanuel was taken to the opera, after being shocked to learn that the price of the dancer who appealed to him was fifty gold louis, Napoleon, in a gesture of diplomatic courtesy, told the Italian king that the bill would be added to his own account. A frequent customer, he kept a private room backstage.

What is the atmospheric shift? A certain formality is shed. The crown cast aside for a moment. The emperor after all has no clothes. Before he undresses, reflecting the mercantile frenzy of the times, his aide cleverly bargains with the dancer's mother. This is how it was usually done. What would it cost to have this girl? To use her body? For one night? A week? Exclusive privileges? How much? The body of empire stripped.

Yet the unveiling has a ceremonious quality; it is cloaked with a kind of dignity. There would be no way to avoid it. Going to the theater, whether for drama, dance, or opera, you would be swept up in the ceremony yourself. You even become one of the performers. Approaching the vicinity of the theater, on the boulevard du Crime, for instance, famous for all the murder mysteries and melodramas playing there, or drawing up in your coach to the newly built Opéra Garnier in the fashionable first arrondissement, you will be observed by the others. What are you wearing? Who is on your arm? What is the expression on your face?

Entering the foyer of the theater, you are also entering a hall of mirrors where everything you say is echoed, every gesture reflected back a thousand times. Who will greet you, who will pay you deference reflects your position in society. If you are powerful or powerfully attractive, heads will turn. If they turn, your position along with your reputation rises. Even the architecture of the arena echoes the order of society, those at the fringes invisible in the highest balcony, the bourgeoisie in the orchestra, the emperor in his box.

As he enters, if you are in the audience, even if you oppose his policies, you will rise to applaud him. And he for his part will do his best to appear regal, which in the waning days of royalty cannot be simple, especially for an emperor with just a fraction of Napoleonic and no royal blood. The rumor is that even the first Napoleon took lessons from the great actor Talma, who had played many emperors, to learn how to effect the right bearing. His nephew has learned the same postures. As pompous as they seem, you yourself enter into the performance, pretending to believe his gestures, at the same time as you remain discreet in your knowledge, because of course it is an open secret, that as the play closes he will make his way backstage to secure his goods.

But why, given the power he exhibits, must the procurement take place backstage at a theater? Certainly emperors can command private visitations. They do not have to attend the ballet or opera for such reasons. But you know the answer. Everyone requires the right atmosphere for desire. Mood is everything. This is why theater is necessary. The glittering crowds. The ceremonious entry. The gilded box. The curtain rising slowly. The music. A leg turning beneath pink gauze. And afterward the furtive entrance into what is a secret world, the mystery behind the proscenium, the thrill of possessing those who are so powerful in that magic half round, commanding the stage, goddesses, nearly ephemeral despite all that flesh, fleeting, like shooting stars.

And as the young dancer he has chosen comes to him in his private room, there is this too: that he who is the most powerful man in the state, who is the state and who could from time to time feel overburdened by exactly the power he has sought and gained, who could even feel bored by the close air of his cabinet meetings, the confined arena of the court, who could, once all this power is his, still be longing for something larger, could even be, at times, disappointed with his throne, as if no one were sitting in it, as if the palace were somehow empty and he had been tricked and could long, even passionately, even irresistibly, for this young woman with all the glamour of the stage still clinging to her, to carry him into a more magical world, into a mythic realm of mysterious powers, powers he can feel as she touches him, glittering at the tips of his own hands now, rising in his hips, his royal penis, shining now too, with another authority altogether.

Yet considering the young dancer, despite the honor of making love with the emperor, I imagine a certain authority has left her body. How old can she be? Perhaps sixteen or seventeen. She is pretending to love the emperor's attentions. But inside something in her has gone still. Does she feel betrayed? Somehow the envelope of his body around her is more tightly sealed because her mother has brought about their union. She is not even straining in the direction of an escape. No route appears, even in her imagination. Was she embarrassed by the haggling over her price? Possibly, especially if, like Bernhardt, she received an upper-class education, learning in the process that such transactions are not moral. But this mortification, if it occurs at all, is balanced by other considerations. She is old enough to understand economy. Grateful, perhaps, that her life is more comfortable than others she knows, the children in the apartment next door, for example; with her mother's skill they might even be able to move to a larger apartment. What has vanished, then, inside her? It would be simply her desire. Not the exchange of money but the power he has over her because of it. None of the glamour of his throne can change that.

Still, something in her likes the glamour. She is just a girl. Fingering his gold buttons, running her nose through his epaulets.

As she runs her hands over his hips to excite him and as he mounts her, she feels nothing in the rosy depths of herself, nothing that rises to meet him as he enters her. Yet all the while he moves, red in the face, breathing over her and sweating, she diverts herself by thinking of the new dress her mother might buy her.

Years ago I had a lover with whom I was passionately in love. Her body, her way of being, her style, all of this continually drew me. I wanted her almost from the first moment I saw her. In the first months of our affair, which was a brief one, we were passionate in bed. And then one night a change occurred. It was the first night of a weekend away. She was treating us to the hotel. We had a long dinner. Then we went to our room. I was weary and eager to sleep. And this angered her because she wanted to make love. She mentioned the room and how she had paid for it and suggested I should give something back to her by making love that night. I refused. The next day was taken up with a long quarrel. Bit by bit, as her approach shifted from seduction to demand, despite my love for her, my passion left me.

Whether the aim is to buy what you desire or to use desire to accumulate wealth, money easily corrupts love. In the century when Marie Duplessis lived, courtesans, especially those who became rich, were painted as preying on respectable men, draining away their resources, using them with cold calculation, and afterward discarding them at a whim. In his celebrated novel, *Nana*, Zola provided a classic portrait of a ruthless heroine. Though the judgment was somewhat mitigated by the sad and meager circumstances of her birth, it was harsh. And his conclusion was hyperbolic. Along with the Goncourt brothers, Zola believed that courtesans were causing the ruin of France.

Still, every exaggeration contains a seed of truth. Courtesans could be ruthlessly avaricious, and many men were ruined. Yet the truth goes deeper still. The ravenous courtesan can also be read as a symbol. Her greed was a mirror of society. Greed was the driving force of European economies in the Second Empire. In these avaricious times, a courtesan was just like any other ambitious businessman, eager to accumulate a fortune and rise in class. Bloodsucking on the path to success was a common strategy. Desire of all kinds was stimulated, then as now, to turn a profit. And in the process, many bodies were used and discarded—the bodies of wealthy men, the bodies of women, the bodies of laborers, the body of the land—to make fortunes.

Still, desire is never as simple as it seems. Deeply rooted in both body and soul, the secret aspects of a man, hidden wishes in a woman, a past forgotten, an inner territory neglected by reason, will be known by attraction. The men who sought after courtesans were not just buying flesh. They liked them for something else they represented, something the revolution had failed to win. The effect was theatrical in its own way. Costumed and given the proper accoutrements of class, courtesans paraded the streets of Paris in fine coaches as if they had been wellborn. Yet though they replicated upper-class women, as in a mirror, the image was reversed. Dressed like ladies, they did not act like ladies. Though they looked as if they were proper, they were not. The French have a word for an attitude that is a perfect mixture of insolence, wit, rebellion, and grace, *insolite*. This was a large measure of their charm, how well they could carry off the charade and still carry on outrageously. The eroticism depended on parody. The whole demimonde was, in fact, a kind of cabaret through which proper society could be mocked and rebellion expressed, as long as the rebellion was constrained to what we call the after-hours.

Wandering the neighborhood where so many of the great courtesans, *lorettes*, and also actresses lived, I found an antique shop

almost directly across from Notre Dames des Lorettes, the church
that unwittingly lent its name to concubinage. The proprietor
there was so old, it seemed almost as if he too were one of the
artifacts on sale. Here amongst an odd assemblage of things, I
found a leather box, and of course I opened it. Resting there, as if
untouched since the day they had been pulled from the fingers of
their owner, was a very old pair of ladies' white gloves. I thought
immediately of a photograph I saw in the book I was reading
about the life of Bernhardt. In this picture she is small, about six
or seven years old, and she stands next to her young mother,
Youle, who was already a well-heeled courtesan. Youle's hands,
one of which was on Sarah's shoulder, were gloved. So close was
the resemblance to the antique gloves I found, it could have been
the same pair.

When I was a girl, gloves were still worn as a sign of being a
lady. I was given several pairs by my grandmother. White for day
and black for night. In general I disliked them, save for one very
long and scalloped pair that was supposed to be worn in the
evening. I found these glamorous. I have a photograph of the
French actress Arletty wearing black, elbow-length gloves, dressed
for the role she played as a nightclub performer in *Le jour se leve*. It
was filmed in the late thirties, and by this time the gloves, which
once signified membership in the upper classes, had also come to
stand for a certain kind of provocative sexuality. Even today, they
still have an allure. The neighborhood of the *lorettes* borders and
fuses with a neighborhood called Pigalle. It was to the Place Pigalle
that the famous modern painters, Manet among them, would come
to hire models for the day, laundresses and *grisettes* hoping to earn
enough to keep alive. Now the neighborhood is known for its prostitutes and sex shops. On the same day that I visited the antique
store I walked up to the Place and looked into the windows of one
of these shops where there were several pairs of very long gloves in
a range of Day-Glo colors.

■   ■   ■

So many artifacts from the culture of my childhood can be explained by this shadowy history. Though the truth is coded. I remember one film, for instance, which I saw when I was about ten years old. It was called *Gentlemen Prefer Blondes*. On the surface it was a silly story, especially if you did not understand, as then I did not, its very thinly veiled references to the fact that in America too showgirls were courtesans. Marilyn Monroe, dazzlingly funny with a studied stupidity, and Jane Russell, sharply perceptive and more buxom, played two dancers. The only mention made of financial transactions was that the women were supposed to be looking for rich husbands. Though the financial arrangement was there by inference in the famous song, "Diamonds Are a Girl's Best Friend."

In America of the fifties, we would have called the film naughty. My grandmother would raise her eyebrows and then wink at anything described this way, which gave whatever it was a desirable glow. The sense was that just over the edge of convention, a forbidden world existed that was glamorous and fun. Accordingly, when you thought of Paris, the dancers of the Moulin Rouge, the cancan, cigarettes, red wine, plunging necklines, heaving bosoms, too much rouge, and a whale of a good time would come to mind.

Of course, Paris was not exotic to the Parisians. But Parisian nightlife was. The more exotic the better. Just as later, the sensational dancer Josephine Baker was wildly popular, not despite but precisely because she was African American. Of the variety of courtesans who peopled the demimonde, Asian, African, and Jewish women were especially prized. In this half world all the usual boundaries were drawn simply to be crossed. Women who did not wear underpants would lift their legs to show you what they had beneath their skirts. Men swore and smoked cigars in front of them. The women themselves smoked and swore. Occasionally one would dress like a man. And there were men who dressed like women. Beneath a tuxedo, you might find pink lace, or a black line would edge a man's eyelid, his lips reddened.

And this half-real world provided still subtler ways for a man to experience himself as a woman. I am thinking of Agénor de Guiche, for instance, remaking Alphonsine Plessis in every detail. How she should dress. How she should apply her makeup, what perfume she should wear. What color ribbon should be put in her hair. His fingers feeling the fine texture of the fabric he has chosen for her. I can imagine him now, instructing her how to brush her hair, gazing into the mirror in which her face is reflected.

So many secrets were revealed in this half-world. There were women who loved women and men who loved men. *Gay* we say now, and that this was the word once used for courtesans is hardly coincidental. No wonder George Cukor, who was gay, was able to work so well with Garbo. Or that Charles Ludlam made such a convincing Marguerite. By the time I saw him play the role, he was a fat and balding middle-aged man, dressed in gaudy ruffles, flouncing about the stage, and the first act was so hilarious I was doubled over in laughter. But after the intermission, as I found myself weeping, I turned to see most of the large audience in tears too. He was as moving in the role as any woman I have seen. And he knew it. In his performance, as Ludlam wrote, an audience could see a man playing a woman and "feeling what people formerly thought only a woman could feel. . . ."

In this he captured a secret well known to the gay world. Something courtesans had to know too. What you observe when you exist at the periphery of vision. Because you are seen as illicit, you are entertaining. It is easy for you to make your patrons laugh. But do they know that with their laughter you have been given the most forbidden intimacy of all, the glittering shards of what they have tried to destroy in themselves? A second act will inevitably follow. A tragic one. Understanding they will never acknowledge the nature of this intimacy, you can trust them only to abandon you, just as they have done with themselves.

As miraculous as the small rebellion seemed, everyone come together, men and women, rich and poor, identities fused, rules relaxed, the marks that division had made on the soul were still there. Time is not so easily undone. The roles, however, were often reversed. A rich man, for instance, in the privacy of an upstairs room, might ask a woman, born into poverty and in every way his social inferior, to lie on top of him, to give *him* orders, or even to beat him with a whip. But despite the reversal, the pattern of dominion remained in place. As what was hidden surfaced and everything was turned inside out and upside down, it was a continuous carnival and, like a carnival, would vanish in the daylight because it was theater, not reality.

Yet what is reality if it does not include impossible dreams and wild fantasies? That story, for instance, of a pauper who becomes a prince is certainly as real as desire. What occurs on a stage, reaching as it does into a hidden territory of want, can reach a deeper order of truth. I am thinking of *Paradis*. This is what the highest balcony, so near the place where the theater met the sky, was called, Paradise. Because these were the cheapest seats, the poor would sit here. They came often to see the murder mysteries playing at theaters on the boulevard du Crime. The endings of these dramas must have given them small moments of triumph. For while they knew that in real life the causes of early death from overwork and hunger would go unnamed and that those responsible would only prosper, here they could count on seeing a crime solved and justice done.

As with all illusion, though it vanishes theater is also real. If you are an actor you will become your role. For a few hours you actually are an emperor, a murderer, a slave. Feelings of omnipotence, of rage, of oppression will course through your body. At the end, wearied just as if you had actually lived through the events depicted onstage, you will need hours to come back to yourself. And the same will be true if you are in the audience. As you watch a performance, your mood will also change as well as, perhaps, your soul. Now you are a woman who against her own common sense has fallen in love. Then you are the man who has fallen in love with her. Then you are his father, pleading for the honor of his daughter. Then you are the courtesan again, overcome with grief, hope waning in your heart, repentance dawning, death enclosing you. Here in the theater the longing for communion that lies at the heart of revolution is, if only momentarily, realized.

Sitting in the theater that first night, when thunderous applause announced that this play was to have a long life, there must have been wealthy men who were weeping. Many would have gone to prostitutes; some kept a courtesan themselves. Even condoning the moral lesson of her death, a man might still cry. Was he weeping for the young women that he had known so intimately? Or perhaps a great-grandmother, a mother, a cousin, possibly a casual acquaintance, someone he had employed, or even the beggar on the street whose eyes resembled someone he once knew, no matter how slightly?

Or was his pity for someone else? One more intimate than a lover. Prominently seated in his box, for which he has paid with his extraordinary achievements, he is taken back to the boy he was, thirty or forty years ago; it is not his mind that remembers so much as his body, wincing with the thought of poverty, heavy with an unnamed grief. Looking now from a short distance, one so close it is not measurable, yet far enough to perceive what otherwise he never allows himself to remember, he watches the other story of his rise, how he made his fortune, how he got his success, the sacrifice he made of himself, who he had to become to succeed, what he had to relinquish. A certain lightness, a litheness, and even though he was ashamed for having it, a certain loveliness was once his that, because of course it had to happen, had perished.

Perhaps this is why he cannot get this woman out of his mind. A woman who does not exist. Who lived for a moment on the stage. He has fallen in love with her. He sees the play many times. And then the opera. He has even learned some of the arias by heart.

La vita uniti trascorreremo
We will be happy living together

De' corsi affanni compenso avrai
Your grief will vanish now I'm beside you

La tua salute riffiorira
New life will blossom, you will be well

Sospiro e luce tu mi sarai
Your light and spirit will grow here inside me

Tutto il futuro ne arridera.
Trust in the future, all will be well.

I wish I could play the great music here that Verdi wrote for this scene. You would not be able to resist it. As with sacred music, you would be enchanted, swept away from yourself and yet, at the same time, into a larger self, glorying in the change. Though, there are days when I cannot bear to hear this music. I do not want to feel the grief of it. What has happened to us all.

Alphonsine Plessis, Marie Duplessis, Marguerite, Violetta, Bernhardt, Duse, Garbo, Melba, Callas, Ludlam. As I write I can feel the presence of each of them as well as the man in the audience who, despite the fact that I invented him, must surely have existed, must exist even now. He is Camille as I am he. He may be a man, but nevertheless as he watches the play he becomes small, seductive, frail. Just as the playwright did when he wrote the part, becoming Marie Duplessis, becoming his own mother too, and even his great-grandmother, all the while discovering memory, compassion, himself.

And isn't this what theater is in the end? Not just spectacle but a ritual of exchange in which one thing stands for another and everyone becomes someone else. The actors onstage become the characters they play. A young man becomes old before our eyes. A kind person plays a mean one. A beautiful woman becomes plain and shy. A young man becomes a monkey. Under a heavy costume, three men appear as one horse. The lighting shifts, the scenery changes, the atmosphere is different. Everything changes continually. The mean become kind. The old die. The monkey reveals his wisdom. And just as these transformations take place, you too become other than yourself, become everyone, everything you witness. Your mood changes, your opinions shift, you suffer transformation from the recognition. It is a kind of miracle you have experienced. The transubstantiation of flesh. Bodies and spirits are being traded, and by this transaction your soul is allowed a larger breadth. You are awed by the wide arc of it. By all that can be held there. The detail, distinct and infinitely complex, a vastly abundant variety, and, wildly improbable as the mystery still is, all of it undivided.

Erotic Bodies

Eros, weaver of tales

SAPPHO

THE SKY

Darkly blue and covered with clouds whitening in the moonlight, black profiles of the trees; I imagine green; slick road, warm lights pocketed in the nighttide of the hill, and I am swimming, my blood dark, my mind whitening, floating over the turns, as I think of you.

EYES

It is not a penetrating gaze I turn toward you; it is I who am entered through the dark openings in my eyes.

HERE

When you are in the room, I can feel you inside of me, around me. If I turn to look out the window, put my hand on the chair, pick up a piece of paper, shut my eyes, open my eyes, take in a breath, speak, listen, taste the food on the table, you are in everything, everywhere.

HANDS

Tips of the fingers. Moving lightly. Barely touching. Almost grazing, lazily, a small trail that remains, a quickening shimmer, as the touch moves to the back of my ear, over my shoulders, down my neck, spine, settling at my hips, resting there, the palm sinking into me.

BED

Place of sleep and dream, place of waking, a thought quickening under my skin. Not what you said. Not what you did. Not the image of you. But who you are. A dream of you in my body.

LIPS

Your lips light like little wings, fast over my face, eyes opening, shutting, the flutter, the infinitesimal flights, the air disturbed so slightly, the wind subtle but infinite over my skin.

WATER

Like a lake in the body. Your words, my words. Like rain.

SHOULDER

Curling forward, inward, as if to cradle you as you speak.

SLEEP

I cannot see your face in the dream. I cannot see you at all. There is a rush of bodies. No one I know. We are all walking. Moving up a hill, over a green field. Nothing else happens. Except for the atmosphere. It is like the inner lining of my body. Soft, red, pliant. What I feel when I am awake and thinking of you.

PULSE

Low like a hum. Like a bow drawn over an instrument at the bottom of the scale.

HIGH

Then rising, pitched, soprano, whistling as pure as air through the peaks, opening a passage to the pinnacle, until there at the summit breaking, going that high, then hushed.

ARMS

Sinking in, your hand resting in my hands, forearm brushing my forearm, your breasts against mine, closer and closer still, inside.

THE HONEY

The honey of it, the pleasure, even to think your name, the sweet rise, the warm spread of the knowledge, the swelling of the space, the undeniable impulse, the opening of my mouth, arms, hands, heart, pelvic bones, my mind when you come near.

LINES

Marks. A white place on the skin. What cannot be hidden. Time. What will become visible.

MEMORY

The others with us. Here. Peopling the stories you tell. The stories I tell you late at night or in the morning, a mother whose mouth you have, a father whose eyes I have, a child who has the color of your hair, a child who has my mother's beauty, husbands, lovers, friends, names whispered like music, bodies of memory in us.

BREATH

The bright beauty of it. How it lights me from inside. How it could burn me up, how it could eat and swallow you easily, how it does, how I disappear, how I am small in the face of it and changed, how large we become, how as it carries us, everywhere, how everything rushes through this moment, the transpiration. Your breath. Mine.

SONG

How every place touched by you or the thought of you, or the sound you make speaking, or the way you move near, hips and belly and feet and every mouth, every opening, how toes curling with the feel and want of you inside of me, how vision softens, ears wait, reddening with the sound, the song, how every place you touch sings.

Four

And sing me before you go the song of the throes of
Democracy.

WALT WHITMAN, *"By Blue Ontario's Shore"*

. . . you find
her everywhere (or did find)

in cathedral, museum, cloister,
at the turn of the palace stair.

H. D., *"Tribute to the Angels"*

APRIL

At the edge of pain, the slight ache in your shoulders, which will soon
grow stronger, running up and down your spine and into your legs,
making it difficult for you to walk, hard even to sit up, is desire. Not
the kind of wish you can put into words. Not a request. Something
more like knowledge. This body, the body of pain, a body of continual
effort and broken motion, is not the only one. There is another body.
Not just the stronger body which was yours just a few hours ago, but
an earlier body, still here. Though it will elude you, you can almost
feel it now. Soft like warm air, with an inner skin of sweetness, fluid
as water.

APRIL

The body that will not let you forget, finds any opening, the slightest crack in consciousness, to remind you, this is not all there is. Try as you might, you will never stop wanting this body.

Democracy

I knew where I was in one sense. I had written three weeks earlier to request admission to the Hotel Paiva. Since the house was once the residence of one of the most famous courtesans of the Second Empire, Thérèse Pauline Blanche Lachman, the marquise de Paiva, known simply as Paiva, and because this particular building is one of the grandest of the period, a veritable symbol of its decadence, I was eager to see the interior. Yet, entering the gray, auspicious structure, which, though ornate, seems almost hidden as it recedes from the street only to rise behind a bank that obscures its entrance, I took several moments to catch my bearings.

I was prepared for the luxury. I had read about the layers of gilt and gold, marble, onyx, intricate wood carving, malachite piled like too many layers of a dissolute wedding cake, about to fall from its own weight. When she began work on the building in 1885, Paiva's plan had been to build the most beautiful house in Paris. She hired a fleet of artists and craftsmen to carry out her wishes. The painter Hébert, the sculptor Gérôme, and Baudry, who had fashioned the extraordinary ceiling of the Opéra Garnier, among them. The result was excessive, even for a time when excess was common.

But I was not prepared for the other effect, driven by the avalanche of sensuality within its walls, an almost electric air of power. Coming from the Champs-Elysée, which as it swells along the sightlines of Hausmann's triumphal way is almost always brilliant with light, crowded with cars, and overwhelming in its raucous modernity, moving through the dark and narrow passageway alongside the currency exchange, and climbing the stairs, I entered a somewhat plain lobby, placed to admit members of the Travelers, a very exclusive men's club, which occupies the premises now. My guide, another woman, witty, with an ironic appreciation of the history of these rooms, led me through an ornate anteroom into the grand salon. It is an immense space composed of two rooms, one smaller than the other. But in the massive mirrors that face each other from opposite ends, countless chambers appear in a seemingly endless reflection of every golden detail. The echoing glimmer reminded me of Versailles.

Even through the dust and debris of construction that was there that day, the pure force of the room was staggering. And as we made our way into the gentlemen's bar, once Paiva's dining room, then climbed up the onyx staircase, passing the landing watched over by statues of Dante, Virgil, and Petrarch, and moved into the courtesan's bedroom, its golden ceiling dripping with gilt pendants, its fireplace malachite, and stood in her bathroom, which looked like a sultan's *haman*, covered in splendid Turkish tiles, the power only increased.

Here as in the American financier's palace, Trump Towers, the presence of money is unmistakable. But it was not just the opulence that impressed me. It was something more. As I sat for a while alone in the bar and gazed at the paintings of lushly nude women, each framed by golden triangles, peaked by what looked like the insignia of a Roman emperor that in turn crowned every doorway, I began to realize that this opulence told a story. A familiar tale and in one way a democratic myth of transformation, with a hero who goes from rags to riches. Except in this case the hero was a woman.

At the heart of this plot, her body, a succulently rounded object of desire, is displayed everywhere. You can see her likeness in the two large sculptures languidly balanced at two ends of the fireplace in the grand salon or painted on the ceiling, as Night pursued by Day, or again in the astonishing wood carving on the dining room ceiling, out of which a golden nude seems to float. But it is not just the image of her body that draws you. Without modesty or shame, these rooms reveal not only how Paiva made her fortune, but the intensity of desire that drove the bargain. Surrounded by the extraordinary earth-colored swirls of polished stone, the glittering touches and swaths of gold, the rich patinas of wood and tile, at the edge of consciousness yet with an almost unnerving intensity, you will begin to feel as if you are being embraced by a beautiful woman, her soft skin, her gleaming eyes, her cushioning lips. As a certain heat rises from these walls, you can almost feel yourself entering the interior of her body.

It is a body that promises so much, a promise I can feel in my own desire. There is the wish for sensual pleasure, of course, but sexual desire is made from so many different wishes, humble longings for love, longings that are venal and small, longings that lead us past ourselves. And now when I follow the path of my desire for the courtesan's body, I am drawn as if toward another larger chamber. An almost infinite place, containing everything.

Something of this infinity was lost when the greater promise of revolution failed. You can feel the plenitude of it in the swell of her breasts, as Liberty, lusty with a visionary passion, leads the people over the revolutionary battlefields of France. A grandeur, a sweeping largesse. I felt the glow of grandeur as a child in my first study of the American Revolution. Separated from my sister and father, moved back and forth from my mother's to my grandmother's house, I found the ache of loss and loneliness well met by this story. It was not the opportunity to rise in fortune but the eloquent assertion of the intrinsic value of democracy that became a fertile part of my imagination. Assemblies before which fiery speeches were made about freedom. Declarations signed in protest. The right to life, liberty, and the pursuit of happiness. The people as one body dreaming, moving into action, speaking.

Later Thomas Paine and Thomas Jefferson would become heroes to me, but in the dawn of my political education, Patrick Henry was my favorite figure. I remember standing in front of a classroom, my shyness suddenly lost, as with great fervor I told the story of his refusal to submit to tyranny. *Give me liberty or give me death!* my voice rang out dramatically. Only eleven years old, I was still ignorant of the intricacies of the political debates that raged in the fifties. But the idea that this man would sacrifice his life for something larger than himself appealed to me. Though I would not have been able to say this at the time, that he would not compromise his soul gave me an idea of amplitude that could carry me past my own small grief.

Democracy became my passion. I memorized so many of Roberts' Rules of Order that in school meetings I was deferred to as an expert on democratic procedure. I brought my enthusiasm home in the form of a constitution that I wrote in longhand through which I delineated my rights as a citizen. Confusing regency with presidency, the document referred to my grandmother as the queen and my grandfather as the vice king. I was completely unaware of the pun. Years later my sister and I laughed at the odd titles and their accuracy, how my grandmother was the real ruler of our family, how my grandfather was so clearly a subsidiary light. And with his evening bourbon and his cigarettes, he clearly qualified as the vice king too.

I was not unique in my enthusiasm. Certainly, as we came of age, democracy was the shared passion of my generation. We wanted to enlarge the boundaries of the democratic process. The most popular cause we championed was freedom of speech. Through the fifties McCarthyism had been slowly undermining the Bill of Rights. But I suspect there were other reasons for the popularity of this issue. A strange and banal silence in the atmosphere was part of it. The public atmosphere was like an upper-class dinner party, hampered with stultifying rules about what could or could not be said.

And in my own life, there were still other reasons. The ideals of democracy, which I learned at school, had somehow pierced the cocoon of my separation, dignifying my existence, even gracing my ability to speak. It was not just the right of expression I had been given but the sense that speech mattered, that wherever there was speech there would also be a larger body included in the conversation. With this understanding, I gained the feeling that though I had lost my family, I was part of a greater matrix.

The matrix, however, had limitations of its own. It could not hold all of my memories. The movement of private knowledge into public discourse is not simple. What stories can be told depends on how they are received. Even the language you will need to be able to describe your experience, the particular use of the word *abuse,* for instance, or *neglect,* must evolve from shared perceptions.

I did not repress the memory of my mother's drinking. But keeping it secret, I suppressed it. I did not tell anyone about the drunken scenes that kept me awake at night. Unable to separate my memory from the shame of drunkenness, I feared the humiliation of disclosure. Then one night, the story came out. I was fifteen and living with my father. Because he was a fireman and staying overnight at the firehouse on one of his regular shifts, I was home alone when two friends came over with a six-pack of beer. After an hour, Bill had to leave, but Marianne, my best friend, stayed, and we finished all the beer ourselves, drinking until we reeled. Perhaps it was our drunkenness that triggered my grief. The memory of those nights with my mother thick in my throat, I began to weep. My friend held me, as frantically she asked what was making me cry. It was then that I told her of the nightmarish hours I had spent with my mother when she was drunk, what she said to me, the cruel precision of her insults.

The healing was not just in my speech but also in her response. Her father alcoholic too, she understood my sorrow. In every sense of the word she received what I told her. I remember waking the next day with a new ease. The weight of the story had lifted, gone, in a sense, where it had to go.

Everyone feels the need to describe experience. Of this there is no doubt. But why the need exists is still unexplained. There is, of course, the fact that when knowledge is kept silent, it loses potency, fades, or even moves backward, erasing itself. And there is this too. In the process of telling a story, you will come to understand events on a far deeper level. This is as true in public discourse as it is in a private life. Every society repeats stories about itself, fashioning a history that will frame the present.

Democracy relies on the telling of stories. If a people are to govern themselves, they must know as much of the truth as they can. But something more is gained in the process. The constant exchange of stories that democracy requires is itself a profound experience. Unexamined memories, forgotten regions of the psyche and the soul must be continually explored for the form to remain alive. In my lifetime I have seen democracy begin to expand, not only to include those who have been excluded, but to provide a listening arena, a vocabulary, an intelligent reception for stories that have been buried. Not just stories of the disenfranchised and the marginalized, but marginalized and disenfranchised histories even in the lives of the accepted and the privileged.

Thinking of this process it occurs to me now that just as stories serve democracy, democracy must exist for the sake of stories too.

Perhaps some strange unexplained physics exists, the physics of narration, by which stories are drawn together, like atoms with a positive charge. It is after all only when they are assembled that stories can partake in that alchemy by which one common account will be made. A story we will all hear, and that, as it moves through our bodies, will change us.

Though I cannot describe the effects yet, telling my own story has changed me. And adding the legend of Camille has only deepened the change. From the circumstances of her life, not only can I see the nature of my own circumstances more clearly but, by a mysterious process of transformation, my own story has gained another significance. It bears now on larger questions, not simply what I am seeking in my own soul but what society seeks. How then shall we live? By what ideas of the body, of democracy, and even economy, shall we be guided? The story has become much longer, really, than any I can tell. What I write here now is just one passage in the longer narrative that we all share.

This is a story that is continually being created. In the last several decades, for instance, a new chapter has been added to the common narrative, though the subject is familiar. Just as tuberculosis and cholera were once strong in our collective imagination, with the advent of AIDS, the life of the body in sickness and death has entered public discourse again. But now accounts of open sores and tumors and night sweats and severe chills, bleeding that will not stop, lacerating pain in the joints, wounds that do not heal, brain fevers, and swellings are being given from a different point of view. The storyteller has changed. It is not just governing bodies and boards of health or social critics who speak, but those who are ill themselves.

I have the sense that something momentous occurs with this slight but significant change in perspective. Though the message comes from the sick and the dying, the transmission is vital, even quickening. As if a memory lost to the culture were returning. And with it perhaps, though it is scarcely visible now, a new direction.

When I was growing up, there were a number of organizations that spoke for the needs of the ill. Heart and lung associations existed then, and foundations for cancer or muscular dystrophy, illiciting sympathy and aid. But in the mid-1980s a radically different kind of alliance appeared. Men and women diagnosed as HIV-positive or already ill with AIDS began to create their own ideas of what the medical procedures and social policies that so affected their lives should be.

The most visible group affected by AIDS, the gay community, had assembled before to protest discrimination against homosexuality and because of this, protest networks already existed. There were already leaders, accomplished activists who, because society had marginalized homosexuality, knew how to bring hidden stories to light. Stories that were also about the body, though these stories were about desire and pleasure.

The halt, the lame, and the blind banded together. It is an image that confounds our idea of strength. Still, there is a steady and even luminescent power in the union. I have felt the effect myself. In the year before I had my most serious collapse, I attended a meeting of a small organization in San Francisco, the one founded by Marya and Jan, to give voice to those who are ill with chronic fatigue immune dysfunction syndrome. A dozen or so men and women, most of us ill with CFIDS, sat around a long table in a small room in city hall. Before the official meeting began, there was the usual casual conversation. We all knew we could speak openly there about the tempest raging in our bodies. Some were more severely ill than others. Because the illness had reactivated a childhood case of polio, Jill was in a wheelchair. Jan and others had suffered from serious seizures. But all of us had been to the same general terrain, and together we could bear witness to this landscape of affliction. We were, in a way, like a group of embattled soldiers. Because of what we saw and endured, an immediate intimacy developed among us. Even when I was not well enough to attend meetings, the memory of that room, intense with a shared knowledge, sustained me.

Storytelling. The art lies at the heart of democracy. And perhaps it is at the heart of existence too. Often, the longing I feel to describe the events I have witnessed is so compelling that I wonder at times if it is not entirely personal. The thought occurs to me that perhaps events themselves want to be described. The flaw of the conjecture is immediately evident to me. I have given the human attribute of desire to a thing, a phenomenon where no person or animal capable of desire resides. Where nothing, in fact, lives but a passing configuration of incidents, a tremor, for instance passing through muscle, nerves sending a strange signal, or a moment when fear is felt or a certain slant of light, brushing the trees, settles in bright corners of a shaded landscape and then in your eyes. Yet still I could swear that I can feel a desire to be known coming from events themselves, a resonant wish that makes me want to describe what I have seen or experienced. It is as if time and space were like a pageant, peopled by moments no less alive than you and me, who are ourselves really only passing events, temporary congregations of cells, chemicals, atoms, moments that call out to be seen, remembered, told.

As soon as I could, I began to attend meetings again. A small group convened to discuss political strategy. How to alter the public mood, which so diminished the gravity of the disease. To press the Centers for Disease Control to study the epidemiology of the illness, for instance, a study that had already been mandated and funded by Congress, or to encourage research. After some time the group metamorphosed into a foundation, and for a while I sat on that board. The first few meetings were almost celebratory. Especially since for many of us who had the illness, even to arrive at the meeting place was an accomplishment that made us heady with joy. It was less for ecological reasons than simple survival that we crossed the bridge to San Francisco in one car, calculating who was the strongest and most able to drive and, regarding parking, the number of blocks the weakest could walk. It was a kind of comic pilgrimage. At least we laughed at ourselves, giddy with our small victories.

I rarely had much to contribute. But there is one occasion I remember vividly. I was asked to describe what it was like to live with my illness to representatives from the city's office of public health. Though in the larger struggle for recognition, my testimony did not play a particularly significant role, in my own mind the moment was like one of those scenes from a play where a long-delayed confrontation finally takes place. At last I could tell my story in the public arena. There may have been only two haggard officials actually present, but to me they represented that vastly anonymous and usually unreachable audience that has so much power over all our lives, society.

If at times all of us feel disempowered in a world run by giant corporations and governments increasingly beyond the reach of the people, the sense of disempowerment increases exponentially when you are ill. It is not just the frailty of illness that weakens you, though physical weakness certainly deepens the feeling. To be a patient in the labyrinth of modern medicine is to become disenfranchised at an almost primal level. Regarding your own body, it will seem like almost any other opinion carries more weight than your own. As you are told what in the range of your complaints has meaning and what has none, or even at times what you ought to be feeling, your own knowledge weakens.

The most common, seemingly innocuous procedures of medicine serve to strip a patient, not only of dignity, but also of the capacity for autonomous judgment. Asked to somehow describe complex symptoms in the small boxes of an admitting form and to answer yes or no to questions for which only a far more nuanced response would be truthful; made to repeat your complaint several times over, once to a receptionist, once to an aide, once again to a nurse, many of whom seem vaguely disinterested and none of whom are allowed to tell you anything about your condition. Dressed in a gown that leaves you exposed and cold, even if you have a flu or bronchitis or pneumonia. This must have been what it was like to wait at court for an audience.

The disenfranchisement only continues in the process of diagnosis. But here the problem is not just with medical procedure. Trying to express what you feel in your body, you will confront a paucity of words. European languages lack the vocabulary you need to describe physical sensations with any precision, especially symptoms that are painful or uncomfortable. This alone will leave you fumbling in a fog of vague impressions, certain that what you feel remains unnamed. And then there is the hierarchic order of medicine, the doctor often acting more like a lawyer with quick and pointed questions. Some of his questions may baffle you. Others are easy. But still your efforts to describe what you feel will all too frequently be frustrated by an invisible veil of preconceptions, ideas in medical books, maps of the body, prejudices regarding who gets which disease and why, who should or should not be believed. And all along you suspect that while you labor to paint a portrait of a territory your doctor has never experienced in his own body, he will weigh laboratory results far more heavily than your testimony.

When what you know is ignored, the dismissal can be psychologically painful. But the invalidation of the patient's knowledge can also have disastrous effects on your health. It happened to a friend recently, a middle-aged woman just a few years older than I. For a full year she complained to her doctor about a pain in her leg that steadily worsened. When she would tell him she was worried, time and again he assured her that the pain was not caused by anything serious. He diagnosed sciatica at first. And then when the physical therapy he ordered did not help, he wrote her a prescription for Valium. Finally, as she became increasingly disabled, it was difficult for her to climb up onto his examining table. But rather than noting the growing severity of her condition, he told her to hurry up. "There are people who are *really* sick who need to be seen today," he said. It would be months before she finally received the right diagnosis, this time from a young doctor on the emergency ward who could feel the problem with his hands. A malignant tumor had eaten through her femur.

There are many doctors who listen more closely and with greater compassion. Yet within a system that diminishes the significance of a patient's testimony, everyone tends to err in the direction of ignorance. Surprisingly, it is physical experience itself that is ignored. Even with the most sensitive practitioners, you will seldom be asked to give full witness to the life of your body. And because on an unspoken level of mind, you learn how to treat yourself from the way that you are treated by others, especially authority figures, the effect of this narrow focus can be to limit the range of your own attention. Many times after visiting a doctor who did not listen well, I have found myself turning away from the habit of awareness, trying to ignore what I feel myself. The eventual effect, if you are in pain or discomfort, can be a subtle resignation, the sense that nothing could or perhaps should be done to help you.

The resignation is similar to the resignation the working poor will sometimes feel. As if the hard circumstances of their lives were inevitable somehow. Which is also how society often makes them feel. The similarity is perhaps understandable if only because, just as stories are the stuff of democracy, economy is an extension of the body. Who shall prosper, who shall not, who shall have pleasure, who shall be deprived, even, at times, who shall live and who shall die. You will certainly feel economy as continuous with your own body if you are fighting to survive.

And the circumstances of poverty and medical neglect share this too, something I have felt just underneath my own resignation: the sense that my body was somehow at fault not only for being ill, but also for having an untreatable or even unnamed condition, for failing, in fact, to fit into the profile of what is an abstract body, the one that medicine creates from studies and statistics.

Dissociated, kinesthetically akimbo, as if pasted together from instructions written in a foreign language, strangely uncoordinated, this Frankensteinian body can at best provide only a distorted mirror of experience. When my doctor, who was intuitively astute, offered the diagnosis of an immune disorder to me, because she had not experienced the illness herself, her only recourse was to read a list of symptoms that had come down, like pronouncements from Sinai, from the Centers for Disease Control. But I could not recognize my own condition in this construction.

A few years later, at a conference for medical professionals that the CFIDS foundation organized, I discovered how this strange list of symptoms came into being. When we read the list a few months before, we were confounded by the symptoms the agency had chosen to list. Rarer symptoms were listed first, some prominent and common symptoms were left out entirely, and the experience of the illness, its gestalt, its felt quality, was not on the page. Midway through the conference, when the representative from the CDC had finished her presentation, someone from the audience rose to ask her how the agency had come up with the official protocols for diagnosis. She answered the question almost casually. The symptoms, she said, were chosen and listed randomly.

Random choice. The image I get is of wandering symptoms, like characters in search of an author, disparate and shapeless with nothing at the center. The method may make sense if you are doing a survey. You would want to pick names from a telephone directory almost blindly, for instance, if you are studying public opinion and wish your results to be uncontaminated by your own opinions. But in the life of the body symptoms are never experienced randomly. They come in clusters and, grouped together, form a kind of coherence that can be sensed. The cluster of symptoms, for instance, that you feel when you are coming down with a flu. As one sensation is added to another—headache, fever, fatigue—you begin to grasp the nature of your affliction.

Though if you did not know the name for it, you would not be able to diagnose yourself as having the flu. This is where a doctor's knowledge is crucial. In the realm of healing, perception is achieved through collaboration. It is a democratic process of a kind. Even to name the symptoms, doctors and patients must work together. A doctor may ask you to describe what you feel, for instance, but if you have learned no words for the symptoms you are experiencing, you may not even have delineated them. While I was very ill, I found it difficult to read. But though I am dependent on reading for my work, I never listed this difficulty as a symptom. I assumed it occurred simply because I was so fatigued. Even when a friend with the same illness told me of the cloudy spots in her vision, blotting out letters, words, sentences, I did not realize that I had the symptom. But later, after talking with her, the spots appeared again, and finally I could see them. It is a phenomenon I first understood from Wittgenstein, the philosopher of language, who pointed out that a sunset will not even be perceived until the word for it is learned. We need words not only to describe what is observed but to observe at all.

And there is this too, bearing both on medicine and democracy. What you are able to say or even know about your own experience depends in some mysterious manner on the attitude of the listener. Truth comes into being by call and response. The curiosity of the listener is like a magnet, pulling testimony from an inarticulate obscurity. And as with any tale, when the listener has heard the story, the process of telling will be healing in itself.

Knowledge is the medium of love. This must be one reason why telling a story seems so important. You will not feel loved if you are not known. And when you love, you are eager to know as much as you can about the one you love. The exchange is not static. As friends or lovers pass stories back and forth, the nature of their relationship changes, and in the mix they are altered too. In a sense, by speaking and listening we bring ourselves and others into being.

Everything that is expressed between patient and doctor matters. Even in the most impersonal transactions, a relationship exists that will affect you. The mood may not be measurable, but it is consequential. When you are suffering in your body, an impersonal or cold attitude can seem almost like an assault. In her famous work, *On Death and Dying,* Elisabeth Kübler-Ross includes an interview with an eight-year-old child who said she dreaded the visit of one of her doctors because he was always so cold to her.

I will never forget one experience I had coming out of exploratory surgery during a bout with a pelvic infection. Though I was hardly awake, I was in such intense pain that I was frantic for help. But because the anesthesia had not fully worn off, I found myself unable to speak. Yet when, with the greatest of efforts, I was finally able to mouth the word *pain,* first inaudibly, and then with several attempts, loudly enough to get the attention of a nurse, she looked at me as if she did not understand what I was saying. Again I labored and at last succeeded in creating a sentence, "Take away the pain." In response, and with an icily philosophical manner, she explained to me that any medication she might give me would not take the pain away but would only mask it in my mind. Unable to tell her that I knew this but wanted the medication nevertheless, I was afraid that I would be left to struggle with obliterating pain alone. And, even in my body, I was shaken by the absence of compassion in the tone of her voice.

In crisis, the body has an instinctual reaction to uncaring. It must be an ancient feeling, a fear pitted deep in flesh. You feel the danger in a wordless flash, as if your body has inherited the knowledge over millennia, that without care you will perish. During my long sojourn with my illness, I did everything I could to prevent the visits of one friend who, perhaps through her own denial, could not comprehend how ill I was. Because of the disjuncture in the seam of knowledge between us, it was excruciating to be in a room with her.

The wish to be known, to be seen. This is a physical longing as much as any other. That I experience the longing so strongly comes less from deprivation than expectation. I was fortunate enough to have a father who met this need. He gave me the feeling that he understood me. Though the knowing was not of an analytical nature. It was a kinetic coherence he reflected back to me. I felt I was being myself in his presence. And also becoming who I meant to be. He would pick me up for our weekend visits and ferry me to some activity of our mutual choosing. Our taste was eclectic, catholic, broad-minded. Whatever was in town interested us. Boat and tackle shows, stock car races, the latest movie, Griffith Park, and Ferndale, the circus. He taught me to ice-skate and row a boat and body-surf. As I grew older, he would follow my interests. I learned to ride horses, and then we rode together out into the wilder land at the edge of the San Fernando Valley. When I learned tennis, we would go to the courts together. And when my interest turned to art, he would take me to museums, waiting patiently as I stood, sometimes for endless periods, gazing at the paintings that I liked.

On our way to wherever we went and during our return or while we would stop for dinner, we would talk about a range of subjects. I spoke to him about art, the light in impressionist paintings, the intensity of van Gogh, or in skating, how I preferred going fast to making figures, or my latest thoughts about democracy, the movies and movie stars I liked, or what was happening in school, with my friends, the little dramas in our family. He respected whatever I said, considered it, responded evenly, as he would have done to an adult. I could feel the intelligence of his reception even when he did not speak. Sometimes we engaged in friendly debate, but he was always more than fair, letting my mind make small accomplishments of reason. And as he weighed the reactions I had to the other adults in our family, he would let me know that he too had seen what I had seen. Only later did I realize how well he listened and that listening the way he did is an art. Now I know that his listening carried me through many forms of grief. Years after his death, the atmosphere remained with me, sustaining me far more than I have realized, until this moment, as I tell the story.

If my father taught me to trust my own perceptions, I know that there are parents who do the opposite. The lessons can be harsh. I am thinking of the pedagogy by which German children were raised for at least two centuries before the last world war. Some of the methods seem cruel. A lock of hair tied by a long string to the waist to correct slumping posture. An infant beaten for crying. But the punishment did not stop there. The child's soul was also abused. As the psychologist Alice Miller has written, a child would be told that the punishment was *for your own good*. The lesson would confound your ability to trust your own experience.

Deprived of your own authority, you will be tempted to look toward another authority to tell you what to think. The same process that occurs between parents and a child or governments and citizens also occurs in a doctor's office. Whether the attitude of your doctor is abusive or simply paternalistic, if you are not seen and heard, your faith in yourself will be shaken. Somewhere in the breach between your own knowledge and medicine's ability to apprehend it, you cease to trust the knowledge of the body. As you pass your authority to others, whether it is a doctor, a nurse, a laboratory, or hospital, you are hardly aware of the loss.

And this too is a collaborative effort. You may be very willing to forfeit your authority. Illness is wearying. To have someone else take charge, someone who knows more than you, can be a relief. If you have been sick for a long time or searching unsuccessfully for a cure, you will want to believe a doctor who says he can cure you. Even if you grow worse under his care, you will tend to deny what your own experience tells you. After Marie Duplessis's death, Liszt told this tale. He referred her to a doctor popular among society women, but under this man's care she grew worse rather than better. Yet she did not question his procedures until she grew gravely ill. It was only then she discovered that, using an experimental treatment, he had been slowly poisoning her with strychnine.

Faced with pain or the fear of death, everyone tends to look for omniscience if not omnipotence from their doctors. And the reverse is also true. The ability to heal others is associated with divine powers. I am thinking of Charles X, the king Alphonsine observed as he retreated through Normandy. He was crowned in the year that she was born. Following tradition, he chose the ancient cathedral at Reims as the site. Then, like so many kings of France who came before him, once the crown touched his head, to seal the legitimacy of his reign, he reached out his hands to touch the heads of his subjects who suffered from scrofula and who believed they could be cured by a royal touch.

To place yourself in someone else's hands can be soothing. It would be like surrendering to a lover. To trust is part of the pleasure. You can feel the healing in your flesh; it is like being blessed. Still, not every lover can be trusted. The transgression may be subtle. The way a lover looks at you, for instance. Not meeting your eyes, perhaps, or sizing up your body as if it were an object. Then you may find yourself growing unresponsive, as if your body knows that to yield would be to betray yourself.

Fundamentally, medicine has a diminishing view of the body. There is an unspoken pornography at the root of the philosophy that diminishes flesh: the idea, inherited from science, that matter, including the human body, is of its nature spiritless. A thing. Perhaps the container of the soul, but only that. You can feel the tincture of the thinking when you are a patient. It is perhaps why so many of us are afraid of hospitals. Like certain ideas that the rich have about the poor—that the poor are less intelligent, for instance, or less sensitive—this philosophy leaves the way open for cruelty.

By the same tradition, not just the body but bodily knowledge too belongs to a lower order. Not only is the patient's testimony by definition subjective and therefore scientifically inferior to the seemingly more objective opinions of professionals, but sensual evidence itself is deemed by science to be untrustworthy. Francis Bacon, father of the discipline, puts it more bluntly; ordinary experience, he writes, is "a loose faggot, and mere groping in the dark." Once head of the Star Chamber that tried witches, he must have been aware of the pun. Faggot. The term was used then to refer both to homosexual men and the kindling used to burn them for the sin of sodomy. You can almost feel the breath of an unnamed fear and loathing in his language. And what was the fear? I suspect it was simply all that the body knows.

This philosophy is not necessarily argued today. But it is embedded in many unquestioned practices and tendencies. The rejection of experience, for instance, may account for the fact that so little attention has been paid to the needs of the dying. While medicine has been intent to save lives, the quality of experience at the end of a life has been ignored. The director of a hospice for patients dying of AIDS in New York told me that until recently, for instance, no attempt had been made to make a distinction between symptoms of AIDS dementia and Alzheimer's disease, though the treatment for each of these conditions would be different. Before their advocates stepped in, the prevailing attitude was that since the mental condition of the patients had deteriorated so much, treatment made no difference.

The conjecture may be a bit capricious, but still I cannot help but wonder at the balance history has wrought here. That it would be gay men who are restoring bodily experience to the discourse. As patients gain power within the practice of medicine, this is the knowledge that returns. I witnessed the effect in the meetings I attended. Along with the fact that we as patients were shaping medical policy, I could sense the first beginnings of a still more radical change in the rooms where we met. The air was electric with it. Though we sought the results of laboratory experiments and the analyses of experts, the force that had driven us together, that drove us through all our meetings, was another testimony. It was the experience of the body that gave us vision.

■ ■ ■

Is it any coincidence that that poet of democracy should also be the poet of the body?

> *One's-Self I sing, a simple separate person,*
> *Yet utter the word Democratic, the word En masse.*

> *Of physiology from top to toe I sing....*

The return of bodily experience to public consciousness has great implications not only for the democratization of medicine but also for democracy itself. All that a people must be able to do in order to participate in government, to discern problems and test the truth, to make choices, is connected to the knowledge of the body. Those who lose the authority of experience can no longer govern themselves.

Since the turn of the century, the reclamation of bodily knowledge has developed simultaneously with the evolution of democracy. Just as psychoanalysis was beginning to mine the psyche, another movement began to explore the territory of physical experience. I encountered the somatics movement as a young woman. Since I was born in California, it would have been almost impossible to avoid. I can see why the movement would take hold quickly in the West. Moving in this direction, manners, convention, even conventional ideas had to be relinquished. Along the way inevitably one would encounter new and strange notions of the body from Indians, the Navajo concept, for instance, that sickness can be healed through a painting made with sand. Then there was the proximity to Asia, offering a different map of the body, drawn with points and meridians through which electrical currents pass. The process of discovery only intensified after Esalen Institute was founded. Here on a ground fed by sulfurous springs that flow into baths placed exquisitely at the edge of the sea, for the last four decades the generation of visionaries who founded the somatics movement—Ida Rolf, Gerda Alexander, Charlotte Selver, Moshe Feldenkrais—has taught students how to value and refine sensual experience.

On paper some of the lessons may seem trivial. To move your leg back and forth and around, for instance, or to press hard into a muscle that is cramped. But in the flesh the effect is formidable, something like one of those dreams during which you discover rooms in your house you did not know were there before; chamber after chamber of physical existence and its meanings will be revealed to you.

One year when I was visiting Esalen for a conference on the philosophy of the body, I met a teacher, healer, philosopher of movement from whom I began to understand how to witness the life of the body in a new and far deeper way. Perhaps because of the effect of her own work, Emilie Conrad, who is still strikingly beautiful in her fifties, has a vivid presence. This is a powerful quality. Thinking of Paiva again, I imagine that much of her magnetism lay with the quality of her presence. The contemporary saying would be that she was "in her body." So much so that to be near her would put you in yours. Bernhardt had this quality too. During rehearsals of *L'Aiglon,* when she would stop in the afternoon to have her cup of tea, the whole company would stop with her just so they could watch her drink it. "Everything this woman did was extraordinary," Paul Poiret would write later.

Like Bernhardt, at an earlier point in her life, Emilie liked to wear exotic clothing, close to costumes. But now as the work she does moves closer to the core of bodily experience, she dresses with simplicity, though she is stunningly elegant, the workout equivalent of early Chanel. Her speech, still holding traces of a Manhattan accent, is remarkably direct.

Drawn by the resonance of our work, we became friends. I began to study with her, discovering through my own movement an astonishing range of experience, at once sensual and full of an implicit significance. Many times I have tried in conversation to describe the experience but without success. Still, because this is part of my story, I will try to set down something of what I learned.

The movements she leads you toward are not ambulatory or purposeful in any way but are made for their own sake. Eschewing habitual patterns, which dull your awareness, and instead exploring movement outside of the realm of habit, you will find a larger experience, vast really, with unimagined riches, like an undiscovered continent, a new world of the body. Except that the idea we have of *body* is too bounded. Because as you experience movement in this way, you begin to find the supposed dimensions and laws of physicality changing. You might feel a kind of weightlessness, for instance, while for twenty or thirty minutes you lift your legs above your head, or a new flexibility as you move muscles you did not even know you had. Introducing sound as a form of movement, you become aware of vibration as motion, your body vibrating like an instrument, momentous changes even in the small actions of your tongue, your throat. Or feeling the muscles along your spine or in your chest and stomach roll, curve inward, the space inside you expanding, you discover your body is infinitely more fluid than you thought, as if you are made of another substance than what you imagined. Through it all, the sense you have is not unlike the vision the impressionists captured in nature, seeing the light that is also grace, finding the greater life of the body.

Knowledge of the body. A crucial part of the work is awareness. You will be asked to stop and take in what you have experienced. And when doing so, you find that witnessing your body, its intelligence, the astonishing range of response, ingenuity, generativity within it, is itself a kind of motion, or at least a force, the force of perception. Heisenberg's principle applies in this dimension too. To see the life of the body is to affect it. And in a sense, the body creates itself by self-reflection from moment to moment.

■ ■ ■

We are all always both knower and known at once. The coupling
has its excruciating side. Indulging in the illusion of separation, I
have been angry at my body many times for interrupting my life
with illness. But something else is also possible. Turning my attention toward sense, movement, sensation, taking in the great
breadth and complexities, the intricacies of physical experience, I
feel a kind of relief in response and then gratitude, as if flesh were
glad to be known, a steady stream of what feels like love saturating
the substance of my existence.

A week or two after I returned from Germany I began to make
small entries in my journal, trying to trace the arc of events in my
body. Years before, I had been asked by a doctor to keep a record
of symptoms. The request seemed bothersome, and I failed the task.
But this was different. As if my gaze were softened somehow and
by seeing I could make an alliance with my body.

MARCH

*Sitting in the glare of the late afternoon sun, as it strikes through
clouds, bright over the water, I can feel parts of myself gone. If a picture were made of me following the path of nerve endings, legs, feet,
hands, lips, parts of my face would be invisible.*

Bearing on democracy and economy alike, the life of the body is
molded from idea and circumstance. Not only your idea of what
happiness is but also how you earn your keep, how many hours
you work and at what pace will shape experience. We live in a
busy world. I know what it is to be hurrying, to feel that there is
never enough time. In the rush to do the impossible, I often feel as
if I am in transit. Settling nowhere, barely experiencing anything.

"Getting and spending, we lay waste our powers," Wordsworth wrote, near the beginning of the nineteenth century. The loss must have been felt as a great irony then. To climb the ladder, you would have had to exploit your own body, using every sense and sensation for one purpose, marshaling all your efforts for success. Yet if you landed among the successful, though as a reward for all your struggles your opportunities for sensual pleasures would have multiplied, your capacity to fully experience them would seem to have suffered. Once wealthy, you might be able to acquire the most luxurious possessions. Run your hands over the finest textures. But still something more valuable would seem to have escaped you. The whirlwind of your desire taking you nowhere in the end except to feel a vague hunger, a vague loss, though you would not be able to say exactly what is missing.

I am thinking once more of the prosperous gentleman in the theater. As he weeps, he is moved by the sacrifice the young courtesan has made. She has given her life for her lover, his family, and his career. But I am also seeing that he must be crying for himself too, knowing all he has had to sacrifice for his ambition. In a sense he has given up his life too.

Though after the play is over he might be able to buy his life back for a few hours. With a courtesan. Or a chorus girl. Purchase a period free of the bondage of his success. Some precious, purposeless moments. Half goddess, half siren, the fallen woman would represent all that was irresistibly present and still unobtainable, what was passing through his grasp, moment by moment.

It was present as a promise in Paiva's mansion. The hope for a place that might reflect the grandeur of experience if only you would give yourself fully to it. But such a mansion exists. It is everywhere. Moving at a different tempo from the one followed by modern economies, if you sink deeply into any given moment, the moment itself will lead you beyond yourself, as your life merges with every other life.

■　■　■

You can hear the sound of this larger dimension in Verdi's music. Hauntingly beautiful, as the voice alternates between frenzy and wonder. *Dell' universo intero,* Violetta sings, repeating the words of her lover. When the chorus takes it up the sound will become majestic, *the entire universe.* And if you are touched beyond your comprehension it is because indeed the whole universe does seem to exist here in these intimate, frivolous moments. To feel everything, everyone here around you, within you, this is the strange, unpredictable truth of experience. The more you are present to any given moment, the more it will expand beyond any boundaries you have imagined.

JUNE

Tried to sit in the back. It usually restores me. The sun, the shade, those rare old deciduous pines. But I couldn't do it. The illness damaging something in my body, what one takes for granted, the capacity to receive. As if too much sound, movement, light were coming at me. I could not take it all in.

Of course I am entering a realm of pure conjecture, but thinking of this stange expansion, I find myself wondering why the bodily desire to partake in a larger meaning seems so strong, even rivaling the instinct to struggle for survival. This desire is met along with other bodily needs in the simplest of daily events. I am thinking of the way we take a meal together, for instance, sitting at a common table, telling each other stories, to feed and be fed, to listen and speak inextricably mixed, as among us a shared body of meaning takes shape. Though the notion may sound fantastic, still the tendency toward convergence cannot be denied: every experience is like a hall of mirrors, reflecting intimate memory, distant events, histories woven into image and sound. Even the plainest words you might choose to describe what you have known, *subject, slavery, sickness, death,* contain worlds of meaning, which stretch way beyond the present, over space and into the past, the future.

And it is not just stories that come together. Events themselves have an almost uncanny way of coalescing. At times the coincidence seems particularly just. In my search for the history of Camille, I read this story, for instance, from the life of Alexandre Dumas *père*. It explains how, during the revolution of 1830, the uprising that deposed Charles X, Dumas was able to capture the entire fusillade at Soissons. He found he had inherited an unpredictable emblem of power. That his Haitian grandmother had given him coffee-colored skin proved beneficial. As serendipity would have it, the color frightened the wife of the commandant. Forty years earlier, she had experienced a slave rebellion in Haiti. When she saw a black man brandishing a gun, she cried, "Give up, give up, it's the second revolution of the Negroes!"

Despite moments of justice, history can often seem unjust if not chaotic. I do not believe in predestination, nor do I think every event is fated. But still, as I tell these stories, drawing disparate plot lines into one net, immersed in the mood wrought by convergence, I sense traces of a deeper order, one that cannot be said to exist yet in human affairs but to which nevertheless the human soul responds, with a mixture of regret and longing.

And is this not also why we hunger for stories? A good story will give you a sense of a deeper order beyond your understanding, lending you a sense of confluence between your own life and larger meanings that you may not even be able to explain. When I was young, as I watched a small luminescent box with rapt attention while a gray-toned image of Greta Garbo playing Camille fluttered and expired in the arms of her lover, I understood only too well all the gestures of love and loss. But there was something else too in the scene, giving me the sense of a mysterious meaning in life, one that I could not grasp though I could feel it. This was death itself. And the aftershock of absence that, even now, seeing the film, stuns me into a wondering largesse.

Every illness contains something of death. The loss of a capacity once thought irrevocable is like a little death. And any weakness you feel in your body will be redoubled by the perception of weakness, which comes perilously close to the knowledge that you will have to die someday. The fear can even keep you from your own experience.

The death of someone you know can frighten you too. Even hearing of a death, you will feel the event in your own body. Your heart almost seems to stop in resonance. If the relationship you had was intimate, you will find it difficult to rest, eat, sleep. But at times this constant state of agitation can become a kind of opening—there is no other way to describe it; every moment seems to enter you with an astonishing clarity, and, of course, you appreciate the simple fact of existence more.

I did not experience this clarity when my father died. I was sixteen years old. The news that he had been killed crossing the street came to me from a stranger who was standing on our front porch when I came home one evening. It was just before twilight. The man had been sent by an association for the families of firemen. Hearing his words, I went into a kind of fugue state, transfixed but not quite able to cross over from disbelief into grief. At the funeral I was counseled not to see his body. The motive was to protect me, but now I know the advice was wrong. It took me years to fully grasp the simple fact that he had died.

In the intervening decades I had many dreams where he appeared, on a street corner or the foyer of a theater or in a neighborhood yard. Usually, I discovered that he had never died but only had gone away, hidden himself, assumed another name, another identity. In most of the dreams I was glad to see him again. He was usually ashamed he had left. In one dream he tried to make it up by bringing me a toy dog. Only then did I realize I was still a child. But in all the dreams, his visits were short, and before long he would disappear again.

A few years ago a very close friend, with whom I shared my home, died in the same way, violently and quickly, hit by a motorcycle while she was crossing the street. I was at the hospital waiting while an attempt was made to save her life. When they gave us the news that she died, I asked to see her. The sight of her body, bandaged, lifeless, located me in loss. I could accept the reality of her death. And this allowed me to begin the hard and amazing work of grief, a paradoxical path by which loss takes you past yourself into a wider network of existence. It is interesting that the enigma of a nothingness in which everything exists should be accessible through the body, through the physical experience of death. It is as if, through matter itself, the greater body of nature begins to teach you a wild and tender reason beyond your comprehension, except that somehow your body understands.

The process must be similar when you are dying. When I was very ill, in certain rare moments I could feel an unutterably peaceful stillness, which led me toward an acceptance, not only of my own failing body but of death too. It is only in modern industrialized societies that the process of dying has lost its meaning. In older cultures the ending of a life was understood as an auspicious time.

As I write I am seeing the last scene of *Camille* again in still another way. As if the scene were about death itself. Not a heroic death, as in war, for instance, but a natural one. An ordinary death from disease. When I think about it, I can see that Camille is the artistic ancestor of the weekly television dramas I sometimes watch, the dramas that take place in hospitals and emergency rooms. Open-heart surgery, the red meat of the muscle jumping in the hand of the surgeon, a white bone visible, fluid rushing from the mouth of an unconscious man. Since Camille coughed and spat blood onstage, the lens has opened wider and wider, admitting a tide of corporeality into public life. And yet over the same period, death has receded from visibility in another way, the dying moved from private homes to hospitals, and mortality has been put at a distance.

Looking back over the last century, I can see now that history has been moving in opposite directions—both toward and away from the life of the body. In one way, with its heavy morality, *Camille* bespeaks a desire to control and eclipse this life. But the play also signaled a greater embrace of physical existence. I am thinking not just of the bodily desires and events portrayed onstage, but of the actress famous for performing the role. Though her movements seem melodramatic to us now, Sarah Bernhardt was famous for her realistic gestures. In her time, her manner seemed shockingly natural. The realism drove her audiences wild. She was at the crest of a wave, a rebellion against the mannerisms that had restricted corporeal knowledge.

It is there almost as an underground aquifer, underneath the artistic movements of the nineteenth century, a stream of images and words moving toward the exploration of the body. When Bernhardt was sixty and still commanding the stage, a young dancer called Isadora Duncan recently come over from America began to shock Parisian audiences with the way she danced. Revealing less flesh but more of her body, she traded the traditional ballet costume for a sheer flowing dress that allowed her to move more freely. "But look," she said, "under the skirts . . . are dancing deformed muscles. A deformed skeleton is dancing before you." Breaking free of balletic positions, her dance edged further and further into a motion emanating from the center of her body. Her authority subjective. Her source her own experience. Hour upon hour in her studio, alone, her attention would be turned inward as she sought, she said, "the human spirit through the medium of the body's movement."

Is it a casual coincidence or part of the same coalescing inclination of events that a year earlier, a few months before the century turned, Claude Monet painted *Le bassion aux nympheas, harmonie verte, Lily Pond, Harmony in Green?* As if emerging from clouds of reflection, a bridge arcs over a pond, wood, water, lilies, rushes, trees, fusing with the sensuality of vision. Not just the pond but the capacity of the eyes to feast on light revealed. The same wave that was resurrecting movement was also renewing sight.

On the birthday when I turned thirteen, because impressionism was my passion at the time, my father gave me a book of reproductions called *The Impressionists and Their World*. Monet, Manet, Renoir, Pissarro, Toulouse-Lautrec, Redon, Gauguin, Cézanne, van Gogh, Sisley. There are just eight paintings by Monet pictured in it, the pond not among them. Half of the reproductions are in black and white, and the ones in color are badly done, the characteristic brush strokes faded in these copies. But I treasure this book. By now I have several volumes of impressionist paintings with far better reproductions, but, never thinking to weed this one from my library, I have kept it forty years.

I have held onto it partly as an artifact from the first years of my emergence into the world of art and intellect. The fact that the impressionists were painting perception itself amazed me even then. And that they caught the changing nature of reality. The haystacks, for instance, that Monet painted, at different hours of the day, with different angles of light. For me, then as now, this work captured what I myself experienced at the ocean at sunset, light bleeding over the water, or in the Sierras, trees brushed by the morning sun, the motion of a spirit in things that Isadora Duncan was discovering through her own body.

But the real reason I have kept the book, I suspect, is because of my father. It is a testament to the way he loved me. The way he understood me and encouraged my interests. He was by no means a perfect parent. All the flaws in his character affected his ability to care for me. In his own more subtle ways he abandoned me, even as he made me a kind of partner to a loneliness he had about him. Yet I was lonely too. We had both lost everyone. My mother, his wife. My sister, his older daughter. Like the last residents of a vanishing village, we were everything to each other.

The light in impressionist painting is full of joy. But if you gaze for a longer time, you can see a delicacy there in the way the light bursts and then dapples and then expires into shadow, like someone coming to life and then dying. The world the impressionists painted no longer exists. As the last century moved toward progress, not just a way of life, but much of the countryside itself was disappearing. Though where you live, whether you have land or not, trees, farms, vineyards, orchards, cannot be separated from the way you live. So many people moved from the countryside to the city. Peasant economies suffering collapse. The old matrix woven between community and land disappearing.

I wonder if the impressionists were aware that they were capturing a quality of life that was passing. Though I know the atmosphere of the nineteenth century must have been more exciting than elegiac. There were so many new inventions. I am thinking of cameras, for instance. They appeared just before Marie Duplessis died. One photograph of her exists today. We are used to the invention now. But in the beginning, as a journalist suggested at the time, the photographic image must have inspired the hope that mortality itself would one day be suspended. The possibilities would have seemed endless. Telegraph wires diminishing space, steam trains and then automobiles saving time. There would soon be electric lightbulbs and gas heat. Then as the century turned, even gravity gave way as Orville Wright took a machine into the air. The motion was so fast. The changes so great. The cost would have gone almost unnoticed. No one talked about pollution. Though there were a few men and women who saw that something was being lost. Among them Henry David Thoreau, who was writing *Walden* in 1847, the year that Marie Duplessis died. He saw what was vanishing, "As if you could kill time without injuring eternity."

Of course this kind of eternity cannot be experienced in one life alone. It exists in the continuous cycle that is part of nature, one generation following another. An eternity, which can be sensed, however, by all of us, in any given moment. I know this because I have felt it as part of a mix of sensual impressions in the course of a day. And whenever I have sensed this eternity in the world around me, I have been better able to accept the inevitability of my own death.

The *Grande Horizontale,* they called her. Half unclothed, lips parted. There is something eternal about her. She may be supine, but her recumbence is like the recumbence of the earth. Could it be that sequestered in hidden chambers of the minds of the men who sought her, she stood for the natural world that was vanishing? She is in a way a goddess, a goddess of continuous abundance. Despite the advantages of progress, there must have been some regrets. At the dawn of the mechanical age, her body emerged everywhere. Here adorning a bar, there a cornice, embracing windows, holding up doorways, grape leaves twined around her shoulders, breasts,

legs. The myth can be read on the walls of Maxim's, where courtesans spent so many nights with their prosperous benefactors.
Paintings of succulently nude women bathing in a lake, dancing in
a forest under the moon, sitting under trees, limbs like branches,
branches growing over skirts.

La dame aux camélias. Lady of the Camellias. This death too,
the death of nature, would have been felt as Camille slowly expired
on stage. Something wild and beautiful that had to be sacrificed if
we were to keep moving in the same profitable direction, toward
that place where, secretly, we hope to escape death. But there is a
price to be paid. "We know not where we are," Thoreau wrote, of
the way we live now.

There are many different ways of knowing. As a child in school I
learned that the air we breathe, what we eat, comes from the earth.
But early in my life I was given another lesson more directly.
Whatever grief I had or loneliness I felt could always be eased
when I would hike or ride a horse into the hills around Los Angeles, which were still untouched then, or swim in the ocean or camp
with other girls in the High Sierras. I did not know why once in the
water or surrounded by trees, I had no thought of alienation or isolation. Now I can talk about the intricate weave of natural life, the
interlacing of cause, effect, the mutuality of survival, which is a
great part of the beauty of nature, whether grand or delicate, its
coherence. Yet something else was there in my experience. I felt it
in my body. Washed in waves, the odor of seaweed or of pine, hay
or horse manure, the smell of Sierra red soil inside me, I could feel
myself being woven into the whole of it.

It was not a feeling I had in the city where I was born. Through the
intricate ways that so many events and ideas resolve themselves
eventually into flesh, this city too has become part of my body.
Bodily knowledge is continuous with the whole play of existence.

Los Angeles is a sprawling place, diffuse in an unpleasant way. There is no center, no there there, as Gertrude Stein once said of her vanished home in Oakland. The heavy warm air gives the city a sensual presence, but the architecture, the streets, the freeways dissect and splinter any sense you may have of a single whole.

Not every city, however, is incoherent in this way. I am thinking of Paris, which is part of my story too. Perhaps it is because of the way the Seine runs through the middle of the city or the sameness of the stone, much of it quarried in earlier years from the surrounding countryside. You can feel the city the way you would a landscape, as one continuous whole, coherent in itself. And, as if lending themselves to this wholeness, there are goddesses all over Paris, elegantly sculpted in stone or in wood, gilded or polished, crafted but still wild, working together to weave the city into one fabric. Any way you turn, you find her there. Taking the forms of the Mona Lisa and the Venus de Milo, the two magnetic poles of Louvre, she charges the world of art with her presence. As the virgin, she awaits visitation in every church, even defining the geography of France at Notre Dame, which is point zero, the place from which all distances are measured. Our Lady.

As I wander through the city, I detect the wake of her presence everywhere. A goddess whose sway can still be felt in the soft lights of the bridges that swim in the water at night, in the melting colors of Aubusson tapestries and the shining fabrics to be found on the rue Jacob, in the whispering lacy trees of the Bois de Boulogne, the delicate blue and white flowers that shift and sigh at the heart of the Palais Royal or the heavy musk of burgundy, odor of the soil, the color of blood, and, of course, the madeleine, that sweet taste, dipped in tea perhaps, the sound of the word recalling Mary Magdalene, prostitute turned saint, sacred body of passion, with the same name as Mary, mother of the son, God's Mother, *mother.*

■ ■ ■

I can feel the pull of the place in my body now while I write. But I am also remembering my own mother now and the place where she lived after my father and she divorced. At the age of seven, I was taken by my father to visit her there. Because I had not seen her in seven months, she seemed like a stranger to me. We met her at the lunch counter where she worked. She gave me what was then my favorite meal, a hot dog, and this made me happy for a while. But later when we went together to her small apartment, a single room smaller than the one I had shared once with my sister, I was saddened. The bed and a bureau were shabby and nondescript, the furniture of a rented room. It was as if I could see all the loneliness and despair of her life in that cramped space, a place that came to stand for all isolation in my memory.

Though now as I near the end of my story, I am beginning to see that although loneliness is real and painful, isolation is an illusion. Society, like nature, is one body really. Each life reverberates in every other life. Whether or not we acknowledge it, we are connected, woven together in our needs and desires, rich and poor, men and women, alike.

I am thinking of the chorus in *La Traviata*. Verdi has been criticized for including it, as if a chorus were inappropriate in so intimate a tale. But there is always a chorus. Even in the most private moments, the presence of the larger society can be felt, the force by which we sound our lives. And the reverse is also true. *Amor e palpito dell' universo intero.* Love is the pulse of the entire universe.

Is this another reason why, as the courtesan dies, we weep in the last scene, not only because she dies but because of the nature of her sacrifice? She has given her life for her lover. Of course it is a familiar injustice that a woman should give up her life for a man. But if, in a different part of the mind, Camille expresses the hidden

desires of a whole society, there would be still another dimension
to the tragedy. Another unsatisfied longing. The longing we all
share to give ourselves to others.

In her account of the belle epoque, Cornelia Otis Skinner describes a
remarkable event that was repeated during the many boisterous
nights that prosperous gentlemen spent with courtesans at Maxim's.
After a few hours of drinking and general carousing, these men
would begin to throw fistfuls of valuable coins. Then the courtesans, who hardly needed the money, would dive for the change.
Several years later, in 1932, when the restaurant was renovated,
hundreds of gold louis were found in the seams of the old uphol-
stery. The dispersal would not have been motivated by charity. I
suspect the money was thrown more like a gesture in a ritual dance,
the body loosened from its strictures, expanding toward a larger
body, the common ground of existence.

It would be like the gesture Charles X had made when he placed
his royal hands on the heads of those who were ill. In the old way
of thinking, a king has two bodies. The first, his own, is small and
bounded. But the other, immortal, graced, and infinitely capacious,
belongs to the entire nation. And this is why he can heal his subjects. Touched by his hand, you are touched by everyone. The common body.

The belief was not restricted to France. It belongs to many ancient
healing rituals, in Native American, Tibetan, and African traditions.
The kingdoms of Benin, for instance, which once stretched from
Ghana to Nigeria, had ways of summoning the presence of the
whole community, the land, all creation, past and present, the spirits of ancestors, to the task of healing anyone who was ill. These
practices were carried by slaves to Haiti and became part of
Vodoun. Is it possible that Cessette Dumas passed something of this

wisdom to her son, Alexandre-Thomas, who would carry the message on, even as a whisper, across the water?

What I learned from Emilie Conrad has something of this wisdom in it. As a younger woman, she spent several years in Haiti, studying Haitian dance and the ways of Vodoun. This education changed her experience of life. The common body. As I was studying with her one afternoon, after an hour of movement—my eyes closed, the room filled with other students doing the same work—a kind of miracle transpired, though in a sense it is an ordinary experience even if you are not always aware of it. Without any conscious effort, all of us seemed to be moving together. The sounds we were making formed a single music. It was a profound state of trust, one I recognized from an old and unfulfilled desire in my body, now met. This is the greater life of the body.

To sacrifice yourself for others would be one way to enter this greatness. But since the desire to give is an expression of the body, perhaps it is not your body so much as a limited idea of who you are that must be relinquished. As the courtesan dies in Cukor's beautiful film, the lens of the camera is softly focused. Dressed in light, flowing clothing, Garbo seems to float into and fuse with her surroundings. But everyone blends, her lover, his father, and everything converges, tears and light, promise and loss mixing freely in the air.

This is the answer I have been seeking. What of my own soul was lost to illness. My trust in the common body. Though I know now I never really had that trust. What I had was a kind of suspended disbelief, a hope. Though the hope was tied in a strange way to the feeling I carried from my childhood that I was the errant one, the one who failed, the one who was wrong to desire. I was a motherless child in a way. The loss of a mother is profound. You will feel deprived and unprotected, of course, but something even deeper is lost to you. This body that is gone, her body, was the first body you belonged to, your very existence, flesh and bone, inseparable from hers. And thus when this trust is broken, connection itself suffers. She is point zero, the place where the geography of the heart begins.

All of us are motherless now in one sense. The coherence of nature dissolving. Human community dissipated. And there is this too: the effect of the social order on motherhood. Though her mother never left her, my mother was motherless too. Brilliant and talented, she and her mother both struggled against the expectation that they sacrifice themselves to their children. In a world that provides little protection for children, this is what mothers are asked to do. My grandmother could not give herself away without a resentment that spoiled the gift. She had wanted to be an actress. And who knows what other suppressed longings she had? Thinking of my mother now, I know she was restless. She wanted more passion in her life as well as more spaciousness in her soul. I think this is one reason why she drank so much. She was always trying to retrieve herself.

For centuries women's lives have been pressed between the impossible choices presented in two tales, one of a virgin, the other of a whore. But stories are often more capacious than those who tell them. Despite the vaunted theme of sin and redemption, the figure of Magdalene has always drawn me. Because she was the saint of prostitutes and courtesans, last year, in the heavy heat of summer, I traveled to St.-Maximin, a small town outside Aix-en-Provence, so that I could see the procession that takes place there every year on her saint's day. The Basilica of St.-Maximin claims to possess her skull. Once each year for just a few hours before the procession, this skull is displayed in the sanctuary. Dark with age, it is encased with glass and surrounded, almost ghoulishly, by a golden upper body, neck, and luxuriantly long hair cascading in gold over the shining shoulders. The sight is transfixing. I could not stop staring at it, and after a while I found it beautiful. The effect is to frame the body, in this case bone, so that bone becomes more than itself. Or perhaps, again, the bone becomes what it really is. Radiant. Full of Mystery. Holy.

I walked carrying a candle with the other worshipers as we went from the basilica to the Dominican convent less than half a mile away. There a small choir of nuns sang beautifully before a monk gave a kind speech, quoting, I believe, the Beatitudes. *Blessed be ye poor, for yours is the kingdom of God. Blessed are ye that hunger now, for ye shall be filled.* The reliquary was covered for the march in a golden mask, which was dramatically removed when it reached its destination. Then it was set at the edge of a small square, just a few yards in front of a beautiful sculpture of the other Mary, softly green the way old copper or limestone can turn with age, with quietly muted lines, holding the infant, of course, and looking more young and vulnerable than she usually does. Turning to take in this vision of the two, I felt as if I were being touched by something far more ancient than the church, soul and body, birth and death, passionate and compassionate love all in attendance.

Many times I have written about how my mother inexplicably vanished or, drinking, returned briefly as someone else, frightening and malign, pulling me into the delirium of her nightmare. But there were elements, causes, marginal inscriptions in the experience I had not seen before. Somehow to know my own loss of her, I had to include another story in the mix.

And the choice of the story I have used to accompany my own was perhaps predestined in some way, shaped by the archaeology of my soul. Though I did not know it at the time, I must have been drawn to *Camille* not only for the subject of the story but for where it takes place. My mother loved Paris. She never saw the city, not even once in her life. She knew it from books and the old postcards she would collect or that I sent her. From these she had learned as much about the city as I knew. When in her fifty-ninth year she began to teach herself French, the shelves in her small tract house began to fill with books in this language. Long ago I realized that when I was very young it was she who gave me my love of this city. I remember waking at the age of seven in my grandmother's house with an image from my dreams of a city through which a wide swath of blue ran, a map I must have seen in one of my mother's books. It would take me years to understand that this dream expressed my desire for her. And that my trips to Paris were all attempts to recover her body.

Arriving at Charles de Gaulle, watching out the window for the cab to pass the modern sectors at the end of the Seine, I move to the edge of my seat when the Pantheon comes into sight. Despite the tiredness of a long flight and the sense in my body that it is still night, I begin to feel the familiar elation. I can hardly rest, so eager am I to immerse myself.

But this immersion has its peril. Because of the intensity of my particular desire, what happens to me next is what happens to almost everyone who visits Paris. As anticipation and pleasure fill me with elation, everything I see takes on a chiaroscuro of unrevealed mystery. The more I see, the more shapes of experience and shades of understanding just beyond my reach beckon to me. I read the map, turn it upside down, stop at a café, then summon my last drafts of energy and press on, walking on feet that are burning now, or legs close to folding under the effort, not to, as tourists say, take it all in, because I know in Paris that this is never possible, but to grasp an elusive state of being, signs of which can be found around every bend, tantalizing me, and which, like an exhausted lover on a chase, I want with an increasing passion but never have.

And now I have come to see that this continual failure is perfectly suited to my story. Probing my desire to find my mother in this city of endless glimpses, I have come to see that still another, even deeper pattern of loss, fraught less with anxiety this time than with a ceaseless, agitated search, has inscribed restlessness in my body and become part of the story of my illness. Not just the loss of my mother. Or even of my own experience. But a more fundamental unfulfillment belonging to us all. A larger life not fully lived, like a public square unfinished, evocative of possibility.

Was my mother also seeking the promise of herself here? The disappointment belonged to everyone in the family. My sister's longing, my own, my father's too in some sense, hinged on that promise. The central tragedy of my family, one that began to occur long before I was born, was my mother's destruction. Wholly aside from our own suffering, the process of her demise was harrowing to witness. She was beautiful; she was rebellious. Her eyes have that gleaming, almost haunted, quality you will often find in photographs of very attractive or gifted, wild, or dissolute young men and women from the twenties and thirties. Jack London, who drank himself to death, had this look in his eyes. It is as if they reflect a captivated light, glimmering from the secret recesses of dark pools.

What harmed my mother is not clear. The mystery remains as ineluctable as she herself was. Her retreats were withdrawals even from herself. Qualities would rise up in her, illuminate her face, her eyes, then die back, disappear. Her wit, her intelligence, her charm, a kind of brilliance of being, odd in a person who claimed to be shy, a composed directness, her sexuality, aqueous, playful, were present only provisionally and briefly or as incipience risen and then crushed as if by an unnameable weight. One could only glimpse who she was, and in this way one suffered the loss of her, almost from moment to moment.

This too is in my body and I suspect in my sister's also. A leaning out as if to catch what can never be caught. No one is ever lost without consequence to others. Loss and longing move from body to body, expressed in one place as sorrow, in another as illness, then as destruction, and everywhere as desire.

In the end perhaps Paris has finally given my mother to me. Placing these streets, the histories of the place, alongside her life and mine, a kind of chemistry has occurred. I cannot entirely explain it. I only know that weaving the events of my childhood and the crisis I suffered in body and spirit with all these other stories, stories of illness, revolution, love, my own story has transmuted. And because the canvas is broader now, the tragedies not my own anymore, just as I hoped, the mood has become slightly more playful and the ending of the story, larger than my own, is perhaps less predictable.

SEPTEMBER

Rereading my own words, as I think of my mother, lonely and probably afraid in her rented room, I am imagining a choir lush and powerful like a chorus from Verdi, singing around her, a chorus that echoes my grief, too.

Perhaps, looking back from a far distant future, these histories, including all their contradictions and complexities, will appear in one glance as a harmonious dance. But since I write now from a closer perspective, putting the pieces together is more precarious. I must read between lines, study patterns, styles, interpret moods as auguries, present old photographs as clues. My method is less objective than intuitive. I follow what strikes me or, rather, what follows me. And now, as I feel closer than ever to understanding the descent of my own body and soul, I am drawn to a pair of images taken at the turn of the last century, juxtaposed on a page from a book about Isadora Duncan. One is of the dancer in an artist's smock. It was taken by her brother in 1900. In it she has an authoritative stare, as if she has dared to go somewhere no one else has gone before and returned to tell us what she knows. Next to this is a picture of her brother, taken in 1902. Here he is rapturous, looking toward the future, toward us, as if he has caught a glimpse of the possible. A possible beauty. In his hands he is holding a book. The caption tells us he has been reciting Whitman. Though since it does not give us a citation, I will have to guess at the words he has read. This line may be among them. It is a question really: *Will the whole come back again?*

Because, of course, it is not just nature that is fading. There is a promise that has waned. Whitman's words sound wholly elegiac today. And that famous image of Liberty, a woman or a goddess, one breast revealed, leading the people, a worker as well as a gentleman moving with her as she makes her way through the battle, seems gloriously impossible. The song of the body, of the field, of the woman and the man, of the ship builder and the sailor and the farmer and the mother and the prostitute, the song of democracy.

Democracy. From the texts that I read in school about the founding of America, I learned many phrases that would serve me. Government by the people, of the people, for the people. Freedom of assembly. Freedom of the press. Freedom of speech. I have put the latter to long use. But one phrase eluded me. I was not taught it. It was not included in the textbooks of the fifties, a period when, like today, the term *free enterprise* was far more popular in the press. I found it recently while I was reading again about the early days of modern democracy. The words were used by the whole political spectrum, from Alexander Hamilton to Tom Paine: *the common good.* Once, they expressed the goal of the American Revolution. I suppose the meaning is implicit in the phrase *for the people*. And it is not entirely lost. The vague suggestion, for instance, that policies favoring the accumulation of wealth by a few will eventually benefit the many through trickling profits. But the spirit of the old vision is somehow lost. I suspect it was more than a trickle that was intended. You may be able to sense the dimensions of the loss by listening to the rhythms of a text rendered from this older sensibility: *for God hath so tempered the body that there should be no schism in the body, but that the members should have the same care for one another.*

The same care for one another. I have never lived in such a world, but as I write these words I know that the longing I feel for it illuminates the path of my descent. And I sense too that it is inextricably mixed with the failure of my family. The state of anxiety that entered my body, the distrust, existed long before I was born. It was there, I suspect, before my mother and father came into the world and even at the turn of the century when my grandparents were born. Because none of us really seemed to have the vision. Tatters of it were evidenced at holidays, when we would all come together and live for a day as one, exchanging gifts or cooking, sharing what we had, our lives. Otherwise we were atomized. Separate and stray in our effort. It was not just that my father was disenfranchised in the family, less powerful somehow, having less say, because he was a working man. Nor was it the lack of generosity my grandmother showed toward us all with what financial resources she had. Nor was it the whirling narcissism of my mother's madness. Rather, all these were secondary events, metaphenomena, not exactly consequences of but efforts to fill an emptiness at the center. Just as the country did not cleave, we did not cleave to our mutual survival. And in this, we were bereft of mutuality.

As children, my sister and I were fiercely loyal to each other. But over the years the old pattern took its toll. Love each other as we do, we have not been able to sustain each other, to help each other through crisis, even in the ways we are able to do for friends. And in this way, unwittingly, we have betrayed each other.

I can feel it in myself now. A longing in my body for a kind of fluidity, a relaxation of boundaries, for trust to be the medium of my existence. A desire for commerce aimed not at profit but as a way of being, as in the ecology of a forest, a valley, or the larger body of earth, which contains us. Can a political body long too and, even unaware of its wishes, consume itself chasing phantoms of desire?

The lack of mutuality was not unique to my family. At the time I graduated from high school I could feel the injustice, the inequality of the divide between those who were so rich and those who were desperately poor. Though in the period following the Second World War, the middle class was growing, and there was an unspoken hope in this growth. In those years almost everyone of every political persuasion expressed shock at the severity of the divide in other countries. Now the divide grows severe here too. And I have come to understand the ruthlessness of it on another level of my soul. Though I never experienced destitution, the suffering of want became more vivid to me through my own fear. What happens if you stumble, make a mistake, fall ill?

As my generous friends came to the end of their abilities to help me, I struggled to my feet. For several months I would spend my days meeting the simplest of my needs. Preparing food. Then resting. Cleaning up the kitchen. Then resting. The pace was laborious and slow. But finally I was able to work for small periods. A small grant was given to me. Later more money was raised. I crept by inches back from the brink of a worse fall. But I could not easily forget what I had learned.

■   ■   ■

I am thinking again of the passionate pull between Camille and her lover. How once separated, they could not forget each other. The respectable young man with so much promise. The fallen woman who had been so poor as a child.

SEPTEMBER

Pain in the joints, bone tired, and the old fear, the question, always rising with alarm, how will I sustain if I fall ill again?

Any way you care to see it, a certain wholeness remains. Our fate is shared. Every story we tell simply makes the whole more evident. Those of us who are ill now, immunity disordered or even ravaged, like canaries in the mine offer still another vision of a common, precarious future.

NOVEMBER

The fear is there, but it subsides in the telling. To have told the story. Though the story isn't finished.

Democracy. The story told over and over again of a soul healed through illness is perhaps metaphorical of a path we take together, to find redemption through the body. There is a dignity to material need. The process is so simple. A drink of water. A meal. A bit of rest. Despite my shame, I can finally see that there is a nobility, even an unwitting altruism, in the asking. It is through this sacrament, caring for one another, that every narrow fate will find its emancipation.

DECEMBER

Looking at that picture of my mother swimming, I think how beautiful. The drops of water, clear as glass, mixed with her beauty, the dark of the water, her dark good looks.

Through the telling of her story, I have become so close to Marie Duplessis now that I find myself hoping there were times when she was free from history. Moments of love and loving, when she was loose and able to cry, to express all that had been held back. What her body thought. The floor of pleasure still sounding in her. Her lover stroking her arms. Then pulling her in close. The feel of him surrounding her, as she became soft and awake in embrace, her mouth to his, tongue to tongue, and the fullness of speech there, the silent knowledge of skin and flesh, blood and bone suffusing the atmosphere, a luminous hymn of being, the host around her finally arrived with the song she ached to hear.

JANUARY

Not just what is unspoken but hope too exists between the lines.

The failed promise of our visions, our unspoken desires. What has not yet come into being will always be elusive. If I were to try to describe the quality of the woman my mother might have been, I would say that above anything else she would be like water. This was not her principal effect. She was shy and held back, but still you could feel the intensity of another force within her. She might lean toward you momentarily or hold her breath observing the delicacy of a moment, anticipating your response, quick to notice a telling detail, her intelligence liquid, traveling into your thoughts, comprehending the subtle wave of your intent, answering with a gesture still more subtle, quietly transparent.

FEBRUARY

It is still amazing to me how much a book has a life of its own. It becomes part of your body as you write, waking you early in the morning with the desire for completion, the need to come all the way into being.

Though I have felt trust and experienced many bodies moving as one, the feeling is not my constant state. It is always temporary. And in this writing I am beginning to understand why. Through my own difficulty, but also guided by the life of another woman who died almost a hundred years before my birth, I have seen that trust is not an isolated phenomenon. Except for fleeting moments, either we create it together or we will not have it at all. It is a medium we make from our lives. An atmosphere from which no one can be left out, because if anyone is, then abandonment exists as a possibility for us all. It is a sensate, living bond between us. Till death do us part. In sickness and in health. And now this is both my hope and my consolation. Neither the loss nor the continuing desire is mine alone.

The Body Electric

Life was thus an almost utterly improbable event with
almost infinite opportunities of happening.

J. E. LOVELOCK

STAR

A star bursting. Collapsed from its own weight into waves of dispersion. The earth turning in the waves, fire and ashes, then cold and dry. Until the day when elements met, touched, and, light passing through them at just the right moment, fused, transformed.

TRACES

You swear you can feel it now. Traces of this history, lingering here. A subtle force that pulls you out. You can feel it on the surface of your skin. That and a mysterious suspension; as you move you are almost floating. And then suddenly you are stopped by an instant of comprehension. All the delicate junctures between foot and earth, mouth and air, eye and light full of anticipation.

THE STORY

The story continuing in your body. A rush of energy up your spine, soft vibration of pleasure, the sinking collapse of weariness, chest caved in, skin sagging, then the long quiet night, after which arms and legs stretched out of the dark, you are newly alive in the morning.

NOT YET

Repeated and repeated every day with only the smallest visible changes. Though you are older. But with each year you can feel yourself folding more and more into each moment. Into the whole. You notice this, for instance, your hands opening like a crab, the web between thumb and forefinger a small wave of flesh, and there in the motion, an idea, crab nebula, vast space, burst of light, something not yet arrived.

NEW

Or you feel the hint of something new in the tempo. Heart drumming. Feet moving in time, words forming with each beat. *That sense of descent,* you hear yourself saying and then stop, the words singing from and then echoing back to your body, a kind of music now, in the making, *hurtling downward,* and before you begin the next phrase you are dancing, possessed by perfect timing.

NOW

The electric moments of all creation still in your body. Despite everything, be it grief, be it fear, making you glad. The story of how it all began being told inside you. And your own birth and your own death, every passing and all that is coming to be in your body too. The entire wave, washing through you, in you, even at this instant, taking you now.